HOPI TALES OF DESTRUCTION

COLLECTED, TRANSLATED, AND
EDITED BY EKKEHART MALOTKI

NARRATED BY MICHAEL LOMATUWAY'MA,
LORENA LOMATUWAY'MA, AND
SIDNEY NAMINGHA JR.

UNIVERSITY OF NEBRASKA PRESS
LINCOLN AND LONDON

Portions of this book were previously
published in Hopi and English as
Hopi Ruin Legends: Kiqötutuwutsi,
narrated by Michael Lomatuway'ma, Lorena
Lomatuway'ma, and Sidney Namingha Jr.
and edited by Ekkehart Malotki (Lincoln:
University of Nebraska Press [for Northern
Arizona University], 1993).

Library of Congress Cataloging-in-Publication Data
Hopi tales of destruction / collected, translated,
and edited by Ekkehart Malotki; narrated by
Michael Lomatuway'ma, Lorena Lomatuway'ma, and
Sidney Namingha Jr.
p. cm.
"Portions of this book were previously published
in Hopi and English as Hopi ruin legends:
Kiqètutuwutsi, narrated by Michael Lomatuway'ma,
Lorena Lomatuway'ma, and Sidney Namingha Jr. and
edited by Ekkehart Malotki . . . 1993"—Verso t.p.
Includes bibliographical references.
ISBN 0-8032-8283-4 (pbk.: alk. paper)
1. Hopi Indians—Folklore. 2. Hopi Indians—
Antiquities. 3. Legends—Arizona—Second Mesa (Mesa)
4. Legends—Arizona—Third Mesa. 5. Second Mesa (Ariz.: Mesa)—
Antiquities. 6. Third Mesa (Ariz.)—Antiquities.
I. Malotki, Ekkehart. II. Lomatuway'ma, Michael.
III. Lomatuway'ma, Lorena, 1933– IV. Namingha,
Sidney, 1935–1983.
E99.H7 H684 2002
398.2'089'9745—dc21
2002003601

Contents

Preface

Myths, legends, tales, and other kinds of oral narratives are a significant part of the vast expanse of expressive folk culture. Summarily referred to as oral literature, they must be regarded as true examples of "verbal art" (Bascom 1955). Unfortunately, the performance of this verbal art has experienced a dramatic decline. Worldwide, whole bodies of oral literature are vanishing into oblivion.

One of the bitter ironies of Western culture is that it began to appreciate the special qualities of oral literature at the very time when such orality was beginning to vanish. Persons who spoke only European languages were either oblivious to other languages or made it a policy to suppress them, thereby eradicating rich and ancient cultural traditions. Few cultures have been able to resist this onslaught.

This deplorable development also holds for the Hopi Indians of northern Arizona. As Terrance Honventewa observed in 1984 at the third annual Hopi Mental Health Conference, "Today, that precious and expressive language is in danger of extinction. Many contemporary tribal members speak little or no Hopi at all. Therefore much of the folklore, religion and other cultural treasures are already being lost."[1] Along the same vein, Emory Sekaquaptewa reports that in an informal survey of high school students conducted by the Hopi Health Department in 1986, when the new Hopi High School was opened at First Mesa, 85 percent of respondents claimed to be unable to speak or understand Hopi.[2]

With the disuse of the Hopi language, functional storytelling, which requires a narrator and an audience in a face-to-face encounter, suffered equally and is nearly extinct in Hopi society.

All the ruin legends presented in this volume were collected in the Hopi vernacular from what I call "story rememberers." They differ from the large body of Hopi oral literature in that they revolve around some actual historic event. Overall more fictitious than factual, the legends provide explanations for the demise of villages that now lie in ruin. In spite of their mythic trimmings, which do not make them "history" in the modern sense of the word, these destruction legends are culturally important. In the absence of authentic historical records they shed light not only on the Hopi past but also on the Hopi psyche. For this reason, Harold Courlander considers them more significant than scientific findings: "Apart from the excavations and conclusions of anthropologists, the oral tradition . . . is a more revealing instrument in some ways than the archaeologist's shovel. For out of the oral tradition, we get insights about values and motivations that are not visible in potsherds" (1971:15).

Due to the mixture of mythic, legendary, and historic events that distinguish the narratives of this collection, I will classify them as "mytho-historical" in nature. The qualifier "mytho-" is not intended to designate these legends as sacred or venerable, nor is it supposed to conjure up such associations as "false" or "fantastic." It is chosen with the sole purpose of reminding the reader that the historical accounts compiled here are distinctly laden with actors and agents from preliterate Hopi mythology, all of whom are endowed with greater-than-human faculties: gods and goddesses, culture heroes and evil sorcerers, terrifying spirits, animals capable of speech, and others.

To Hopi audiences, the events portrayed in these narratives once constituted true, factual history, regardless of whether they were perceived as rational-possible or irrational-impossible. They served the Hopis to reinforce the bonds of ethnic and cultural identity and to create a sense of continuity. Christopher Vecsey has factored out some of the most salient functions that pertain to the role of mythology in society and individual life. His perceptive observations also apply to the mytho-historical narratives presented here. According to him, they

> tend to anchor the present generations in a meaningful, significant past, functioning as eternal and ideal models for human behavior and goals. They can teach moral lessons to children and adults alike, communicating cultural messages and representing the community's philosophical positions to its own members through a revered vehicle of tradition. [1988:24]

They

> can bind a community in a knot of belief and common consciousness, glorifying ancestors and heroes of the recent and distant past, imaginary and historical, who can serve as paradigms for conduct. They

can authorize institutions or call for their alteration, marking off a culture as an accepted way of life. They can contemplate unsatisfactory compromises in social life, provide safe outlets for deviant desires, and serve as ideological weapons by one portion of the population against another. [24]

In light of the above observations this book constitutes what might be called an oral history primer. The following ancient villages, each briefly characterized by its unique historical fate, are contained in the primer: (1) Sikyatki: Destroyed by Hopis from Qöötsaptuvela at the request of its own village chief to terminate intravillage animosities resulting from an unjustified life-and-death race demanded by the sorcerer faction in the community; (2) Hisatsongoopavi: Destroyed by an earthquake triggered by the Water Serpent gods residing in the local village spring when implored to flatten the land for greater planting convenience; (3) Pivanhonkyapi: Destroyed by fire at the request of the village chief to cleanse the community of its evil ways brought on by a gambling craze; (4) Huk'ovi: Abandoned due to an act of sorcery perpetrated by a Hopi girl against neighboring Pivanhonkyapi; (5) Qa'ötaqtipu: Destroyed when a fire, initiated by its chief to avenge a crime committed by neighboring Matsonpi, consumes Qa'ötaqtipu instead; (6) Hovi'itstuyqa: Destroyed by enemy raiders when persuaded to do so by a man from Tupats'ovi who loses his wife through adultery committed by a man from Hovi'itstuyqa; (7) Awat'ovi: Destroyed in 1700 by a contingent of Hopi warriors from Oraibi, Mishongnovi, and Walpi at the request of its village chief when Awat'ovi's residents, twenty years after the Pueblo Revolt of 1680, readmit Spanish missionaries, thereby creating a state of *koyaanisqatsi* (social chaos) among the town's population.

For reasons of linguistic preservation as well as cultural authenticity and sensitivity, the seven narratives were presented both in English and Hopi in the original 1993 hardcover edition. To make the book more affordable and accessible to a wider audience, the Hopi versions are omitted in this paper edition. The reissuing of these tales of village destruction and abandonment comes at a time when the history of the Puebloan societies of the ancient American Southwest is being radically revised, with the newly emerging image being "brutal, grim, and unpopular" (Lekson 1999:67). Ruth Benedict's (1959[1934]:79) utopian assessment of the Pueblos as an "Apollonian people" who abhorred all excess and violent behavior reflected the majority opinion held and propagated by social philosophers during much of the twentieth century. By extension, this view that native Pueblo Indians were paragons of peace who lived their lives in complete harmony with their environment was also attributed to the Anasazi, their prehistoric ancestors.

A first inroad into this academically conceived "Pax Anasaziana" of agriculturists innocent of violence and warfare was made, quite cautiously, by David Wilcox and Jonathan Haas (1994). Five years later, Stephen A. LeBlanc (1999) laid out, in much greater detail and with broadly based theoretical underpinnings, the framework of a rather different Southwest. According to him, the great Pueblo period, which lasted from the 10th through the 15th century, was one plagued by constant strife, raiding, and warring among its indigenous inhabitants. Indeed, he reaches the conclusion that warfare was "a driving force behind much cultural behavior" (LeBlanc 1999:307). This, in the eyes of Stephen Lekson, made the Ancient Southwesterners "much like other societies, including our own" (1999:68). Most recently, Polly Schaafsma (2000) has contributed to the demolishment of the "peaceful farmer" model of the Pueblos in her analysis of rock art and kiva murals of Arizona, Utah, and New Mexico. She convincingly demonstrates that a great deal of this prehistoric art contains imagery symbolically lodged in the ideology and cosmology of warfare.

This postulated climate of chronic violence and conflict is augmented by a growing body of archaeological evidence for cannibalistic practices among the ancient Anasazi. On the basis of this evidence, the case for cannibalism, argued primarily by Christy G. Turner and Jacqueline A. Turner (1999) but also independently proposed by Tim White (1992) and Shane Baker (1994), can no longer be categorically dismissed as part of human behavior in the prehistoric Southwest. Counter-arguments challenging the validity of a cannibalistic explanation for many of the mutilated bone assemblages are advanced, for example, by Andrew Darling (1999) and William Walker (1999). However, their suggested alternative explanations of "corpse pounding" (Darling 1999:735) following the execution of witches, or "bloody purges of black magic" (Walker 1999:52), only add to the gruesome picture.

Hopi Ruin Legends, characterized by Lekson as "Homeric tales of warfare and tragedy" (1999:71), confirms this revised assessment of the Anasazi past from a Hopi point of view. At the same time, these legends also belie the stereotypical interpretation of the Hopi tribal name as "peaceful." As I have shown elsewhere (Malotki 1991:45) and point out in the introduction to "The Annihilation of Awat'ovi" in this volume, this romantic notion, generated primarily by white America, is unjustified both on linguistic and historic grounds. While the Hopis view themselves as Hopiit (civilized ones), they too partake of the darker side of humanity. That they do once again illustrates the gulf that typically exists between our philosophical and religious ideals and actual behavior. Recognizing this universal truth will ultimately bring about a better understanding of the human condition and lead to the conclusion that we are all endowed with the same bundle of negative and positive traits that characterize *Homo sapiens sapiens.*

The actual destruction stories, constituting original, unexpurgated Hopi source materials, owe their existence to the remarkable memory of several individuals from Third Mesa and Second Mesa villages who were sincerely committed to seeing this portion of their cultural heritage preserved for posterity. Concerned about the accelerating loss of their native language and culture, they also volunteered the ethnographic information contained in the introductory chapters accompanying the tales. These introductory chapters provide general background information, analytic comments, and other pertinent observations designed to complement the reading of the legendary accounts. While not intended to be exhaustive interpretations of the legends, three of these chapters provide detailed discussions of major cultural topics: *powaqa* (witchcraft); *koyaanisqatsi* (social chaos); and Paalölöqangw (the Mythic Water Serpent).

Unfortunately, three of the four contributors to this book are already deceased. My greatest gratitude belongs to the late Michael Lomatuway'ma, my friend and research assistant of many years. In the early and mid-1980s, when I amassed the bulk of my Hopi oral literature corpus, he contributed extensively to this work. Hence, four of the seven legends preserved in this book are his. They relate to the end of Huk'ovi, Pivanhonkyapi, Sikyatki, and Awat'ovi.

Lorena Lomatuway'ma, Michael's wife and initiate of the Maraw society at Hotevilla, told "The Downfall of Qa'ötaqtipu." In addition, many of the ethnographic details in the introductory segments are hers. Both a sweeping command of her native language as well as an intimate knowledge of Hopi culture eminently qualified her to assist me in preparing this volume. Her enthusiastic sharing of linguistic and cultural insights to this book is acknowledged with great gratitude.

I am equally indebted to her late brother, Sidney Namingha Jr., who narrated the fate of Hisatsongoopavi (Ancient Shungopavi). He was greatly respected as a song poet, both in his native Hotevilla and in Shungopavi. He also recalled the song attributed to Pavayoykyasi, which allowed me to incorporate it into the "The Annihilation of Awat'ovi."

The events leading up to the demise of Hovi'itstuyqa, finally, were narrated by a man from Second Mesa, who preferred to have his name withheld. He was endowed with a near-encyclopedic familiarity with Hopi culture, and his death was a great loss not only for Hopi scholarship but for the Hopi community at large.

The English renderings of the legends as well as of the ethnographic passages in the introductory sections are all mine. They attempt to steer a middle course between too close and too free a translation. Once again, I need to credit Lorena Lomatuway'ma for all the help she rendered during the lengthy translation process undertaken several years after Michael's untimely death in 1987. For any errors or other shortcomings in the final English versions, however, I alone am accountable.

That the book *Hopi Ruin Legends* in 1993 finally became a reality was due to the efforts of a number of people. My foremost thanks must go to Eugene M. Hughes, president of Northern Arizona University, and Henry Hooper, associate vice-president for Academic Affairs, Research and Graduate Studies. Karl Webb, dean of the College of Arts and Science; Nicholas Meyerhofer, chair of the Department of Modern Languages; Ronald W. Langacker, professor of linguistics at the University of California, San Diego; and Kenneth C. Hill, editor-in-chief and director of the Hopi Dictionary Project at the University of Arizona, were enthusiastic in their endorsement of the manuscript. Ivan Sidney, at NAU the special assistant for Native American Programs, Office of the President, also strongly advocated publication of that book as a means of preserving both cultural heritage and the Hopi language. Each one of them deserves my sincere gratitude.

As always, my English prose greatly profited from the writing skills of my friend Ken Gary of San Diego. He provided an editorial facelift for the entire manuscript. Valuable editing suggestions were also thankfully accepted from Stefani Salkeld of San Diego for the English story versions and from Charles O. Rand and Claudette Piper for the introductory materials to the legends.

Finally, for the preparation of the typescript, I need to thank Louella Holter, associate editor at the NAU Ralph M. Bilby Research Center. Her care and skill in completing the task were most impressive.

NOTES

1. "Prophecy in Motion," *Report of the 3rd Annual Hopi Mental Health Conference* (Kykotsmovi AZ: Hopi Health Department, 1984), pp. 67, 68.

2. Emory Sekaquaptewa, personal communication, August 1991.

HOPI TALES OF DESTRUCTION

ONE

Hisatsongoopavi: Devastation by Earthquake

INTRODUCTION

This is the first published account of the legendary demise of Hisat-songoopavi (Old Shungopavi).[1] Originally, the village was simply named Songoopavi (Sand Grass Spring Place) after the adjacent spring, Songoopa. By attaching the epithet *hisat* (old, ancient) to the place-name, the narrator merely points to the fact that the ancestral village site on the eastern foothills of the mesa is not identical to the location of the present-day village of Shungopavi on top of one of the spurs of Second Mesa. Modern Shungopavi is one of the most populous Hopi communities and remains a stronghold of Hopi culture. No other Hopi village can boast an annual ceremonial cycle more intact. No other Hopi village replenishes its religious societies by inducting new initiates to the same degree.[2]

Historical as well as archaeological evidence indicates that the residents of Hisatsongoopavi moved to the top of the mesa in the late 17th century. Following the Pueblo Revolt of 1680 against the Spanish yoke, during which the people of Shungopavi razed the mission San Bartolomé and killed its resident priest Fray José de Trujillo,

> the Pueblos began to quarrel among themselves. The Apaches and other semi-nomads, noting the Pueblo dissensions and withdrawal of Spanish arms, spread fresh devastation over the land. No wonder then that the people of [Old] Shungopavi soon abandoned their mission village and built the one they occupy today high up on the mesa edge. [Holterman 1955:35]

Potsherds retrieved from the middens adjacent to the ancient mission are archaeological proof that during the period between 1629 and 1680, Old Shungopavi was clustered around the mission (Hargrave 1930:2).

While many of the Hopi potsherds from this time show distinct Spanish influence, others represent genuine Spanish Majolica ware. Among the sherds identified by Ross Montgomery as foreign imports while working at Awat'ovi with the Harvard Peabody Expedition, "one came from Valencia, four from Puebla, and two from China" (Holterman 1955:33).

From a study of sherds and other archaeological remains collected in the foothills of Second Mesa, Lyndon L. Hargrave posits the existence of two additional Old Shungopavis prior to 17th-century Mission Shungopavi: 13th- and 14th-century Shungopavi and 15th- and 16th-century Shungopavi (1930:3). He determines that the original habitation site was established "before 1250 A.D. and occupied until the early part of the 15th century," when the natives relocated closer to the spring Songoopa (1930:1). They were residing here when the Spanish arrived in Tusayan, the Spanish appellation for Hopiland. Whether Pedro de Tovar, who commanded a Spanish contingent from the Coronado expedition at Zuni, also visited Shungopavi after reaching Awat'ovi in 1540 is not recorded. The first documented Spanish sojourn at the pueblo took place on April 22 and 23, 1583, when the party of Antonio de Espejo arrived (Hammond and Rey 1929:101).

In 1896, when Jesse W. Fewkes attempted a first archaeological exploration of the ruins of Old Shungopavi, the remaining walls of the mission served as a sheep corral. After Fewkes excavated the extensive graveyards for two days, Nacihiptewa [Nasiheptiwa], the Shungopavi village leader, entreated him to halt the digging "on the ground that such work would blow away rain clouds and thus deprive them of rain for their farms. He likewise stated that disturbing the graves would incense Masauuh [Maasaw], the god of death, and kill the little children" (1896b:536). Fewkes yielded to the request and abandoned the project, convinced that "the necropolis of Old Cuñopavi [was] one of the richest in scientific treasures in Tusayan, and [would] some day yield to the student a wealth of material destined to throw a flood of light on Tusayan cults and customs in prehistoric and early historic times" (536). The artifacts removed during the two-day dig are housed today in the Field Columbian Museum in Chicago.

The mythic narrative recorded here features the deific Paalölöqangwt (Water Serpents) as the agents responsible for the ruin of Old Shungopavi. Endowed with supernatural powers, they are represented as anthropomorphized beast-gods who freely communicate with the village people. The legend thus contains elements typically associated with prehuman mythical times when all living beings, including the gods, freely intermingled.[3] Karl Luckert has coined the term "prehuman flux" for this state of affairs (1975:133). As powerful controllers of *paahu*, that is, all contained bodies of water such as springs, pools, lakes, rivers, and the oceans, the Water Serpents are dreaded as well as revered by the Hopis, as is evident from the following folk statement.

TEXT 1

The Water Serpent is so named because he lives in springs. He vomits up the water. As a result of this action a spring forms. So the water is the Serpent's vomit. This creature is both feared and respected by the Hopi. The Serpents are also at home in rivers and lakes.

While likened in his appearance to the rattlesnake, the mighty Serpent has no analogue in the real world. Portrayed with bulging eyes, dentate mouth, a cephalic projection, and greenish skin, the god is cast as a monster reminiscent of the dragon in the lore of European sagas and fairy tales.

TEXT 2

The Water Serpent is the master of the oceans. He is similar to a rattlesnake but is of gigantic proportions and greenish hue. His head is round with protruding eyes, and his mouth is studded with teeth. On top of his head he sports a horn that is bent backward. In addition, his head is crested with a bunch of ocher-stained feathers, similar to those worn by members of the Snake society, and a fan of eagle tail feathers. Around his neck hangs a necklace made entirely of seashells.

This combination of different attributes from various animals (mammalian horn, avian feathers, reptilian body) makes for a hybrid, composite creature, thereby emphasizing the greater-than-human powers of the Serpent deity. Overall, the deity represents one of the most powerful embodiments of fertility and fecundity in Hopi religious imagery. The vegetal fertility association of wells, the abode of the god, is obvious. Furthermore, the horn as an excrescence from the god's head is a widely diffused symbol of male sexual potency.[4] Finally, there is the phallic icon of the snake itself as a potent emblem of genital energy that fertilizes fields in the form of rain and thus produces life-sustaining crops.[5]

Curiously enough, it is the monster's furry skin that, in the eyes of the Hopi, gives the god the rather innocent-looking appearance of a cat.

TEXT 3

They say the Water Serpent looks exactly like a cat. Just like a cat he has ears and whiskers. In addition, he has woolly fur like a cat. Those who have seen a Water Serpent claim that a yellow Serpent lives in Hotevilla. For this reason yellow cats are at home there.

The Hopi belief that all springs are inhabited by Water Serpents, that is, receive their life-sustaining flow from the presence of the god Paalölöqangw, has two implications. First, new springs can be created by burying in the ground a *paa'u'uypi* (water-planting instrument) containing a Paalölöqangw specimen. An instance of such an act of spring generation occurs in the present tale when the shaman from Walpi removes one of the Serpents from Songoopa Well and transfers it to a new location near his home village. Conversely, withdrawal of the animal from its abode leads to the extinction of the spring. This belief is confirmed in the following anecdote that describes the theft of a Paalölöqangw and the ensuing consequences.

TEXT 4

Long ago, the Oraibi people had a spring. I guess, a flowing spring. It was down on the plain on the southeastern flank of the mesa at a place called Masqötvasa. One day, a man from Shungopavi found out about the spring and went to the place in search of it. He had a canteen with him when he found it. Upon placing a little Water Serpent into the vessel, he scooped water into it four times. Thereupon, he took it home and transplanted it to a location below the [present] village of Shungopavi. After digging a hole in the earth, he put the canteen inside. From that day on, he went there to check on it. Soon the area was saturated with moisture. So the man built a dike, behind which the water collected. He named the spring Songoopa, and from that time on the villagers of [Old] Shungopavi drew their water from it.

Two years later, the water hole at Masqötvasa dried up. And now the Shungopavi man fell ill. I guess he was full with the water from the spring, for he was all bloated up and had a big belly. By the time he was near his death, his entire body was wet with moisture. Now his eyes started bulging out and the flesh of his body took on the appearance of the Serpent's skin. I suppose the man had contracted the disease of Paalölöqangw. In this way he was punished for his theft and died.[6]

Because of his fundamental linkage with water, the Hopis implore Paalölöqangw for rain. This supplication is achieved by tying ingredients of his furry skin into prayer sticks made for the god's supplication.

TEXT 5

If anyone comes across a Water Serpent at a spring, that person will step up to him and rub his body, if one has the courage. The furry skin that adheres to the brave one's hand is then taken home. There it is used in fashioning pahos. As a rule, the rains come then.

The reptile's aquatic connection also explains why he is held as one of the totems of the Piikyas (immature corn) and Patki (parted water) clans.

TEXT 6

The Water Serpent is a powerful deity. That's why people pray to him for rain. Members of the Piikyas and Patki clans have him as a totem.

The Horned Serpent god of the Hopi pantheon readily brings to mind Quetzalcoatl, the famous Plumed Serpent of the ancient Mexicans of Teotihuacan.[7] The question that immediately arises at this point is whether the Hopi Paalölöqangw cult possibly represents a distant echo of any of the Middle American serpent religions. As far as Quetzalcoatl is concerned, Hamilton A. Tyler suggests that "at most the two gods were distantly related by belonging to the general family of snake gods" (1964:244). I tend to agree. Quetzalcoatl, a culture hero and bringer of civilization and learning, at one time became the most important religious personage in pre-Columbian Mexico. His cult, which was embraced by the Toltec ruler Topiltzin in the Tula of the 10th century, was a beneficent one that did not demand "to be fed frequently on the warm blood and still-beating hearts of human sacrificial victims" (Leonard 1967:59).

The Hopi Paalölöqangw, on the other hand, is notoriously associated with human sacrifice.[8] He cannot claim the aura of a culture hero either. It is the god's overt connection with human sacrifice, however, that makes him a plausible candidate for an offspring of a Maya-type Water Serpent. Luckert believes that Middle American Serpent religion reached the Hopi Indians "in at least two distinct waves. The first wave is still pulsating in the Snake dances of the Snake-clan tradition; the second wave has survived in the Feathered- or Horned-Water ceremonies of the Water and Maize clans" (1976:150). The Maya serpent cult was practiced, as Luckert shows, not only at the tops of the pyramids, but also at the famous cenote at Chichen Itzá, whose waters rose and fell with the Water Serpent's breathing and blowing (146). In addition to the thousands of sacrificial offerings, which include ceramics, jewelry, jade ornaments, copal incense, masks, bells, and other objects of gold and copper, the treasure level of the sinkhole has yielded many human skeletons. While Edward Thompson, who excavated the well for nearly seven years (1904–11), reported (in Willard 1926:114) "upward of ninety" detached skeletons, "the remains of possibly a thousand victims" were more recently uncovered in the archaeological exploration of "Expeditions Unlimited" (Ediger 1971:276). The skeletal materials were both male and female and seem to have comprised all age groups. The widely held assumption that only virgin maidens were sacrificed in the cenote must therefore be considered inaccurate.[9]

When Luckert referred to a connection between the Hopi Paalölöqangw ceremonies and the Mayan Serpent cult, this legend featuring the sacrifice of a beautiful virgin girl to the Serpent gods in the village well was still unrecorded and unpublished (1976:156–166). In my view, it further supports his theory about the Middle American origin of or influence on the Hopi cult.[10]

In addition to being the nurturing god of all the springs and pools across the land, the Hopi Paalölöqangw also has a dark side. He is believed to be the bringer of floods as well as the producer of earthquakes and landslides. In the present story, the sacrifice of the virgin girl is carried out to halt the destructive earth tremors triggered by the Serpent.[11] L. S. M. Curtin (1971) has recorded a folk episode from a Hopi Indian that, from all indications, features a witchcraft plot against the village of Shungopavi. The scheme involving an earthquake is set in motion through a sorceress who provokes the Water Serpent by immersing herself in the local village spring. In the Patki legend of Palatkwapi, a combination of flooding and shaking of the earth subsides with the immolation of a little boy and girl (Nequatewa 1967:85; Parsons 1926:185).[12] Text 7 illustrates the appeasement of such a flood-earthquake combination for the village of Oraibi.

TEXT 7

Long ago, I guess, there was a flood somewhere at Oraibi accompanied by an earthquake. In order to stop the disaster, the people decided to sacrifice the grown daughter of the village leader. For this purpose, they dressed her in the finest clothes.

Having done up her hair in butterfly whorls, they put a black woolen dress on her and placed a cape around her shoulders. Everything was new, nothing had been previously worn. Next, they fashioned prayer sticks that were placed on a wicker plaque. Thereupon, the girl's father took his daughter to the spring at noontime. Upon arrival there, he explained to her, if she were to be offered to the spring, both the flood and earthquake would stop. The girl agreed, without any protestations or sign of fear. As soon as the two stood at the edge of the spring, the Water Serpent emerged right in the center of the spring.

As the Serpent stood there at his full height, the father said to his daughter, "All right, go in now." With that, he placed the tray with the prayer sticks into her hands. Whereupon, she entered the spring. The moment she stepped in, the water began sloshing and whirling in spirals. The Serpent then vanished into the depths with the girl.

Now the village leader returned home again. True enough, it was not long before the earth stopped shaking. The people were now able to live again. Soon the flood waters receded, until all the water had dried up.

Soon thereafter, the Water Serpents too departed. There were none left in the spring. By accepting the sacrifice of the girl, they had committed a wrong. They left because of their own transgression. For this reason people say the water is no longer flowing there. It was the Serpents that had sinned by taking the girl under.

Apart from legendary sources, hardly anything is known about the practice and function of human sacrifice in prehistoric Hopi society. Fred Kabotie, in an interpretation of a Mimbres pottery design, intimates that in the past, under extreme conditions of drought and famine, a human life was considered a legitimate sacrifice to obligate the rain gods to send their life-sustaining moisture. According to him, this one-time custom is still reflected in the act of feeding *hooma* (sacred cornmeal), a substitute for the human offering, to the kachina gods when they arrive at a Hopi village to stage a rain dance:

> Drought has been one of the worst foes of the pueblo people since unknown time. Long duration of dry weather brings disaster to people of the Southwest. When Earth Mother is dried up for lack of water, famine takes its toll of men, women, and children. When the Rain Deities, the holders and keepers of one of the sources of life, fail to respond to prayers, it is felt that to obtain rain from them is worth more than any worldly possession, even more than human life. [Kabotie 1982:75–76]

Kabotie continues, "In the pantheon of the Kachinas of the Zuni and the Hopi peoples there is a certain class of Kachinas who, by their potent power to make rain, require a human sacrifice. The offering to the Rain Deities is interpreted in terms of the white corn meal" (75–76).

In this respect, the Hopi purpose of the human offering closely resembled that of the Mayan cenote ritual. As Alfred M. Tozzer has shown, the latter "was primarily a rite for rain" (1957:214). Thus, the human sacrifice functioned as the ultimate intercession for rain, that is, life-sustaining moisture.

A second important function of the human sacrifice, as can be gathered from Hopi oral traditions, seems to have been that of placating the fury of the water gods.[13] Furthermore, as the two following Hopi folk statements reveal, the act of human sacrifice could also be used as an incentive for the water god to do the very opposite, that is, to unleash his devastating powers. Once again, this scenario seems to be limited, as occurs so often in Hopi oral literature, to the socially aberrant manifestation of *koyaanisqatsi*, a way of life that is marked by corruption and turmoil.[14] This state of affairs always calls for the most drastic remedy in Hopi mythology. The evildoers responsible for *koyaanisqatsi* must be eradicated.

TEXT 8

Once in a while, a village leader somewhere becomes so disgusted with his children [the villagers], that he has to draw up a scheme against them. In order to purify their hearts, he usually resorts to sacrificing one of his own children. In return, the Water Serpent will shake the earth [causing an earthquake]. At other times, it will start raining without cessation. As the water fills the land, the village gets flooded. This is what people say.

TEXT 9

Occasionally, a village chief, upon realizing that his children [the villagers] are out of their senses, will plot something to their detriment. As a rule, he then sacrifices either his son or daughter. After making prayer feathers for either one of them, he places the offerings in a tray. Upon taking the victim to the spring, he tells it to enter the water. As soon as the victim has done so, the water starts whirling around. Then the Water Serpent pulls the victim under.

Destructive forces of an apocalyptic magnitude are expected to come to pass on the doomsday of the Hopi world. Again, the purification of evil Hopikind is carried out by the Water Serpents who are released by the avenging Pöqangw Brothers. Text 10 assigns the cleansing powers of devastation to one Serpent, Text 11 to two.[15]

TEXT 10

The tradition of some Hopis has it that the Water Serpent inhabits the oceans and that the two Pöqangw Brothers straddle him.[16] All three of them keep watchful eyes on the Hopi. It is said that if the Hopi ever reach the point of utter disintegration, the brothers will issue certain instructions to the Serpent. "All right," they will say, "that is enough!

You were instructed to turn this land over if ever these our children did not come to their senses." Since Old Spider Woman will also share this knowledge, all four of them will say, "Well then, it looks as if they're not going to heed our warnings. If they will not listen, then let it commence." Pöqangwhoya and Palöngawhoya, holding pahos in their hands, will break these now and cast them aside. Then they will direct the Water Serpent, "Come, it is your turn." Following this order, the Serpent who possesses enormous strength will start to writhe, causing the entire world to turn over and the land to be flung into the sea.[17]

TEXT 11

Two Water Serpents are holding the world in balance for us, one along the northwest side, the other along the southeast. On top of them sit the Pöqangw Brothers. If by the end of this world the people have not desisted in their evil ways, the brothers will let loose the Snakes. They will then stir, as a result of which, chaos and pandemonium will reign. Owing to the Serpent's movement, the waters of the ocean will start to boil, and the entire land will be shaken by earthquakes. The earth will then turn over, taking with it all mortals.

To avoid the god's wrath in the form of dreaded earthquakes, prayer sticks are constantly fashioned for him.

TEXT 12

The Hopi make pahos for the Water Serpent lest he become angry or irritated in any manner. Were this to happen, the Snake would cause earth tremors by moving his body.

As might be expected, a number of stringent *maqastutavo* (taboos) regulate Hopi conduct at springs. Contamination of the precious water source must be avoided. Hence, playing by or in a spring, including bathing and swimming, are strictly forbidden.

TEXT 13

The following taboo is addressed to children. When children are asked to get water, people say to them, "Don't horse around at the spring. Don't play in the water. Because the Water Serpent lives there. If you soil his water, he is bound to pull one of you under." Because this has happened in the past, we forbid our children to do these things. A child that does not obey contracts the disease of the Serpents and swells all over his body.

TEXT 14

It is also a taboo to enter a flowing spring. If someone does so and takes a bath, that person gets infected with the disease of the Water Serpent and swells up.

TEXT 15

One does not drink from a spring directly with the mouth [rather than using one's cupped hands], or one gets sucked in by the Water Serpent.

TEXT 16

Whoever swims in a flowing spring fills up with water. This happened to a little boy once. He was taken to the hospital, and they opened him up and drained the liquid from him. However, he got full of water again. For a while he was all right, but then his stomach started bloating again. The boy was drained several times, but his condition did not improve. In the end, he became completely dehydrated. This is what typically happens [to a transgressor of this taboo]. For this reason, people are warned not to swim in a spring.

Of all the taboos, the ones with the most dire consequences are those that prohibit behavior that might tempt the Serpent sexually. Thus, a strict dress code is supposed to prevent a woman from exposing her genitals to the god.[18] Any kind of flirting or love-making in or near a source of water is equally intolerable.

TEXT 17

They say that a woman who goes to a flowing spring for water must tuck her dress between her thighs prior to entering the spring. Or, she can wrap herself tightly into her shawl before she scoops out the water.

TEXT 18

A female who has intercourse at the spring bears a snake to the one who impregnates her.

TEXT 19

When a boy meets a girl, he must not be together with her at the spring. They are not to touch each other when there. For after the girl engages in intercourse and gets pregnant, she becomes filled with water. As a result, her stomach is tremendously bloated. Eventually it bursts, and the girl dies.

TEXT 20

One does not flirt with a person at the spring. The person who engages
in such an activity becomes desirable to the Water Serpent. The
Serpent carefully watches a person's behavior. Living in the spring,
he sees what two people do. Thus, when a boy reaches under a girl's
dress to feel her up, it is the Serpent that subsequently copulates with
the girl. It is as if he breathed on her, whereupon she gets saturated
with the water. A female so breathed upon gets impregnated by the
Serpent.

In addition to presiding over the waters of the earth, Paalölöqangw is also
attributed with powers of fecundity. Alexander M. Stephen characterizes
him as one who "nourishes the germs, supplies sap to those of vegetation,
and life blood to those of animals" (1940:102). This fertility aspect of the
god is acted out by the Hopi in a number of puppet dramas. In these
dramatizations, the god is portrayed not by a mask but by an effigy that
is manipulated like a marionette. Ceremonial Paalölöqangw performances
are staged in a variety of forms. The *Kuysiplölöqangw* (Water vessel snake)
features single serpent marionettes rising from water jars. Other, more
elaborate dramatizations are described as *Paalölöqangwt timu'yyungqam* (the
Water Serpents who have offspring) and *Paalölöqangwt naanaywaqam* (the
Water Serpents who are fighting). The manifold aspects of these theatrical
exhibitions have been reported in great detail in Fewkes and Stephen 1893
and Fewkes 1903 for First Mesa, and in Geertz and Lomatuway'ma 1987:217–
252 for Third Mesa.[19] Tyler suggests that the fertility mimetically invoked
in these Serpent dramas "seems to be that of the earth" (1964:246). The
Hopis believe that the performing Serpents are actually alive, as may be
gathered from Text 19.

TEXT 21

The Hopi also make the Water Serpent dance. In one performance,
the Serpent emerges from a water jar. This performance is very simple.
Another version, in which four Serpents are present, is more complex.
They say that the Serpents behave as if alive. This latter dramatization
follows exactly the pattern of the Powamuy ceremony and requires
a great many participants. Members of the Flute society are also
involved in this rite.

Text 22 shows that, once again, owing to the strong sexual symbolism
associated with the Snakes, a pregnant woman is not supposed to watch
any of these puppet dramas.

TEXT 22

When a woman is pregnant, she is not supposed to go see the Paalölöqangw performances. If she does, her child will get affected by the Serpent's power. As is well known, a fetus readily contracts disease. There's no doubt that this is true. Hence, women are barred from watching both types of puppet rituals, the one of the "Water vessel snake" and the one involving several Serpents.

Although the present myth casts the Water Serpents in the role of destructive agents, it is ultimately the villagers themselves who set the scenario of destruction in motion. In their overconfident efforts to change the lay of the land, they invoke powers they cannot control. As a result, the entire community suffers the punishment of the gods. To be sure, only the evil instigators of the scheme perish in the disaster, but the story also contains a prophetic warning for the present community of Shungopavi: If the ceremonies are not carried out properly, the fate of the village will be sealed when it is swallowed by the earth to the accompaniment of new cataclysmic earthquakes.

NOTES

1. In the spelling of village sites currently inhabited on the Hopi reservation I follow the conventional, if "distorted," orthographic practice. Thus, for example, Shungopavi will be used instead of Songoopavi, which would conform with the standardized writing system now available for the Hopi language. All uninhabited ruin sites, on the other hand, will be rendered in phonemically correct spelling. In accordance with this approach, Hopi place-names occurring in quoted passages will be accompanied by their appropriate spellings in square brackets.

2. At Shungopavi, the Popwamuyt, Leelent, Tsuutsu't, Mamrawt, and Lalkont (i.e., the Powamuy, Flute, Snake, Maraw, and Lakon society members) conduct initiations on a regular basis. The theft of the altar pieces representing the goddess Taalawtumsi in 1978, however, has brought a halt to the quintessential manhood initiation rites of the Wuwtsimt, Taatawkyam, Kwaakwant, and Aa'alt (i.e., members of the Wuwtsim, Singer, Agave, and Horn societies) (Shannon 1983:33).

3. In a story recorded by Alexander M. Stephen, a youth destined to be the first chief and father of the Hopi is endowed with a variety of secrets and skills by the gods (1929:55). Paalölöqangw, the Horned Water Serpent deity, entrusts him with the faculties of "where and how to dig for water."

4. According to Anne Ross, in Celtic iconography the deity Cernunnos (The

Horned One) was accompanied by a horned serpent, "his most consistent cult animal. The relationship between the serpent and sexuality is widely diffused; to endow the beast with the horns of a potent ram would be to create a highly apotropaic and fecund symbol" (cited in Rawson 1973:84).

5. Snakes, due to their skin-shedding ability, almost universally are linked with the power of healing, rejuvenation, and immortality. That the Hopis shared a similar belief is demonstrated in a folktale entitled "The Man Who Was Buried Alive." In this story the protagonist witnesses how one snake revives another (dead) one by means of magic herbs. The man then applies the same remedy to his deceased wife, with equally life-restoring results. He later becomes a famous medicine man, bringing people back to life just like the Greek savior-healer god Asklepios (Roman Aesculapius) (Gimbutas 1989:136).

6. For similar episodes, see Geertz and Lomatuway'ma 1987:428 and Titiev 1944:425–431.

7. "Plumed" or "Feathered Serpent" as a rendition for the Aztec term Quetzalcoatl is actually a misnomer. A more accurate translation would be "quetzal snake," for the name is composed of the Nahuatl elements *quetzalli*, a reference to the blue-green plumage of the exotic tropical bird, and *coatl*, a generic designation for "snake." In Maya, the concept of Quetzalcoatl appears rendered as Kukulcan.

8. Hopi mythology also contains Middle American memories of human sacrifices to the sun. Thus, in one episode of a hitherto unpublished version of the Hopi emergence myth that I recorded, Old Spider Woman suggests the use of fat from a ritually slain girl to keep the newly created sun spinning properly in the sky. The Aztec belief that life flows from death and that people were created to nourish the sun and earth with their blood and hearts is encountered here with the twist that fat rather than blood of the sacrificial victim ensures the motion, that is, the life, of the sun (González Torres 1985:132). Unlike the Mexican sun cult, however, which demanded the ongoing practice of human sacrifice, Hopi mythology guarantees the continual rotation of the sun by the natural death of mortals, not by the unnatural death of human sacrificial victims. The key passage from the episode illustrating this scenario is cited in full below:

So they grabbed the girl and killed her with their own hands. Old Spider Woman, in her skillful way, somehow applied the girl's fat to the sun. As a result, the sun began to spin again and it became daylight once more. This time, the sun did not stop its motion and reached a point high in the sky.

Thereupon Old Spider Woman said, "All right, it will have to be this way now. The fat of the Hopi will ensure that the sun keeps spinning. Then it will shine its light for you. Therefore, whenever a Hopi dies, the sun will grease itself from the fat of the deceased. In this fashion it will maintain its rotation. This is the reason the sun desires the fat of everybody. Thus, as long as a Hopi dies, the sun will provide its light from the dead person's fat."

The people declared their agreement and said to the old woman, "Very well, it will indeed be this way now. We'll inform all the Hopi who are here about this. And truly, when someone dies, his body will not disappear. Its grease will keep the sun turning, and for this reason a person will have to end his life. So don't be sad when someone passes away, for through his death he keeps the sun spinning for us," the leader explained to his people.

This is why a Hopi must die. For it is because of his death that the sun can travel. This is how things were decided after the people emerged from the underworld. And this is the reason we Hopi have the sun.

9. The fact that many of the skeletal remains retrieved from the well by "Expeditions Unlimited" belonged to children suggested to the members of the team "that the Mayas were not the intellectual pacifists they were once made out to be and that under Toltec domination they developed a child-slaughtering cult to rival the bloodthirst of most other native inhabitants of the Americas" (Ediger 1971:276).

10. There is ample archaeological evidence for a pre-Columbian Horned Serpent cult in the Southwest. This prehistoric evidence, in the form of petroglyphic and pictographic iconography, is especially widespread in Arizona and New Mexico. For an imposing array of horned snake figures from north-central New Mexico, see Renaud 1938: plates 17 and 18. The most remarkable serpent pertroglyph among these, which is found at a site east of the ruins of Pueblo Blanco, is 18 feet long and 2 feet wide.

The Horned Serpent is not limited to the Hopi. He occurs in many of the Pueblo cultures of the Southwest. Thus, he is Kolowisi to the Zunis, and known as Avanyu to the Tewa Indians. In Keres mythology, he is Tsitsshrue or Gatoya, and the Jémez call him Wanakyudy'a (Parsons 1939:184).

11. Harold S. Colton and Edmund Nequatewa report that the spring, Songoopa, which gave the name to the village of Shungopavi, "went dry in the 1870s at the time of a landslide which caused a local earthquake" (1932:54). This local event may well have served as a powerful reinforcement of the Hopi belief in the Water Serpent's connection with earthquakes and landslides.

12. Elsie Clews Parsons reports that the flood and child sacrifice myth of the Patki clan is also "told at Zuni, and . . . derives from Pima-Papago" (1939, 2:970). Ruth M. Underhill provides ethnographic information on a Papago shrine "where it is said that four children were sacrificed in ancient times to stop a flood" (1979:141–146).

13. Interestingly, France V. Scholes and Eleanor B. Adams also mention "relief from hurricanes" as a reason for human sacrifice in the cenote (cited in Tozzer 1957:202).

14. For a detailed discussion of the parameters of this ancient Hopi concept, see the introductory remarks to "The Destruction of Pivanhonkyapi" (chapter 3, this volume).

15. In a folktale recorded by Wilson D. Wallis, which alludes to the same context, Paalölöqangw is portrayed as one that "has two heads facing different ways in almost opposite directions" (1936:12). This may explain the dichotomy in the two versions that I recorded, featuring either one or two Serpents on the "last day."

16. Philip Rawson points out that "in some versions of ancient pre-Classical Mediterranean myth, Okeanos, the immense belt of water said to encircle and bind the world together, was conceived as a vast serpent with human head and horns. This is clearly a transposition onto the cosmic scale of our inner image of the liquid psyche, source of all vitality and fertility" (1973:51).

17. Nequatewa alludes to the same scenario of the world turning over:

Through pools of water and lakes the great Serpents are watching the doings of all people, waiting for the time to come to turn this body of land over and cause earthquake, when the people do wrong, go fighting among themselves. But the two Pukong-ho-yat [Pöqangwhoyat] (the little war gods) who have compassion and sympathy for us all are holding them down so the earthquake may not come to wipe life off this earth. [1936:124]

18. Nequatewa implies that even accidental exposure must be avoided: "Every pool of water or lake, to them [i.e., the Water Serpents] are like skylights in our houses. Through these waters they are always looking upward. Therefore, a Hopi never dares to step across a pool of water. The women are especially cautious because of this idea as they do not protect themselves like the men" (1936:124).

19. Geertz's summary stands out in that the Hopi source materials are fully cited in the vernacular (Geertz and Lomatuway'ma 1987:295–303).

The Legend

Aliksa'i. People were living at Shungopavi, but not in the village currently known by this name. Rather, they were living in the ancient village below this location. Northwest of and a little bit above this community a spring was situated whose name was Songoopa. It was flowing with an abundance of water.

The leaders residing in the village of Shungopavi, however, were facing one problem that constantly occupied their thoughts. The sloping land in their vicinity was no good for farming. There was no place to plant the crops with which they could sustain themselves. To be sure, there was land to the southeast and the southwest, but it was too remote from the village. On several occasions when the men and young boys went there, enemies approached their village and took some of the people captive. For this reason, the leaders wanted to create some farmlands nearby. This was the problem they frequently pondered.

At the spring itself there was life, too. Apparently, some very powerful beings had made their home there. These beings were Water Serpents that had their own way of life. Wherever a spring exists, these creatures can be found. It is due to the Serpents disgorging water that a well springs up from the ground. In this way they supply water for all other living things. They possess the knowledge of providing moisture at any location. And because they were responsible for the flow of the spring there, the leaders of Shungopavi tried to persuade the Serpents to do something for them. They were hoping that the Serpents would enlarge the spring to the point where large masses of water would spill down the slopes in that area.

At first not all of the leaders were in favor of this request. But some of the more obstinate ones persisted and changed the minds of the others. When at long last the Shungopavis all agreed, the village chief and the heads of the different ceremonial societies met at the home of the village chief. With all of them now sharing the same intentions, they were determined to carry out their goal. "Let us begin at once so it won't be too long before the Serpents make the fields for us on which we can plant." The leaders were unanimous in this decision.

"Very well," the village chief said, "let's go fetch some of the necessary things." With that, everybody left the chief's house. Upon returning with the materials required to fashion prayer feathers, they first cut the prayer sticks and then proceeded to actually make the paho. Apparently, some of these Shungopavi leaders were endowed with great powers, for they were familiar with the very type of prayer feathers used by the Water Serpents to produce the flow of the water. Thus, they created exact duplicates of those used by the Serpents. This task completed, the leaders ritually smoked over the trayful of prayer feathers. Whatever wish a person had, he released by blowing the inhaled smoke on the feathers. The men literally blew their desires on them. Finally, before them was a great mound of prayer sticks and prayer feathers.

Next, a person had to be found for the special mission. Everyone knew that the person in question would need to be a member of the Flute society. He would take the prayer items to the spring and, at the same time, inform the Serpents of the men's desires. Presently the leaders found the right person. He consented to their wishes and said, "All right, I'll take your things there for you. I already have someone in mind who can accompany me."

"Yes, indeed, someone should go with you," they agreed.

The two who were to go on the mission now went to fetch their kilts, the type that has no embroidery. Upon their return, they took off the clothes they were wearing and put on the costumes they had brought. Next, they each tied into their hair a plume, symbolizing a cloud, which had also been prepared by the leaders. Then they gathered up the tray of prayer feathers and went out.

They proceeded to Songoopa Spring, and, upon their arrival, one of the men entered the spring. Evidently, he was expected to enter it alone, because his companion waited outside the water. The man entering the spring was the one who swims in it during the Flute ceremony. For this reason the leaders had appointed him to carry out this task. He was familiar with the path into the water, and he now went in along this route. He was chanting a song as he did so. When he reached the entrance of the Serpents' home, he made his way in with the tray of feathers in his arms.

Sure enough, after entering he noticed that there were people living inside, Serpent people. Their number was enormous. The place was heavily populated. These Serpent people possessed the same human form as we, but in addition they had scaly skins that were hanging on a beam attached to the ceiling by ropes. By way of greeting, the Flute member from Shungopavi said, "How are my fathers living?"

The Serpent chief was a man just like us, but quite dark complected. "We live in peace," he replied. "Well, be seated, stranger."

"Yes, we who live southeast of here have come to seek your help. We want you to level the slope that runs along here for us. If you topple the cliff at the top, the earth will become level and we can plant on that ground. That's our plan, thus all these prayer feathers were made for you, and we were sent to deliver them," the man explained.

The Serpent chief just sat there. "Is that so?" he replied. "Hand them over to me," he instructed the Flute man.

Until then, the Flute man had been standing next to the entrance ladder. He now approached the Serpent chief, who took the tray, carried it to a spot where the light was better, and looked it over. After carefully inspecting the gifts he said, "Good, very well." Whereupon, he placed the tray at his feet and smoked over it. When done with this rite, he proclaimed, "All right, we'll give it a try."

With that, he picked up the tray and proceeded to the northwest of the abode where the Serpents' altar was situated. This he adorned by inserting the pahos in it. Since things need to be renewed at some point in time, and the pieces on the altar were quite dilapidated, he was elated that they had received these prayer items. And so the Serpents refurbished their altar there. Sure enough, some of the men who had participated in producing the pahos had been endowed with great powers, for the new altar offerings were exact replicas of the old ones. When all were set out along the altar, the chief handed the Flute member back his tray. Then he gave his word that what the people of Shungopavi desired would become a reality.

The Flute man, who had been assigned this task, had been required to chant a certain song upon entering the spring. But, apparently, at some point within the song he had made an error and had not recited the correct words, because now he was unable to leave. Had he sung the song accurately, he would have been able to do so. Meanwhile, the man who had escorted him was awaiting his return to the surface. But he failed to appear. Quite a bit of time had already passed, so when the Flute man did not emerge from the spring, his escort returned to the village to inform the others. He also went to fetch a few members of the Blue Flute society. After reporting this turn of events at the village, he and the Blue Flute initiates headed back to the spring, where they gathered, playing their flutes and chanting various songs in order to retrieve the missing man. But they did not succeed.

By now, the head of the Serpents had decked the altar with the prayer items he had received. Then all those of high rank who had a place at the altar stepped up to it and sat down next to it. Since they had given their word to help the villagers, they now began to pray for this undertaking. While the priests were performing the ritual, the other Serpents began writhing. As a result, the water in the spring above them started to slosh about, and the ground began to shake. The quake grew in intensity. Soon a portion of the cliff top looming above developed a crack. Finally, it crashed down. At this time, only individual boulders were tumbling down. The Blue Flute society members had not gotten the man to emerge from the spring. As the ground trembled more and more violently, they panicked and fled back to the village. They had, of course, not succeeded in getting the man back out of the spring. It was the intention of the Serpents to make him one of theirs. Therefore, they had purposely restrained him. So the Shungopavis had lost the first man that had entered the spring. Apparently, he had been transformed into a Water Serpent.

The Serpents, meanwhile, were wriggling a bit more, and the earth shook with even greater intensity. The cliff walls along the northeast side now really began cascading down. At the village of Shungopavi, too, the homes of the people started to shake and to collapse. The slopes near the spring still had not formed the desired fields, yet the earth was rocking violently. The cliffs on this side just kept crashing down. While all this was going on, the point along the southeast side of the mesa developed a fissure, which eventually led to that whole cliff sliding downward, too.

Whenever a cliff came tumbling down, the entire mass would land in one huge piece at the bottom. In no way was the ground toward the east side becoming level. Each rock pillar came rolling down in its entirety. This had not been the intention of those in favor of this undertaking. The people of Shungopavi themselves could not stand the earth tremors anymore. They were so frightened by now that they began to abandon the village. Everything was chaos and pandemonium.

Some of the Shungopavis sent word of the disaster to the people of Mishongnovi. They informed them that their own village leaders had initiated this occurrence and that, as a result, the earth was quaking and the cliff walls were breaking away from the mesa. The schemers of this were still in the house where everything had begun, when a man rushed inside. Apparently, he was the chief of the Mishongnovis. "Why did you plan such a thing?" he exclaimed harshly. There was really nothing that he could do to them, yet he still scolded them.

All this time the catastrophe continued. The entire earth kept on trembling. Whenever a cliff cracked, it would crash down. Things could not go on in this manner. The people of Shungopavi were scared, so they sent a messenger to the village of Walpi. There he was to fetch a shaman who had distinguished himself at his trade. The messenger informed the medicine man that he was needed immediately, and he brought him back to Shungopavi. He escorted him to the location where the Shungopavi leaders hatched all of their plans.

When the shaman arrived, he went in to the men and found them still huddled around their altar. Immediately he took out his crystal and peered through it at the chiefs. He saw that every one of them was evil. "What a wretched bunch you are!" he exclaimed. "You've committed a wrong against the people. You seem bent on destroying everyone. Why on earth did you plan such a thing? Every one of you is bad. You had no business doing this. You think you know it all. Really, you Shungopavis are full of vanity," he chastised them. "It was your desire to do a great feat and to experiment with something. You ought to know that you are not to do these things. This world is supposed to stay the way it was created. It does not behoove us to alter it in any way. Some of you must have known this. So why did you persuade the others to go along with you?" he scolded them. "All right, come with me," he commanded them. "If you are willing to do so, the situation can be remedied."

With that, he led them to a place where the earth was cracked and ordered them to step inside. The priests, however, refused. "All right, I want someone to sacrifice his daughter then. Otherwise this disaster won't subside. By coming up with this scheme you committed a great wrong. Therefore, one of you will have to make a sacrifice. The girl to be sacrificed must be one who has just reached adolescence. She must be pure and still be a virgin. You must bring the evil process you started to an end. Hurry and seek out this girl right away. I want you to get the most beautiful one you have."

So a few of the leaders ran into the village looking for such a girl. Since not many people had remained, they had a difficult time finding someone who fit the shaman's description. People had fled in every direction. Finally, they came across a house that was still standing and went inside. It was inhabited by a couple who, by coincidence, had a daughter with the characteristics they were looking for: the girl was adolescent, very beautiful, and her skin was quite light.

The men were going to take her, but her parents did not want to give her up. So the priests explained, "We must give her to the Serpents. That's the only way the spring will calm down. Otherwise, we will all perish."

The girl's parents really treasured their child, but in the end they consented to give her up. Her mother fixed her hair in the fashion that becomes a young unmarried girl. Then she put a strand of beautiful beads about her neck and dressed her attractively, putting a maiden's cape around her shoulders.

When the men brought her to the meeting place, the shaman said to her, "All right, it will have to be you. You'll have to be the one. We must bribe the Serpents with a girl of your qualities. The cliff walls are splitting off more and more."

The houses within the village continued to collapse. The quake had already claimed a number of lives. Each time a cliff came crashing down on a person, it crushed him to death. People by now were clambering to the mesa top and fleeing northward.

Immediately the leaders fell to fashioning more prayer feathers that they would exchange, along with the girl, for their lives. Once again they made a large quantity, which they heaped on a tray and ritually smoked over. Meanwhile, the sloshing of the water at the spring was becoming ever more violent. Finally, the smoking was completed. The shaman from Walpi kept a watchful eye on the men, and when they were done with their task, he said to them, "All right, hand the pahos over to me. We'll be leaving now." Someone placed them in his outstretched arms. "Let's go," he urged the young woman.

After ushering the girl outside, he led her to the spring. As the two were approaching it from the southeast, they could see the waves on top of the water. Every so often they simply rose up. As this was happening, he said to the girl, "Don't be afraid. Just follow me. We'll walk right in."

When they had reached the spring, the shaman made his way into the water, and the girl stepped in right behind him. Once inside, he addressed the Serpent chief without delay. "How terrible!" he exclaimed. "Why did you grant the desires of those evil priests? This quake is now approaching our village to the northeast. I want you to stop it. Get away from that altar," he ordered them. "You cannot grant the desires of the evil leaders while having all the people entrusted to your care. You've known from way, way back that you must not fulfill just any old wish. That was not what you were instructed to do, especially since you are powerful beings. Your sort lives within the springs all over the land," he said to the Serpent chief. "Now, I've come bearing these offerings. If you want this to happen on your own initiative, fine. But you shouldn't do things by the will of those who are evil," the shaman continued. "You knew about this all along. So why did you meet their wishes and accept pahos from them? Here!" With that, he handed the chief the trayful of prayer feathers.

The Serpent chief took the gift from the shaman and carefully looked it over. "If you do not accept this offering, you will die," the shaman warned. "The water here will simply dry up. I take it you don't want anyone to benefit from this spring anymore, for you yielded to these evil desires. So I urge you to take this gift from me. You can also have this girl I brought with me. You have disrupted life here, but because it was their desire, they must offer to you a girl who is still pure. This is the only way they will save their lives," he explained to them.

The Serpent chief replied, "Very well, I'll accept these prayer offerings."

"That's right, take them. Remove the others from the altar, for those were made with evil intentions," the shaman instructed him. "So you who are seated there by the altar move aside," he commanded. The Serpents did as bidden and moved away from the sacred place.

No sooner had they left the altar than the Serpent leader removed the present prayer sticks and feathers from the altar and discarded them below the last rung of the ladder. In their place he set up the ones he had just received. When the Serpent chief finished this task, the shaman said to him, "All right, now take this one," pointing to the girl, whom he had descend to the lower portion of the kiva. There he bade her have a seat northwest of the fire pit. "Sit here," he told her. "You will now remain here with the Serpents. It will be to your merit if not all the Hopis perish. As soon as the evil ones are gone, this episode will be over. This is the only time this will happen. The inhabitants of this spring are not ordinary beings. They are quite powerful, so what is going on above cannot be stopped by prayer feathers alone. For this reason, we had no other choice but to sacrifice you to them. Strive that your life be a long one. Because you have done what no one has done before, the people will remember you and bring their pahos to you. Also, you shall know this: from today and into the future, when two people are having intercourse in the vicinity of a spring, it will be as if the man is having sex with you. The woman will then become impregnated with water, instead of a child, and will die as a result," the shaman explained to the girl. "And you I am going to take along with me," he said, pointing to the leader of the Serpents.

The earthquake now ceased, and from that time on the girl resided there along with the Water Serpents.

Ushering the leader of the Serpents out, the shaman then emerged from the spring. He went in a northeasterly direction and from there north along the northwest side of Walpi. Upon reaching Wipho, he placed the Serpent inside a hole, which he had selected for this purpose. "All right, in this hole here I want you to create a field for us that slopes downward. Make a planting site where the people of Walpi can produce crops. On that new field we will plant and grow whatever we need to sustain our children and ourselves," he commanded him. "And those evil ones in the southwest, whenever they meet their fate, will no longer be on this earth. In this way they will all die," he proclaimed. "And after I have brought you our prayer items, you will use them to bring forth a spring from which the Walpi people can benefit. You will now reside here," he concluded.

"Very well," the Serpent replied. "I will certainly do that. I readily admit I did wrong. I granted the wishes of evil ones and, as a result, almost ruined all of your lives," he confessed.

"Yes, that's the way it is," said the shaman. "As I assured you, I will bring what prayer feathers and prayer things I have."

"Good enough," the Serpent chief answered.

In this manner the shaman found a home for the Serpent. Having placed him inside the hole, he returned to Walpi where he got out his feather box and set to work on the prayer items. While carrying out his task, he concentrated on the desire for life to be good. This done, he piled the prayer feathers on a tray and smoked over them. Once more, while emitting the smoke from his mouth, he instilled in them all his good intentions. When the entire ritual was finally concluded, he took the pahos to the Serpent. "Here, these are for you," he said, upon entering the Serpent's abode.

The Serpent accepted the offering. After looking it over, he said, "This is the way it should be. I can see you worked on this with the wish that life be good."

"That's right," the shaman replied. "But remember, if you do not fulfill my wishes now and go back on your words, you will no longer live."

"Don't worry, I will do what I promised."

And thus the Water Serpent came to live in this place. A year had barely passed when suddenly there appeared some moisture at the site. Soon water began to flow until, in the end, a large stream of water spewed forth. To be sure, the Serpent had first been placed at Songoopa Spring with instructions to produce water there. But because of his failure to properly adhere to these instructions, he was transferred to this site where he produced a spring for the inhabitants of Walpi; and this time, he did it in the correct manner.

From that day on the Walpi people were planting at Wipho. To this time they are still planting there. Meanwhile, those leaders at Shungopavi who had not succeeded with their plan began to die off until no one remained. This is how the destruction of the village of Old Shungopavi came about. Only those few who fled to the mesa top survived. Also among them were the parents of the girl who was sacrificed. The few survivors established a small settlement on top of the mesa, which in time increased in population.

This chain of events accounts for the fault in the present community of Shungopavi. If ever these events should recur, this fault will split open and destroy the village. It is said that if the rituals are not being carried out properly, Shungopavi in its entirety will sink into the ground. The time for this prediction is now at hand. That's why the cliff walls are falling down along the mesa rim of Shungopavi. The process has already started. Only recently a rock pillar toppled over at the southeastern side. South of where the community meeting house was erected is a dried-up dam, along which the fault also runs. Not too long ago a cavity appeared in the dam. Water flowing in is draining into this hole. Where it is draining, no one knows. The children have been throwing all sorts of things into it and finally filled it up. Prophecy has it that all of Shungopavi will still disappear in the crack. And here the story ends.

TWO

The Downfall of Qa'ötaqtipu

INTRODUCTION

The ruin of Qa'ötaqtipu is said to lie somewhere northeast of the Third Mesa village of Bacavi. None of the Hopis I consulted were able to pinpoint its location more accurately since they personally had never visited the site. One clue that seems to lend credence to its geographic placement in the vicinity of Bacavi is the fact that Matsonpi, about a mile northwest of Bacavi, is portrayed in the story as a neighboring settlement of Qa'ötaqtipu. Matsonpi's location, a little mound badly ravaged by pothunters, approximately three-quarters of a mile north of the center of Hotevilla, just below the mesa spur on which Hotevilla is situated, is well known. Its name is humorously interpreted as "Hand-kissing Place." This interpretation, based on the elements *ma* (hand) and *tsoonanta* (to kiss), is linguistically not tenable, however. Nor is a more serious attempt to inject meaning into the place-name. By relating *ma* (hand) to *maqtö* (paw) and *tson* to *tsoona* (to suck), the place-name is said to recall the ancient Hopi custom of dipping a rabbit's foot into salt water and sucking on it during a meal.

Evidently, Qa'ötaqtipu, which translates as "Burnt Corn," could not have been the name originally assigned to the village by its founders. It probably came about when, at a later time, Hopis discovered some charred corncobs there. This discovery may also have led to the assumption that the village was destroyed by fire and inspired the present mytho-historic account.

To my knowledge, neither Qa'ötaqtipu nor Matsonpi has ever been investigated archaeologically, or if they have, the results have not been published. From a cursory sampling of the ceramics scattered around the site, however, there can be no doubt that the village was abandoned long before the coming of the Spaniards in the 16th century. Since Matsonpi existed contemporaneously with Qa'ötaqtipu and received some of its survivors, one can assume that Qa'ötaqtipu was destroyed before the demise of Matsonpi.

The tale of the destruction of Qa'ötaqtipu, recorded for the first time in *Hopi Ruin Legends*, is a typical product of Hopi narrative tradition. Designed to entertain, it contains the average mix of ancient customs, didactic lore, rivalry, violence, crime and punishment, and supernatural magic. Several of the legend's motifs are reminiscent of other destruction tales in this collection. Thus, when one of the two competitors in the life-and-death race unfairly resorts to extraordinary powers by changing into a dove, a similar episode in "The Demise of Sikyatki" comes to mind. The fire that, as an act of revenge, is to burn Matsonpi, is caused by the Yaayapontsa just as in the narrative describing the conflagration of Pivanhonkyapi. And while there the firestorm's threat to Oraibi is averted by the intercession of Old Spider Woman and her two grandsons, here the goddess alone comes to the rescue of the Matsonpis as the fire is about to consume their homes. The story line also contains an interesting twist in that Qa'ötaqtipu, and not Matsonpi, ultimately meets with disaster. It is Matsonpi that transforms the rivalry with Qa'ötaqtipu into a murderous affair and that would thus appear to be more deserving of punishment.

Initially, the friendly challenges between the two villages by means of *wawarkatsinam* (Runner kachinas) end more or less without any resentment on the part of the losers. The somewhat harsh behavior of Matsonpi's Hömsona and Qa'ötaqtipu's Tsiitsiklawqa balances each other out. However, when the Matsonpis challenge the Qa'ötaqtipus to a kickball race and lose, they react with a mixture of jealousy and envy, the symptomatic and almost predictable Hopi reaction in the given situation. This sentiment of jealousy, typically expressed by *qa naaniya* (they are filled with jealousy) in the Hopi original, is one of the most detrimental emotions that governs the Hopi character. As noted in the introductory remarks to "The Abandonment of Huk'ovi" (chapter 5), jealousy is readily attributed to the "bad Hopi" who may operate with witchcraft. Here, too, we immediately witness an escalation to this level of black magic, although the son of the Matsonpi chief is not referred to expressly as a *powaqa* (sorcerer). After the Matsonpis invite the Qa'ötaqtipus to the same kind of race for a second time, they reveal at the last moment that the ante has been upped. With death waiting for the loser, they clearly use supernatural means during the race to influence the outcome of the life-and-death competition in their favor.

When the Qa'ötaqtipu chief, justifiably, it would appear, plans revenge for the unprovoked killing of his nephew, the Matsonpi leader, full of remorse about the crime and concerned about the fate of his villagers, turns to Old Spider Woman for help. That this help is granted comes as a surprise. As a result, the firestorm designed to destroy Matsonpi skips over the village, only to turn on Qa'ötaqtipu itself and burn it to the ground.

THE LEGEND

Aliksa'i. People were settled throughout Hopi land. There were villages far and wide. A few Hopis were also living at Matsonpi and over at Qa'ötaqtipu. Long ago, each community had its own leader. The chief of the Matsonpis was married and had two children, a girl and a boy. The headman of Qa'ötaqtipu also had a wife, but this couple had only a daughter. The chief's sister, however, had a boy. So the chief had a nephew.

Way back then these ancient people were always doing something or other. They organized all kinds of kachina dances, and when the kachinas arrived, they would entertain the villagers. As a rule, they staged the dances during the day. They also held social dances. And every once in a while they arranged for special kickball races. Races were definitely part of their lives. For example, if the kachinas wanted to test the running endurance of boys and men, they came to challenge them to races. These were Runner kachinas such as the Kwitangöntaqa, Kwitanono'a, Tsilimoktaqa, Petosmoktaqa, Nahoykwurukni'ytaqa, and Tsi'rumtaqa. Also the Saytaqa, Tatsiipölölö, Tsilitosmoktaqa, Putskoomoktaqa, Hömsona, and Aykatsina. These and other Runner kachinas used to participate in these challenge races.

In those days of old during the month of Ösömuya, when the weather was not really warm yet, boys and men used to spend much of their time in the kivas. One day, the members of a kiva at Matsonpi were planning to dress up as Runner kachinas and go to Qa'ötaqtipu to challenge its people to races. Since everybody agreed with the idea, they let the residents of the other kivas know. They, too, were looking forward to the event and promised to join in.

From that time on they all practiced running. By the end of the seventh day they were all in excellent shape, so they decided to go the next day. The son of the chief, who was part of the contingent, had only been practicing for a short while but had become a formidable runner. No one ever surpassed him over a short distance. During practice runs, he usually was back at the village long before the other runners returned.

The following morning the runners breakfasted early. Thereupon they all assembled at one place and put on their kachina costumes. And since they were finished early, they took their time on the way to Qa'ötaqtipu. The sun was already past the midday mark when they reached their destination. Upon entering the village, they headed straight to the plaza. There they strutted around, striking commanding poses. Two Kooyemsi kachinas, who had accompanied the group, were hauling their presents around for them. When the villagers became aware of the Runner kachinas, news of their arrival spread quickly.

An elderly man who was the kachina chief came up to them. Long ago it was always him who took take care of the kachinas. That was his task. He said to the viewers by way of a greeting, "Are you walking about, strangers?"

Kooyemsi kachinas, of course, are in the habit of talking. For this reason they were along so that they could speak on behalf of the Runner kachinas. They answered in the affirmative. The kachina chief continued, "Well, you must be about with a purpose. Tell me what the reason for your coming is."

"Yes," replied the two Kooyemsi, "these here came to compete with your boys and men. We came to run and provide some entertainment for your people at the same time. That's why we are here. So let your strong runners come down from the rooftops and race against them."

"Very well," he consented. "All right then," he shouted up to the boys and men, who had gathered meanwhile. "Have confidence in yourselves and come on down from the roofs. You can run against these kachinas for these prizes. I'm glad they brought a great load."

At first, no one was willing to come down. Finally, one volunteered. He selected a Runner kachina and, at a given signal, the two raced off. The kachina failed to catch up with him, so one of the Kooyemsi who was in charge of the presents gave the runner a few. Now the others also started to descend to the plaza. They came up to the Runner kachinas and challenged them. Each time one of the kachinas ran with a villager and could not catch him, he lost and the villager was awarded some of the prizes. One of the kachinas was a Hömsona. He was an excellent runner, so good in fact that he caught all of his challengers. The moment he caught up with one, he grabbed him by his hair and cut a piece from it. When several of the Qa'ötaqtipu runners had suffered this fate, they became scared of the Hömsona. After all, they really treasured their hair. Not one of the Qa'ötaqtipu runners succeeded in beating him. The boy who was impersonating the Hömsona was of course the son of the Matsonpi chief.

After the races had gone on for a long time, the kachinas' presents were depleted, whereupon one of the Kooyemsi indicated that this was the end. The kachina chief said, "Very well, this will be it. You really provided us with great delight. So let me say farewell to you in the proper way, and then you return to your homes with happy hearts." With that he distributed pahos and sacred cornmeal among them, whereupon the Runner kachinas departed.

Upon arriving back at Matsonpi, everybody expressed his happiness. They all agreed that they had had a good time. Everybody shared with his friends how he had fared in the races. This is what the Matsonpis did there, and then life went on for them again.

About two years later the menfolk of Qa'ötaqtipu in turn expressed their intention to go to Matsonpi and have a running competition with its people. So they too began to prepare for the event and get in shape. Day after day they went running somewhere. The nephew of the chief also took part and became very good. Those who accompanied him no longer succeeded in keeping up with him. So with him as an excellent runner, they set a date on which they intended to go to Matsonpi.

From that day on the Qa'ötaqtipus lived in anticipation of the event. Eventually, the time for their departure arrived. Everybody put on his kachina costume, and then they headed out to Matsonpi. Arriving directly from the northeast, they let their cries ring out as they were moving along. The Matsonpi villagers heard them and were sharing the news with each other. Ahead of the arriving visitors, they headed to the plaza. When all the villagers were assembled there, the Runner kachinas made their entry. As they entered, they kept uttering their characteristic cries and strutted about in commanding poses.

The kachina chief walked up to them and asked them what they were doing. Again it was the Kooyemsi who declared that they had come to race with them, whereupon the kachina chief bade the men and boys to come down to the plaza from the roofs.

The menfolk complied and started to compete with the Runner kachinas. They won several races against them, but not once did anyone succeed in beating the Tuutsiitsiklawqa. Whenever he caught up with someone, he tore up the loser's clothes. He really dealt severely with each loser. This Runner kachina was, of course, the nephew of the Qa'ötaqtipu chief. He had dressed in the guise of the Tuutsiitsiklawqa.

After the two sides had raced with each other for a good while, the kachinas finally ran out of gifts and stopped. The kachina chief bade them farewell by bestowing pahos and cornmeal on them, and then the Runner kachinas departed.

Upon their leaving for home, the men and boys at Matsonpi were a little upset that the Tuutsiitsiklawqa had treated them so harshly. And since they knew for sure that the kachinas were from Qa'ötaqtipu, they decided to test their running skills in a kickball race. They started getting into shape, and when they felt pretty good, they thought it was time to inform the Qa'ötaqtipus about the day of the race. This time they sent a messenger, and this is how the news arrived at Qa'ötaqtipu. The one who delivered the message explained that if the runners from Qa'ötaqtipu came over to Matsonpi in four days, they could compete with them in a kickball race.

As soon as the message had arrived, the Qa'ötaqtipu crier chief broadcast it from the rooftop. All the good runners started practicing, and just by the deadline the Matsonpis had set they reached their top form. So they went over to Matsonpi.

The Matsonpis were clearly expecting them. They were all gathered on the northeast side of their village when the visitors arrived from that direction.

As soon as they were all assembled at one place, the Matsonpis described to them the course along which the race was going to take place. Running due northwest, they first would come to a wash. From there they would head southwest until they reached a single juniper tree, which was to be the turning point. Then they would return along the same course.

The Qa'ötaqtipus agreed, whereupon someone shouted, "Taa!" and the race was underway. Sure enough, they headed out in a northwesterly direction. Both groups were equally good and moving along, kicking their kicking stones at about the same pace. Soon they reached the wash, from where they continued in a southwesterly direction. Once again, the two groups were advancing at the same speed, kicking the stone nodule with the same skill. Whenever one group drew ahead, it did not take long before the other drew even and took the lead. In this fashion the rival groups kept passing each other.

Eventually, they reached the juniper tree in the southwest. They circled this, and moved back toward the village again. They did not arrive at the same time, however. The group from Qa'ötaqtipu was a little faster and the first to cross the line that the Matsonpis had drawn. When everybody was back, they assembled in one place and mutually expressed their gratitude.

This is how the men from Qa'ötaqtipu fared in the kickball race. As they returned home, however, it was clear to them that the Matsonpis were upset about losing the race. It was not hard to figure out what was on their minds. Sure enough, no sooner were the Runner kachinas from Qa'ötaqtipu back home than they had decided to challenge the Matsonpis anew. So it was not long before a new message from the Matsonpis came to them. This time it was planned that only two runners would compete, but the messenger did not mention this detail. The men from Qa'ötaqtipu consented to the invitation, and a date was set for some time in the not too distant future.

Once again everybody went to practice running. For some reason the nephew of the chief from Qa'ötaqtipu suspected something and decided not to quit running. Every morning and evening he practiced. He usually ran from his house in a southeasterly direction to an area where the land was flat. The son of the Matsonpi chief, on the other hand, only ran to a point northwest of his house. Eventually, they reached the date which the Matsonpis had set for the race. Once again the menfolk from Qa'ötaqtipu set out. As before, the two groups met northeast of Matsonpi.

When everyone had assembled, the men from Matsonpi revealed to the others that only two would compete against each other. These would be the nephew of the Qa'ötaqtipu chief and son of the Matsonpi chief. At stake would be life or death. Since the Qa'ötaqtipu chief had accompanied his group, he was compelled to agree to the proposition. "Is that so? Is this how it's going to be now? That's too bad, indeed. But we agreed to run with you, that's why we came. So we'll have to go along with these rules, whether we want to or not." This is what he replied.

The Matsonpis once again drew a line in the sand. Then they dug a hole into which the winner was to sever the loser's head. Finally, one of them thrust a knife into the ground by the line. That was to be used for cutting off the loser's head.

Now the two boys chosen to run against each other stood side by side at the starting line. They were, of course, the son of the Matsonpi chief and the nephew of the Qa'ötaqtipu chief. Someone shouted, "Taa!" and the two dashed off. They embarked on the same course that had earlier been used for the kicking stone race. So once more they ran in a northeasterly direction. Upon reaching the wash, they headed southwest. At this point the Matsonpi boy was ahead, but soon the other one caught up with him. Passing him, he said, "I'll take the lead now for a while," and sped on. After some time he disappeared over the horizon. Now the one following him stopped in his tracks. Having arrested his run, he changed himself into a white dove. Evidently, he possessed greater-than-human powers and now was going to race in the guise of the bird. His competitor was far gone, but flying in the form of the dove he was able to advance with tremendous speed. Soon he passed over his rival, without the latter being aware of it. Since he had no desire to show himself in this guise to the spectators, he landed before reaching them. He was far ahead of the boy from Qa'ötaqtipu. Then he changed back into his human shape. Under his own power he was now arriving. When he reached the finish line first, the people from Qa'ötaqtipu, poor things, became unhappy. Surely they would have to return home without the chief's nephew.

A good length of time later the boy from Qa'ötaqtipu also completed the race. Breathing heavily, he jumped over the line, where the Matsonpi boy was waiting for him with a knife in his hand. He could not believe his eyes, for surely he had overtaken the Matsonpi boy. After that the other had never caught up with him. But he did not want to complain. After all, they might all get into a fight and kill each other. This way they would only kill him. This is what he thought, and therefore he did not say anything.

The winner from Matsonpi now said to him, "All right, you must come here to me without any fuss. There's nothing you can do about this. This is what we agreed upon." The boy did not resist and followed the other to the hole in the ground. The Matsonpi now forced him to lie down, grabbed him by the hair, pulled his head back, and cut it off. The blood gushed out so profusely that the hole was nearly full. This is how the group from Qa'ötaqtipu lost the nephew of its chief. Overcome with sadness, the men returned home.

From that time life went on again. But the chief in Qa'ötaqtipu had no intention of letting things remain the way they were. He was determined to plan something to the peril of the Matsonpis. From that time on he lived only with this thought on his mind.

As the days went by, he suddenly remembered the Yaayapontsa. They had power over fire and wind. If he prayed to them, they might take revenge on the Matsonpis for him. Having decided to seek them out, he made prayer sticks for them. When he had finished the amount he was going to take to them, he carried the pahos to their abode. Upon his arrival, he did not see the Yaayapontsa, however. So he left the pahos outside their house and then prayed to them. If they should consent to his wish, they should pick up those prayer sticks, he told them there.

With that he returned home. Four days later he went back to the Yaayapontsa to see if they had accepted his offerings. When he arrived, he could not find anything where he had deposited the pahos. He thereby knew that they had looked favorably on his wish. So he returned home. He had of course not set a date when they were to carry out the revenge. He had declared that that would be up to them. Whenever they would see fit to do it, they could do it. His express desire, however, had been that they punish the Matsonpi with fire.

The Matsonpi chief, meanwhile, was full of remorse about the terrible deed. He knew full well that they had committed a crime for killing that boy merely because they were jealous of his racing capability. By not even trying to intercede, it was as if he had killed the boy himself. Now, after the fact, he was leery of the people of Qa'ötaqtipu. He was afraid that they might retaliate. They had lost that boy and would not just sit still. All he could think of now was when they would strike in revenge.

As the days went by, he got completely worn out with worrying. So one dark night he set out from his house. He went southwest and then a little northwest. There, somewhere, Old Spider Woman was at home with her two grandchildren. It was then that he decided to seek their assistance. Upon his arrival he told the old woman under what circumstances they had caused the death of that boy. He asked her if she could not possibly go to Qa'ötaqtipu and find out what they were scheming. Old Spider Woman, however, already knew that the chief there had initiated something to the peril of the Matsonpis. There was no need for her to check. So she said, "Yes, a terrible disaster has been set in motion for you. They intend to avenge themselves with fire."

"Is that so?" the Matsonpi chief exclaimed.

"Yes," replied Old Spider Woman.

The Matsonpi chief became most unhappy and asked if she could now arrange something so that they would not be harmed. And since the old woman has all the people as her grandchildren she said, "Don't worry, we'll help you. You won't burn to death." Right away she instructed him what to do. "I'll let you know when the day of the disaster comes. At that time I want you to have your crier chief announce to the people to come here to the northeast side of the butte around mid-morning. Tell them to hole up in the houses there. Then nothing will happen to them." These were Old Spider Woman's instructions. Thereupon the chief went home slightly relieved.

Finally, the day came. Directly from the southwest a fire ball was moving their way. Old Spider Woman now informed the chief at Matsonpi about this turn of events, adding that the danger was not immediate. The fire would not arrive before two days. But as it was moving toward them, it would constantly increase in strength.

Having been warned in this manner, the chief kept making prayer sticks. He knew he could not just ask Old Spider Woman and the two Pöqangw Brothers for help without any payment. Also, he was certain that she would not let them down. So he made prayer feathers for them. And since the old woman had also asked for two *taqvaho*, a special kind of prayer stick, he also fashioned those. When he was done, he took everything over to Old Spider Woman and her grandchildren. When he arrived with his offerings, the three expressed their joy about them. They were elated. Then the old woman explained how the crier chief was to make his announcement the next day, for that day the fire was bound to reach them. Upon handing over his prayer items, and having been informed about the coming events, the chief left for home again.

The next day the crier chief made his announcement first thing in the morning. As soon as the people heard the news, they ran off to the northeast, where they holed up. Meanwhile Old Spider Woman went to the southwest side of Matsonpi. There, a little to the southeast, she stuck the first *taqvaho* into the ground and spun a short piece of spider web around it. Then she hurried to a place in the northwest and, dragging her web along, planted the second *taqvaho* in the ground. Around this she wove her web too. Then she started weaving her web back and forth between the two stakes. After doing this several times, she was finished. She left everything the way it was and went home. This is how she helped the Matsonpis.

Not much later the big fire ball arrived. With great might it roared against the woven web, but failed to overcome it. As soon as the fire struck the web, it was hurled over it with great force, and some time later landed on the southeast side of Matsonpi. The people of Matsonpi could see how the flames jumped over them. The heat that radiated from them was terrible, but it set nothing on fire.

Upon falling back to the ground, the fire rolled straight on in a southeasterly direction. Since there was no barrier there to stop it, it simply continued on. Everything in its path fell prey to its flames.

Meanwhile the fire headed directly toward Qa'ötaqtipu, where no one was aware of it. Not before it was at their doorsteps did someone notice it. Immediately he alerted the others. Panic broke out. People did not know what to do first. With only a little bit of food in their arms, everyone ran for their lives. Some were dashing around in search of their children. It was an incredible scene. Somehow or other one person here, one there, managed to escape. Right behind them the firestorm reached their houses and engulfed everything in flames. Thus the revenge backfired. It fell back on the Qa'ötaqtipus and their village was burned. Matsonpi, on the other hand, was spared. The Qa'ötaqtipus had brought this disaster upon themselves through their own evil doings. After all, they had requested the Yaayapontsa to let the Matsonpis perish in a fire.

From village to village the Qa'ötaqtipu people, poor wretches, went looking for a place to live. They got scattered all over. Some moved all the way to the pueblos along the Rio Grande, whereas others sought refuge in Oraibi. Small contingents also went to Walpi, Shungopavi, and Huk'ovi. A few even moved into the vicinity of Matsonpi. The people there bore no animosity toward them and actually admitted them into their community. After all it was clearly they themselves who had committed a great wrong. Thus, some of the inhabitants of Qa'ötaqtipu settled there with the Matsonpis.

From that day on, Matsonpis and Qa'ötaqtipus lived there together. But for some reason the Qa'ötaqtipus did not enjoy their life there. Therefore, all of those who had moved there decided to leave Matsonpi again. One here, one there they would round up their children and set out in search of a new start at another village. In this manner the Qa'ötaqtipus became scattered over many settlements and found new roots for themselves. Their descendants probably still live there with the others. And here the story ends.

THREE

Pivanhonkyapi: Destruction by Fire

INTRODUCTION

The remains of the extinct Third Mesa village of Pivanhonkyapi lie some three and three-quarters miles northwest of Old Oraibi. Its location on a shelf some two hundred feet below the rim of a mesa that projects from Hotevilla is almost equidistant between the ruin of Huk'ovi to its east and Apoonivi, the highest point on the Hopi reservation, to its southwest.

The untranslatable name of the site, for which not even a folk-etymological interpretation exists among the Hopis, may, in its initial morpheme, relate to *pivani* (weasel). However, there is no linguistic evidence for this semantic linkage. Like its neighbor Huk'ovi to the east, Pivanhonkyapi has never been excavated. On the basis of potsherd types, among them Jeddito Black-on-orange and Jeddito Black-on-white "that do not seem to have been in use after 1300 A.D.," Harold S. Colton and Edmund Nequatewa speculate that the site was "occupied in the twelve hundreds" and abandoned before 1300 due to the great drought at the end of the 13th century (1932:54).

Ethnographically, Pivanhonkyapi has become famous for the *Saqtikive* (Ladder dance), which was once staged there according to Hopi legend.[1] The ceremony involved an acrobatic dance act of kachina impersonators on top of implanted pine trees. Several of the deep holes into which the poles were inserted are still visible at the cliff edge.

The mytho-historical chain of events leading up to the annihilation of the village is quite simple. Bored with the monotony of their everyday activities, the residents of Pivanhonkyapi introduce the new board game of *totolospi*.[2] The game catches on quickly. Before long, it becomes such a craze that the entire community is affected. Individual as well as communal responsibilities are neglected. Bent exclusively on fun and good times, people embrace what is commonly termed *kwangwa'ewqatsi* (lifestyle of pleasure). With gambling by both sexes soon leading to promiscuous sex, the uncontrollable situation reaches a climax when the village chief's wife, who is expected to be a model of virtue and decency, also succumbs to the game.

This chaotic state of affairs, marked by the total disintegration of all socially accepted standards and values, is referred to as *koyaanisqatsi* (corrupt life) in Hopi. Composed of the elements *koyaanis-*, which cannot occur in isolation, and *qatsi* (life/way of life), it represents the polar opposite of *suyanisqatsi*, which designates a "life of harmony and balance."

Since, in the eyes of the Hopi, *koyaanisqatsi* generally engulfs an entire community and constitutes a point of no return, only a new beginning can remedy the situation. To eradicate the evil and begin anew, tabula rasa must be created, which regularly implies the wholesale destruction of the corrupt community.

The socially untenable and unacceptable phenomenon of *koyaanisqatsi* is a frequent motif in Hopi oral literature. It figured as the prime factor in motivating the Hopi exodus from the underworld. Having gained wide currency as a result of Godfrey Reggio's movie, the abstract-philosophical concept of *koyaanisqatsi* comprises a wide range of symptomatic ingredients.[3] Most of these are spotlighted in a number of other Hopi terms that try to capture facets of its nature. Thus, *nukusqatsi* declares *koyaanisqatsi* as a "bad life," *nukpanqatsi* as "evil life," and *qahopqatsi* as "uncivilized life." *Tuskyapqatsi* as well as synonymous *honaqqatsi* (crazy life) decry the frenzy that is so characteristic of it. *Natsopqatsi* (intercourse life) focuses on the sexual license it demonstrates. *Kwangwa'ewqatsi*, as was already mentioned above, emphasizes the pleasure principle. Both *nangwu'yqatsi* (life of quarreling) and *qa naavaasqatsi* (life of mutual disrespect) point to the overall disharmony and noncaring that distinguish this mode of living. As *powaqqatsi* (life of sorcery), it focuses on the witchcraft practices and beliefs that are ever present during times of moral degeneration. *Naanaphin qatsi*, finally, says that "anything goes" in the haphazard order of this lifestyle.

Nor is *koyaanisqatsi* semantically a closed, rigid expression, applicable only to the behavioral excesses of legendary times. On the contrary, its content is open ended and flexible enough to absorb any new social aberration. Thus, when defined as *honaqqatsi* (life of drunkenness) today, it refers to the problems of alcoholism and substance abuse that also confront modern Hopi society.

The following folk statements are given as a sample of some of the ramifications of *koyaanisqatsi* in greater detail. To begin with, Text 23 presents an excerpt from a hitherto unpublished Hopi emergence myth in which the curse of *koyaanisqatsi* is described as an ever-escalating social disease.

TEXT 23

Aliksa'i. People were living somewhere down below. A long time ago they were living there, peacefully and free of troubles. It was paradise.

As they were living there in large numbers, they probably greatly increased in population. As the place became crowded, people tired of each other's company and showed no respect for one another anymore. Neither things nor people were respected. They should have known what the good life is like, but instead, they spoke disrespectfully to one another. In many ways, they looked unfavorably upon each other. They also mistreated each other.

Slowly, people were getting out of control. No one had much regard for one another, whether neighbor or stranger. The women began to leave their homes and abandon their husbands and children, only to join the dancers in the kiva and not to return home. They neither cooked nor cleaned house. The married men and the boys did the same. They were chasing around after the girls. While the women each went with several men, the men had several women. In this fashion they were committing adultery. A man had just slept with a woman and already, the next day, he was consorting with someone else. Hence, life was in total disarray. The people were living a life of madness. Evil ways reigned, and people were divided into factions. The same kind of life we're also living today. We should be united as one people, but no one gets along with the other.

For all these reasons, the people of the underworld did not come to their senses. An evil way of life had set in. Thus, with all their bad intentions, they became totally corrupt. Upon reaching this state of *koyaanisqatsi*, the leaders got together and pondered what they could possibly do in order to move to another location.

One reason frequently cited by the Hopi for the development of *koyaanisqatsi* is the breakdown of the native religion, especially as it crystallizes around the institution of the *wiimi* (secret society).

TEXT 24

It is said that because the initiates no longer respect their religious societies, they do not assemble anymore. Prayer sticks are no longer fashioned. The knowledge of how to make them is gone.

Instead of devoting their energies to their religious obligations, people pursue the sweet life. As a result, men in particular neglect their farming duties, which results in hunger and famine.

TEXT 25

When *koyaanisqatsi* corrupts people, they no longer pay attention to their religion. Instead, they keep drifting into a life of greater pleasure. This is what happened in the underworld when they abandoned their religious societies.

When *koyaanisqatsi* takes place, people are only interested in pleasure. The men don't have the desire to cultivate their fields and so don't plant anymore. As there is nothing to harvest, people begin to experience a famine. This is not supposed to happen, so long ago they used to tell us that we should remind each other of these things.

The pursuit of *kwangwa'ewpi* (pleasure) often begins with gambling, as is the case in the present story, or with dancing for the sake of fun, as is explained in Text 26. Unchecked gambling and dancing, as soon as both sexes are involved, typically leads to sexual indulgence and immorality, as is pointed out in Text 27.

TEXT 26

When the people reached the state of *koyaanisqatsi*, they started dancing social dances. All night and day they kept dancing. This dancing served no other purpose than enjoyment.

TEXT 27

After reaching the state of *koyaanisqatsi*, people don't return to their senses. The only thing on their minds is how they can indulge in sex. Deflowering all the unmarried women, they even sleep with the old women.

Thus, when a woman, poor thing, goes to relieve herself at the toilet and refuse area, a man will approach her, seize her, and, after a brief struggle with her, rape her. When a woman goes after water, the same thing happens. Men, whether unmarried or married, grab the woman and rape her.

In spite of the teachings and warnings of the elders, Hopi society today is engulfed anew in *koyaanisqatsi*. This is painfully realized by many Hopi and sadly deplored, as may be gathered from the next two statements:

TEXT 28

When things tip over into the state of *koyaanisqatsi*, everything is wrong. All things are mixed up, and life is bad. The Hopis always say, "*Koyaanisqatsi* reigns when things are done poorly and improperly. This situation leads people to bad ends. It devours them and destroys them." This has been going on since long ago. That is why we were sheltered in this life here on earth. But we're living the same life all over again. Once more *koyaanisqatsi* has reared its ugly head.

TEXT 29

Today, we're more or less living a life of *koyaanisqatsi* again. We have no respect for each other and live according to our own inclinations. The old people have been trying to open our eyes to the right ways, but we don't feel like going by their words and talk back to them improperly.

A great deal of the blame for *koyaanisqatsi* is put on the introduction of alcohol and drugs by white society.

TEXT 30

We're experiencing *koyaanisqatsi* now. Everyone is drunk. Since the whites brought alcohol and drugs, everybody has been going crazy with these substances. That's why we're returning to *koyaanisqatsi*. Goodness knows what we can do to avoid it.

TEXT 31

Today we're looking once more at *koyaanisqatsi*, especially in the form of life led by those under the influence of alcohol. Some people, each time they go to town, roam around drunk there before they return. Women and girls who want to drink prostitute themselves for drinks wherever they are. Therefore, the men also hang around there for them. They are together with just anybody's wife or husband, even if they are clan related. Having abandoned their children back home, they carry on like this. Finally, when they return home, they fight and cause disturbances.

Although the Hopis recognize their own renewed entanglement in the madness of *koyaanisqatsi*, they are equally aware of the worldwide manifestation of this phenomenon. In addition, a great deal of the internal turmoil at Hopi is attributed to white society's greed for land, including its mineral resources, as well as life in the U.S. armed forces, which first acquainted the Hopi with the whites' crazy way of life.

TEXT 32

A few of the elders say that the whites and the other Indians are also living a life of *koyaanisqatsi*. There is always killing and rioting somewhere. Whenever a man feels strong enough, he comes to take somebody's land. We constantly disagree with the whites, because they see the treasures in our land and are bent on causing us to lose this land. Then they dig up the coal in it. They are doing this without the consent of all the Hopi, and so we Hopi are at each other's throats over this.

Furthermore, the whites always manufacture weapons. They say if we have weapons we are mighty and nobody can harm us. Talking like this, they keep calling our young men to serve in the armed forces. Those who were the first to join them really became familiar with the crazy ways of the whites. All of these reasons have brought us to the state of *koyaanisqatsi*.

Once more, as in the previous world, the Hopis feel that the time is ripe to create tabula rasa and make a new beginning. According to one of their prophecies, an avenger will appear who will destroy the wicked and eradicate the current *koyaanisqatsi*. A chance for survival remains, however, only if the old religion is not abandoned.

TEXT 33

We're now experiencing *koyaanisqatsi*. We cannot continue to live like this any longer. For this reason, we are waiting for the one that will purify us or destroy the evil. When he comes, we're bound to notice it. He will deal out punishment to all of us, and we will be walking around crying. No one will aid anyone. It will be total chaos. However, it's been foretold that on the day the purifier comes, the one who will destroy us and take away our lives, those of us who have not abandoned our religion will survive.

The legendary events leading to the destruction of the village of Pivan-honkyapi were recorded previously in English by two other collectors of Hopi narratives, Henry R. Voth and Harold Courlander. While, overall, Voth's version (1905:241–244) and the earlier one of the two recorded by Courlander (1970:241–244) resemble mine, Courlander's second version (1971:157–163) drastically deviates from it. Its entire first half contains an elaborate subplot with a strong witchcraft component. The wife of the village leader's son is abducted by a sorcerer whose evil intentions are foiled when Old Spider Woman, cast in the role of a shamaness, diagnoses the situation with the aid of a quartz crystal and pinpoints the secret location of the abductor. In addition to the general moral sickness prevailing at the village, the story refers to a "society of evil ones" who take women to a place where they can abuse them whenever they want (Courlander 1971:161). Its focus within the overall concept of *koyaanisqatsi* thus rests on the aspect commonly summed up as powaqqatsi (life of sorcery).

All four versions of this legend concur in the motif that, at the request of the village chiefs, the Yaayapontsa become the avenging agents due to the immoral and degenerate lifestyles prevailing among the residents of Pivanhonkyapi. They initiate the devastating firestorm that burns its way across the plain from Nuvatukya'ovi (the San Francisco Mountains, some sixty miles to the southwest), until it engulfs the village.

Not much ethnographic data exists on the Yaayapontsa. Nequatewa exclusively speaks of a Yaapontsa in the singular and characterizes him as a "wind god" (1967[1936]:103). Colton does the same: "He is thought of as a horrid-looking creature with shaggy hair, body painted with ashes, and wearing a breech clout. He is never impersonated and takes no part in any ceremony. He is troublesome and is not liked" (1959:84).

The home of the Wind God, according to Nequatewa, is "at the foot of Sunset Crater in a great crack in the black rock, through which he is ever breathing" (1967[1936]:104). This general location is also borne out in the legend recorded here, although the Pivanhonkyapi chief initially contacts the Yaayapontsa at a place northwest of Oraibi.[4]

Portrayed as repulsive-looking supernaturals, the Yaayapontsa are said to control both the fire and the wind, the latter especially in the form of the dust devil.[5] Courlander's 1970 version, which gives them control over water, storm, lightning, wind, and fire, is not culturally in line with the scheme of Hopi mythology (1970:121). Courlander's depiction of the "Yayaponcha People" in his 1971 publication is equally irreconcilable with Hopi mythography:

> The Yayaponchas were feared, for they were sorcerers with special powers over the forces of nature, and they were wild in appearance, having long, unkempt hair. The Yayaponchas could make the north wind blow, call down storms, and make the lightning strike. They could kill people and revive them, cause landslides by pointing their fingers at cliffs, and control fire. [1971:160]

My informants agreed on the unattractive appearance of the Yayaponcha but were unable to confirm that they control the north wind. The north wind is commonly known as *kwingyaw* and differs markedly from the dust devil activated by Yaapontsa. The Yayaponcha are also not capable of performing the magic feats attributed to them. The feats are typically ascribed to adherents of the Yaya'wimi (Yaya' society). The initial sound similarity between Yaya't and Yaayapontsam, which is also attested to in the variant shape of Yaayapontsat, leads me to suspect that Courlander's narrator confused the two terms and mixed up the mytho-cultural baggage associated with them. This may also explain why the Yaayapontsa are characterized as "sorcerers" by him. Hopi Yaya't (magicians) and *popwaqt* (sorcerers) have certain similarities.

NOTES

1. Colton and Nequatewa surmise that the now-extinct Ladder dance may have been "a spring ceremony held once every four years." In form the ceremony was a kachina dance:

The leader of the Kachinas was a man dressed as a maiden. Four days before the public ceremony, two youths who were to play a leading part in the ceremony made a pilgrimage of 60 miles to the San Francisco Peaks where they deposited pahos in a shrine and from where they brought two Douglas fir trees which they planted in holes cut in the rock at the mesa edge. [1932:61]

According to the two authors, the dance, which in the dialect of Second Mesa is referred to as Saqti, was once also performed at the ancient mother village of Shungopavi. About a hundred yards south of the spring Songoopa lies a gigantic boulder "on top of which can be observed three holes in a row, each hole being about a foot in diameter and between a foot and two feet deep," into which the dance poles were placed (1932:54).

For additional information see also the glossary.

2. For the rules of *totolospi* consult the glossary.

3. The motion picture *Koyaanisqatsi*, which was Reggio's film debut, premiered with its original music score by Philip Glass at Radio City Music Hall in 1982 under the auspices of the New York Film Festival. The nonverbal film, designed as an evocation of modern life in the terms of *koyaanisqatsi* (life out of balance) has received acclaim and recognition at festivals and public performances throughout the world.

4. Voth, in a different tale featuring two representatives of the Yaayapontsa who come trading to Oraibi, situates the place as "about three-fourths of a mile north of Oraibi" (1905:123–124). In an additional story recorded by me, their home is referred to as Yaapontsa.

5. While Colton seems to equate the Yaapontsa with the "Dust Devil," the latter is probably more appropriately identified as its controlling agent (1959:84). Only rarely do Hopis refer to a dust devil as *yaapontsa*. Instead, they prefer to use the more established term *tuviphayangw*.

THE LEGEND

Aliksa'i. There was a settlement at Pivanhonkyapi. Long ago people really used to live there. Oraibi and Huk'ovi were also settled. It was only a short distance to these villages from Pivanhonkyapi.

After the founding of Pivanhonkyapi people lived at first in peace and tranquility. Life was good, and everyone was happy. The boys and men, of course, spent most of their days in the kivas. Engaging in all sorts of activities, they were basically content with their lot. Over time, however, they grew tired of doing the same old thing. Then, one day, one of them borrowed some kind of game somewhere. This game he was now busy teaching the others. As a result, they devoted their time to nothing but gambling. They were actually playing *totolospi*, the first game to be played by the Hopi long ago. So this was going on in the kivas among the menfolk. At first, they only played *totolospi* during the day. At nightfall they usually stopped.

As the days went by, however, the players became addicted to the game and also played during the nights. In addition, people began to watch them at night in the kivas and peek in on them. At first only the young men came, but soon the unmarried women also joined them. Together with the young men they would watch the players through the hatch in the kiva roof. As time passed, the girls ventured inside because they were invited. Finally, the men simply took the girls inside. Both men and womenfolk were playing the board game of *totolospi* now. It was not long before the players quit returning home at the end of the day. Not only did they gamble all day, but also through the night. Whenever someone became hungry, he went home to have a bite to eat, whereupon he returned to the kiva.

Eventually, women who had husbands and children also started going. They too became involved with the game and would only leave to go cook. No sooner had these women made food for their children and fed them, than they ran back to the kiva to play *totolospi*. No other place was of interest to the people.

So the boys and men, women and girls were having a good time. The shouting and boisterous laughter never stopped. All of the participants enjoyed themselves. By now, women and girls would be playing against men and boys. Soon the game reached a point where the participants no longer showed any respect for each other. The unmarried women and young men completely abandoned themselves. No one belonged to anyone anymore. It was total promiscuity. Everyone was in a state of craziness.

Before long, the wife of the village leader also came to participate. To begin with, she merely went to the kiva to peek in from the top. The roof was teeming with spectators, male and female, young and old, who had not entered the kiva. With these the wife of the village leader kept watching the players below. Sure enough, they were happy and were greatly enjoying themselves.

Then one of the players invited the village leader's wife to come inside the kiva. However, she declined. But since she went to the kiva several times, she was repeatedly asked inside. Finally, she succumbed to the temptation, entered the kiva, and sat down on the stone bench along the wall. She told herself she was only there to watch, and this is what she did.

As soon as the players recognized who she was they began urging her to join them. Again, she refused at first, but then she gave in and began playing with them. *Totolospi* really was a great deal of fun. Evidently she enjoyed herself so much that she was not even aware that daylight had returned. Before long, the sun was high in the morning sky, but she did not return home. Soon it was noontime, then early evening, then nighttime, and still she had not gone home.

When it turned dark again, someone called the chief's wife from outside. Her name was Talawaysi. Finally, she heard her name being called and emerged from the kiva. It turned out to be her husband. He said to her, "Come to the house and breast-feed our child. Last night and all day today he has not suckled a single time, and the poor thing is hungry. He won't stop crying, and I don't know what to do."

"All right," his wife replied, "I'll go to him and let him suckle."

True enough, when the woman reached home, the poor baby was crying. So she breast-fed him. The little thing was starved and was gulping loudly as he avidly sucked. Soon he had depleted both of her breasts and was satiated. Thereupon the woman said to her husband, "All right, he's no longer hungry. He's bound to sleep now."

"Good," he replied.

"Well, I'll be going back to the kiva," the woman said.

Her husband remained silent, so the woman left the house and returned to the kiva. There, once more, she began to carry on with the players. It was absolute craziness. People did not bother to come out of the kiva anymore.

Talawaysi too failed to go home just as before. Once again her husband kept pleading with her from above, but she did not leave. Finally, the village leader had no choice but to take the baby to her. Upon entering he said to her, "Here, nurse him."

His wife complied and breast-fed him, whereupon he took the child back home. His wife did not accompany him, which made the village leader furious. His heart sank. "Impossible," he exclaimed. "Things cannot

go on like this! I truly love the villagers, my children, but this must stop."
He resolved to bring them back to their senses.

The village leader pondered the situation. Where could he go? Who
could he ask for help? As he racked his brain, he thought of some people
he could ask for assistance. These were the Yaayapontsa who made their
home somewhere northwest of Oraibi. "I'll go to them," he said to himself,
"and tell them about our life here. I'll give it a try, at least. Perhaps they'll
help me," he thought. "I'll seek them out and beg them to have pity. Who
knows what their response will be?"

This is what occurred to the village leader, so that same night he fashioned
prayer feathers for the Yaayapontsa. Four in all he made, and daubed them
with red ocher. He knew exactly what things were important to them.
When he had finished the feathers, he smoked and prayed over them.
Upon completion of the entire task, he went to bed and slept. Prior to that,
however, he had carefully wrapped up the paho and stored them away.

The following day the village leader took his child to one of his clan's
women. She would keep the little one for him while he was on his mission
to the Yaayapontsa. Then he picked up his prayer feathers, exited from his
house, and set out toward the ledge in the southeast. Northwest of Huk'ovi
he climbed up through a gap. Once on top of the mesa, he decided to
continue straight in a northeasterly direction, choosing a path right along
the ledge. This ledge he followed all the way past Mumur Spring. Just below
Qöma'wa he turned southeast. Going around Ngöyakwa, he stayed to the
southeast of the Pöqangw place and finally came in view of Oraibi. Instead
of going to the village though, he skirted the contours of the mesa edge in
a northeasterly direction. There was a corner there, his destination. Before
long, he arrived. This was the home of the Yaayapontsa.

The Yaayapontsa evidently were aware of his coming, for the minute he
ascended to the roof of their abode, a voice bade him enter. Clutching his
bag of pahos, the village leader descended the ladder into their home. As
he arrived down below and scanned the faces of the residents, he realized
with a shock how frightful the Yaayapontsa looked. They were extremely
ugly beings with blood spattered over their hair and faces. But, much to
his surprise, they welcomed him. "Have a seat, stranger," they said to him.

"Yes, thank you," the chief replied.

The Yaayapontsa then offered him a pipe. This was a custom long ago, to
offer a visitor a smoke. When the smoking ritual had ended, the headman
of the Yaayapontsa spoke. "Well, you must be about for a reason," he said.
"Nobody has called on us for a long time."

"Of course," the village leader replied. "I'm the chief at the village of

Pivanhonkyapi. My children have lost all sense of proper living. They've become corrupt and no longer have anything good on their minds. All they can think of is how to amuse themselves, especially by way of having sex. Things we need for our survival, such as crops, no longer have any meaning to them. Even women with children are neglecting their offspring just to have fun. My wife, too, has joined the lot and no longer returns home. I'm seething with anger and am seeking a remedy to cleanse their hearts. That's the reason for my coming," he said to them. "They've really reached *koyaanisqatsi.*"

"Is that so? Truly, that's deplorable," the headman of the Yaayapontsa replied, just sitting there hunched over. A long time passed until he spoke again. "Very well," he said, "if this is your heartfelt desire, we can surely do something about it. I can see you are disgusted with the situation and are considering how to purge the hearts of your children. We will assist you in this undertaking," he promised.

When the chief from Pivanhonkyapi heard this favorable reply, he handed his prayer feathers to the leader of the Yaayapontsa, who was elated with them. Thanking the chief, the leader said, "I want you to come back tomorrow night. You've seen all my people here. We are a great many. Make some more prayer feathers. Make so many that there are enough for all of us. As soon as you come back with them tomorrow night, I'll have further instructions for you."

Delighted with the good news, the Pivanhonkyapi chief started out for home. Walking back along his own tracks, he arrived at his house again. There he unfolded his bedroll, lay down, and quickly fell asleep.

The following morning the chief ate breakfast, whereupon he resumed his task of making prayer feathers. When he had produced a large amount, he colored them red with ocher. That accomplished, he prayed over them. Then he carefully stashed them away.

That same evening he picked up the prayer items and once more departed to return to the Yaayapontsa. As before, he followed his tracks and soon arrived at his destination. As on the first occasion, he was well received and offered the welcoming smoke. When the smoking ritual was over, he distributed among the Yaayapontsa the prayer feathers he had fashioned. "Now then, these I brought for all of you," he said to their headman.

"Many thanks, indeed," the latter replied. "My people will come up to you and then you can pass them out." One after the other the Yaayapontsa stepped up to the chief from Pivanhonkyapi, and each one was given a prayer feather. The hair of the Yaayapontsa was entangled in big, wild tufts. As each one of them received his feather, he expressed his thanks. No doubt, they all felt happy. Immediately, each one tied his feather to his disheveled hair, where it served as head decoration. Finally, all the prayer items had been handed out. The chief had made just enough for every one of them. All of the Yaayapontsa were full of joy.

Thereupon, their headman said, "There are two forces we control and have knowledge of. Wind, in particular the whirlwind, is one. The other is fire. It's up to you now. We will employ whichever one your prefer," he explained.

The leader from Pivanhonkyapi sat there, thinking. He carefully mulled over his decision. Finally, he said, "Use fire."

"Agreed," the Yaayapontsa responded. They were happy with his choice. "This is what we want you to do now," their leader advised him. "Upon your return you must inform your people, all of them, because they are all crazy, that there will be a dance in four days. Tell them that you want all kinds of kachinas to perform. You will soon find out how many will care to come. You must then also call for us," he added. "You can rely on us. We will be there. My people will arrive in the evening as the very last group. They will be waiting their turn at a place northwest of Huk'ovi, where the gap is. There they will be waiting until all the kachinas are done. At that time I want you to climb on your roof and wave your blanket about. At this signal we will come. This is how you will do this," he instructed him.

"Very well, I will certainly do that."

With this favorable response the Pivanhonkyapi chief started out back home. On the way he headed straight for Huk'ovi. The village chief there was his friend. Upon arriving at his house he entered. His friend was happy to see him. "What a surprise to see you about," he exclaimed. "Come, sit down." The two fell to talking and were still doing so when the crier chief of Huk'ovi also showed up. He and the village head frequently called upon each other. The Pivanhonkyapi chief now explained to them both why he was about at this hour of the day, where he had been, and how he had fared with the Yaayapontsa. "I would like you to come over to my place tomorrow," he invited the two. "If you do that, we can think about the whole thing some more," he said to them, whereupon he went out and headed for home.

He returned to Pivanhonkyapi. Upon his arrival he heard, much to his disgust, that the shouting and laughing in the kiva still had not abated. Once more he took the baby over to his mother to be breast-fed. As it was, his wife was a beautiful woman. But as he entered the kiva with the baby, she looked awful. Her hair was all disheveled, because she had not made herself up. All of the participants in the game looked alike, with their hair wild and messy. No sooner had his wife suckled the child than her husband took it back home and put it to bed himself.

The following day the two men from Huk'ovi arrived. The Pivanhonkyapi chief now laid out his plan before them. "Four days from now I'll arrange for a plaza dance here," he explained. "We will have one kachina group dancing after another. I would also like you to join us that day. Let all the people at your village know that I want kachinas to come from Huk'ovi. Tell everybody that all those willing to dance may do so."

When the three had discussed every detail of the plan, the two chief partners from Huk'ovi went home. The Pivanhonkyapi chief in turn went from kiva to kiva informing the people about the forthcoming dance. Wherever he entered, he said to them, "From today on I want you to think about what type of kachinas you care to impersonate. Once you've made your decision, start practicing. Four days from now we will have a dance, with one group dancing right after another." After this announcement he continued on to the next kiva. When everybody had heard the news, the merriment in the village increased even more. After all, it was the express wish of the village chief himself. There was great rejoicing, and the menfolk set to planning for the kachinas they were going to perform. Everyone was eagerly awaiting the date set for the dance.

Soon it was the morning of the dance day. That day, no one was playing *totolospi*. The people had calmed their gambling frenzy down a little. After all, they knew that a dance was something special. So that day they were not as crazy and came to see the dance. Indeed, the kachinas were arriving. One group would arrive, dance, and then withdraw, whereupon the next group had its turn. Throughout the day they kept up this pattern.

By now it was getting to be early evening. Only one group of kachinas was left. To finish their last dance they had moved to the southeastern side of the plaza, where, traditionally, the final dance sequence is staged.

Now the time had arrived for the village leader to climb on the roof. This he did, whereupon he vigorously waved his blanket in the air. The Yaayapontsa were waiting, and when they saw the blanket, they began their descent on the southwest side of the mesa. The kachinas were still dancing when, for some reason, the spectators began turning their heads in a northeasterly direction. Something seemed to be nearing the village. True enough, from northeast of Pivanhonkyapi some beings became visible. The kachinas were still stomping along the southeastern edge of the plaza when these beings, whoever they were, filed in from the northeast. There was no doubt, they were some kind of beings. The people kept staring at them and passing along the news. They were asking each other what kind of beings were arriving, but no one had any idea.

Before long, the beings approached. Just as the kachinas terminated their performance in the plaza, the beings came up from the northeast. There were four of them, in all, but none of the spectators were familiar with them. No one in his life had ever seen these dreadful beings. They really looked horrible. Their eyes were bloodshot, their hair was in disarray, and their bodies were washed with white mud. They each wore a tattered black woolen dress in the form of a kilt and held something in their arms. "*Aaw, aaw,*" were the cries they uttered as they approached. The thing they held in their hands resembled a shield. Along its edge tiny flames flickered. When the four beings finally reached the spectators, the latter were able to see them better. They noticed that the weird objects held prayer sticks. The father of the kachinas cried out, "Here is one more group." With that he walked toward the Yaayapontsa and, leading them along with great care, brought them into the plaza.

None of the people of Pivanhonkyapi had any idea who the strangers were. The people kept asking each other who they might be, but no one knew what they represented or where they had come from. The four dancers took great care lining up, whereupon the father sprinkled sacred cornmeal on them. No sooner had he done this than the four began to dance. This is how their song went:

Yeeholyee, yeeholyee holyeyeyeyeye
Yeeholyee holye.
We for sure are the children of the sun.
Therefore we provide you here with heat.
For this reason we were asked to dance.
Hi'aa wi'aa wi'aa haa'a'a'a
Hi'aa wi'aa wi'aa haa.
It's inevitable here now
That your homes will be enshrouded in a red cloud.
Through thick smoke
People will be carrying each other throughout the village.
Aa'ahaaha, ii'ihiihi'i.
Yeeholyee, yeeholyee holyeyeyeyeye
Yeeholyee holye.
Look, my mothers, my fathers
Start doing all sorts of things.
They should live a good life.

Instead you allow your children to perish.
Hi'aa wi'aa wi'aa haa'a'a'a
Hi'aa wi'aa wi'aa haa.

A handful of the onlookers, whose hearts were not as closed as most of
the villagers of Pivanhonkyapi, quickly grasped the meaning of the song. It
was foreboding something terrible. Those realizing what it was exclaimed,
"We knew it, this was bound to happen, but we here fail to understand
it." This is what the ones said who were not completely crazy yet. Sadness
came over them. "That's why we kept warning them all the time, but they
simply did not listen."

When the dance ended, the group's song starter handed the village leader
of Pivanhonkyapi his tray of prayer sticks. Next, the dancer in front gave
one tray to the village chief of Huk'ovi. Thereupon, each of the two village
criers received their flaming paho tray. These four men were the only ones
to get this gift. Thereupon, the Yaayapontsa were bidden farewell, receiving
cornmeal and prayer feathers from the kachina father. Then they departed.
This time, however, they did not return toward Oraibi. Rather they went
along the ledge in a southwesterly direction, uttering their cries, "*Aaw, aaw.*"
In due course they descended the path directly southeast of Apoonivi and
then went all the way home to Nuvatukya'ovi, the San Francisco Mountains.

Those Pivanhonkyapis who were still somewhat clear-headed became
quite depressed now. Those beings had really been different, hence those
villagers who were endowed with wisdom and intelligence kept pondering
their significance. They had never encountered beings of this kind. But
one thing was clear: They had not come without a purpose. Their song
contained an important message.

This is what the people of Pivanhonkyapi experienced there. Then it was
the new daybreak. That morning the two chiefs from Huk'ovi reappeared.
Together with the leader and crier chief from Pivanhonkyapi they discussed
the whole matter. Finally, the Pivanhonkyapi leader said to the two crier
chiefs, "Those pahos you received I want you to carry to Nuvatukya'ovi.
Deposit them there on both sides of the highest peak and then come back
again."

"It shall be like that," the two replied. With that, they seized their trays
and set out toward Nuvatukya'ovi. They undertook their task on the first
day after the dance.

That same day, by early evening, the gamblers and crazy ones started all
over again. Once more each of them went to the kiva to continue playing
totolospi. And since the day before they had all dressed early to go see the

dance and had somewhat straightened out their hair, they still looked quite decent.

By this time the two crier chiefs who had taken the paho trays to Nuvatukya'ovi were back home. All four of them now engaged in a ritual smoke, and when that was over, the Pivanhonkyapi chief expressed his gratitude to them. "That's the way it's going to be. All right, from now on we'll be looking for whatever events will unfold," he said to them. "I'm glad we did the right thing. You can go back to your homes now and wait."

Some time later the two crier chiefs departed, one to Huk'ovi, the other to his house in Pivanhonkyapi. That same night, a light from a small fire could be seen shining from Nuvatukya'ovi, from the area around the mountain peaks. No one had any explanation for it. Only the two village leaders knew what it meant.

A new day broke, and then it was night again. By now, the fire was somewhat more visible. Some of those who were at the kiva, but had not entered in order to watch from the top, were yelling and laughing with the players and kept shouting instructions to them with great fervor. That second day the spectators first became aware of the fire. There seemed to be flames licking up into the sky in the vicinity of Nuvatukya'ovi. Every so often they mentioned the fire to the players down below, but no one listened to them. Not being able to hear what they were saying, they merely looked at them and then continued on.

Meanwhile, the fire kept burning, and its smoke began to reach the people of Pivanhonkyapi. There was actually some smoke hanging over the village. The flames were distinctly visible now and apparently advancing on the village. Again the watchers on top of the kiva tried to tell the players, but they would not believe it. They were concentrating so hard on what they were doing that they didn't even bother to listen. So the onlookers shouted down to them, "Come on out and see for yourselves."

"No. You're only saying that to make us stop," one of the players retorted. They simply refused to believe that this news was true. They would not listen. In vain the onlookers tried to catch the attention of those inside the kiva. The smoke was clearly wafting about, but they had no intention of quitting their *totolospi*.

On the fourth day the firestorm was definitely moving closer. The village was beginning to fill with smoke, and its smell was quite intense. Once more the onlookers attempted to warn the players that a fire was approaching. But they still did not believe it. Instead, the boys and men were enjoying the girls and women. They kept embracing and squeezing each other.

The firestorm was coming closer and closer, yet none of those in the kiva believed it. When the fire was just southwest of Apoonivi, one of the gamblers finally came out to eat. As he left the kiva he realized the truth. Quickly he dashed down the kiva ladder again and told the others. He was excited and almost out of breath as he entered. They listened to him, but were hardly able to make out his words. "It's really true," he yelled at them. "There's a fire coming in!"

Now the players came out. By this time the fire had arrived. Leaving the kiva, they scurried all over. Whatever thing people treasured they tried to grab before they ran off, at least those who were among the early ones to emerge. Those who were tardy were caught by the fire. Crying, people were running in all directions. If someone was fond of a person, one held or carried the other and sought escape. Some failed to see each other in the confusion. Only now it occurred to them to run in search of their children. Instead of holding them dear they had neglected them. Fortunately, someone had rounded up the children the morning after the dance and taken them into shelters at Huk'ovi. It was a real nightmare. Some people were still in their houses when the fire engulfed them. A few managed to get away, but most of them were killed by the fire. Several knew of an overhang to which they ran with their children on their back. A few also holed up in remote corners of their homes.

Now the village chief took the flaming paho tray he had received from the Yaayapontsa and placed it in the back room of his house. Right away the fire on the tray grew stronger. Just as it was blazing full force, the fire that had been burning its way across from Nuvatukya'ovi reached the village of Pivanhonkyapi. The two fires now merged and set everything aflame. Racing along from the point where the two had merged, it spread to the people hiding under the overhang. All of those inside died from the intense heat. Thus, nearly the entire population of Pivanhonkyapi was burned to death in the fire.

The fire now embarked on a course that led directly to Oraibi. The village leader of Oraibi spotted it as it headed straight for them. In despair he cried out, "Oh my, there is going to be a disaster. I love my children. I have to ask someone for help." With that he ran to Pöqangwwawarpi, the abode of Old Spider Woman.

Upon his arrival he was about to announce his coming when a voice bade him enter. When he was inside, he saw that Old Spider Woman was at home. She welcomed him. The two Pöqangw Brothers were fighting, throwing each other down all over the place. Their old grandmother got after them, but they did not listen. Once more she yelled at them, this time more forcefully, and now the two quit. Right away, the village leader of

Oraibi informed the old woman why he had come. Imploring her and her grandchildren's assistance, he said, "There is a fire approaching, with whose planning I had nothing to do. I greatly love my children. Maybe with your help they will not be burned to death. This is my wish. That's why I came."

Old Spider Woman assured him of their help. "Don't worry, we'll come to your rescue. Early tomorrow morning, when it is the time to address the sun in prayer, you must get up and make two arrows. Fletch them with feathers of the red-shafted flicker. As soon as you're done, ram one into the ground southwest of Oraibi, the other a little northwest of Atsamali. Now hurry," Old Spider Woman urged him. "The fire is going to be here before long."

The Oraibi chief was happy about the favorable response and returned to his village. There he prayed and smoked for some time. Then he made his bed, lay down, and fell asleep at once. The following day he was up early, at the time when people go to greet the rising sun in prayer. He dressed and then did as instructed by Old Spider Woman. He quickly fashioned the arrows, whereupon he took them to the two locations Old Spider Woman had pointed out to him and stuck them in the ground. Before long the two Pöqangw Brothers and Old Spider Woman arrived.

"You've come?" the old woman greeted the chief.

"Yes, I just got here."

"Very well. Are the two arrows in place?"

"Yes, I stuck them both in the ground," he replied.

With that, Old Spider Woman began to weave a web back and forth between the two inserted arrows. She spun the web really tight. Four layers in all she wove on top of each other and then she urinated on the web. Then she turned to the Pöqangw Brothers and said, "All right, it's your turn now. Chew this mirage medicine and spurt it on the web. It's bound to turn into solid rock then."

These were her instructions to the two brothers. The two did as bidden and spurted the medicine all over the spun webbing. Sure enough, it became as solid as rock.

By now the fire wall was moving in. Already it stood southwest of Oraibi. Thereupon Old Spider Woman explained, "This is how it's going to be now. When the fire comes upon this barrier, it will jump over your houses and land on the other side. That's the way it's going to be. The fire cannot overcome this wall." With this task accomplished, they all went their own way again. The Pöqangw Brothers went home with their grandmother, and the village leader returned to Oraibi.

At this moment the firestorm surged over the horizon. It was headed straight for the rocky barrier. The minute it reached it, it did not jump over the houses, but instead was deflected. Veering off its path, it ran along the northwest side of Oraibi and continued in a northeasterly direction. From there it burned along the southeast side of Bacavi, and then once more rolled in a northeasterly direction. There it climbed up the terrain and burned itself out somewhere near Palapsö. For this reason, the rocks between Pivanhonkyapi and Oraibi still look burned today. The same is true for the area spanning from a point northwest of Oraibi to the southeast side of Bacavi, and to the northeast corner of Paqaptsokvi.

This is how the village leader of Pivanhonkyapi purged the dark hearts of his people. These events truly took place. In this manner Pivanhonkyapi fell into ruin. No one lives there anymore, for the fire killed all the villagers. And here the story ends.

FOUR

The Demise of Sikyatki

INTRODUCTION

The extensive prehistoric ruin of Sikyatki is located about two and a half miles northeast of Walpi, the southernmost of the three present villages on top of First Mesa. Fewkes's contention that the name of the site alludes "to the color of the sandstone of which the walls were built" and hence translates as "Yellow House" is not consistent with Hopi linguistic rules of composition (1898:632, 636). This explanation does not account for the t in the place-name. Compounding the elements *sikyangpu* (yellow) and *kiihu* (house), whose respective combining forms are *sikya-* and *-ki*, yields *sikyaki*, not *sikyatki*.

Since *tuki* (cut) typically occurs in its contracted shape of *—tki* in compounds, a semantic reading of Sikyatki as "Yellow Cut" would be more reasonable.[1] Of course, the adjective *sikya* (bitter, sour) could equally well serve as a modifier element, resulting in "Bitter/Sour Cut."[2]

The most likely interpretation that is linguistically tenable, however, is that of "Cut-off/Divided Valley." It is based on the word *sikya*, which, as an independent noun, denotes "small valley, ravine." This interpretation seems to be confirmed also by Frank Waters, who explains the name as "Narrow Valley" (1963:102).

While most of the crumbled masonry structures of the ancient pueblo have long since been covered by drifting sand, masses of distinctive Jeddito Yellow Ware and its polychrome descendants still litter the site.[3] These pottery types were produced by using an oxidizing firing atmosphere rather than a reducing one and are among the most beautiful ever made in the Southwest. In 1895, Fewkes, by invitation of the secretary of the Smithsonian Institution, excavated portions of the ruin. As was customary at the time, most of the archaeological work was concentrated in the cemeteries. They yielded more than eight hundred pottery vessels, "of which over five hundred were decorated with beautifully colored designs" (Fewkes 1896a:159).[4]

This wealth of outstanding ceramics is one of the reasons Sikyatki has perhaps received more attention than any other prehistoric site in northern Arizona. As Hargrave points out, "Objects of material culture, especially pottery, were in great demand by eastern museums at that time and the superior quality and exceptional beauty of color and form of this pottery created a sensation among collectors of all classes" (1937:63).

Also, among the workers hired by Fewkes was a resident of Walpi named Lesou, who took a fancy to the unearthed pottery and thereby set into motion an interesting chain of events. Lesou was married to Nampeyo, a potter from Hano, the Tewa village at the northeastern end of First Mesa. When he returned home with potsherds from the excavation and showed them to his wife, she became so enchanted with the artistic designs and aesthetically pleasing colors that she soon began to integrate them into her own work (Dittert and Plog 1980:31). Among Nampeyo's most famous creations are the low, wide-shouldered jars whose beautifully proportioned shape was modeled on Sikyatki originals. In copying this inspirational pottery from Sikyatki, she provided a powerful impetus to the deteriorating and disappearing local pottery industry and ultimately initiated a renaissance of Hopi ceramic art that became a great economic boon to the entire community of First Mesa.

While Hopi legendary history contains conflicting claims as to whether Walpi or Sikyatki was founded first, Hargrave suggests that archaeological evidence in the form of pottery remains "prove them to have been founded at approximately the same time, namely about 1425 A.D." (1931:3). Although crude Basketmaker III sherds have been reported from the vicinity of Sikyatki spring, evidence of the subsequent periods, archaeologically known as Pueblo I, II, and III, are apparently absent. Sikyatki's beginning in the 15th century thus falls into the late prehistoric phase of Pueblo IV, which is allocated a time frame between A.D. 1300 and 1600.

Although modern research has yet to determine the exact date of Sikyatki's abandonment, the fact that no Spanish chroniclers mention its name is a strong indication that the village was deserted between A.D. 1500 and 1600, prior to the arrival of the Spaniards (Hargrave 1931:5). As to the reasons behind its abandonment, convincing scientific data are scarce.

Hargrave believes that sufficient archaeological proof exists to support his theory that the Jeddito pueblos to the east of First Mesa were not Hopi and that Sikyatki was part of this Jeddito group (1935). In spite of sharing a nearly identical material culture with the other villages from the Hopi group, as is evident from similar pottery types, the two groups probably were affiliated with different linguistic stocks. Thus, the inhabitants of Sikyatki would have spoken a language different from that of the Hopi at Qöötsaptuvela. This linguistic difference may have been one of the reasons for the feuding that existed between the two villages, as reflected in several of the legendary accounts of the destruction of Sikyatki.

Additionally, Cosmos Mindeleff mentions disputes over land use and planting privileges that apparently arose when a contingent of families from Walpi left Qöötsaptuvela on the northwestern flank of the mesa point and settled on the east side of the mesa, close to territory claimed by the Sikyatkis (1891:24). Finally, Fewkes reports that the ill feelings between the two communities may have been aggravated due to disagreements over control of the water supply (1898:634).

Whatever the real grounds for the abandonment of Sikyatki may have been, one would not expect to find them factually expressed in the oral narratives that were, nevertheless, inspired by them. Of the ten accounts already published, whether in the form of a lengthy narrative or an abbreviated plot capsule, seven feature the First Mesa villages of Walpi or Qöötsaptuvela in addition to Sikyatki. The same is true for my original Hopi version.

Qöötsaptuvela, which is regarded by the people of Walpi as their ancestral home, translates as "Ash Slope." Obviously, this designation does not conform to the customary pattern of Hopi place-name nomenclature. People do not name a new settlement "Ash Slope." Rather, ashes and refuse typically mark a site once it gets abandoned. The name must have originated, therefore, after Qöötsaptuvela's residents left it and began to occupy the top of the mesa after A.D. 1700.

Serious inter-village hostilities with bloody atrocities committed by both sides are reported by Fewkes (1895:576), Cosmos Mindeleff (1891:24–25), George W. James (1917:93), Edward S. Curtis (1970[1922]:189–190), Elsie Clews Parsons (1926:227–233), and Harold Courlander (1982:39–44). While the first three have Walpi and Sikyatki as the opposing factions, Curtis and Courlander have Qöötsaptuvela instead of Walpi. Ruth L. Bunzel's tale (in Parsons 1926:227–233) mentions a village by the name of Polixti at strife with Sikyatki, and Courlander (1982:49–53) mentions a village by the name of Muchovi. The versions collected by Henry R. Voth (1905:244–246), Waters (1963:97–102), and myself basically portray intra-village conflicts of Sikyatki. However, while Walpi in Voth's account and Qöötsaptuvela in mine still participate in the drama of the destruction, though merely as avenging instruments at the request of the Sikyatki village chief, Waters's is the only account that makes no mention of another village. In Bunzel's account, Sikyatki, after causing the destruction of Polixti, is in turn destroyed by combined forces from Samumpavi [Shungopavi] and Oraibi. All three of Courlander's versions agree with Waters on the point that Sikyatki was not destroyed at all but was freely abandoned by its inhabitants when relations with their neighbors became intolerable.

Interestingly enough, the legend recorded here combines plot elements found both in Waters and Voth. Waters's tale, as does mine, features a life-and-death race between two male rivals over a female.[5] However, while Waters's rivals belong to two distinct clans, Coyote and Swallow, in mine only the protagonist is assigned a specific clan association. The antagonist, whose clan status is not revealed, is endowed with the evil and trouble-causing powers of sorcery, as so often happens in Hopi oral literature. In both tales the "good" protagonist triumphs over the "bad" challenger, but while the defeated Swallow faction complies with the Coyote clan's bid to leave the village, the sorcerers in my story refuse to do so. As the ensuing tensions between the two groups escalate and poison the social atmosphere of the pueblo, the Sikyatki village leader decides to purge the evil by destroying the entire community. This episode is mirrored in Voth and, to some extent, also in Curtis. Once more, as is also the case in the destruction legends of Pivanhonkyapi and Awat'ovi, society is at the brink of *koyaanisqatsi* (chaos and corruption), which renders life no longer worth living. Hence, the village chief resorts to the ultimate remedy in the form of total annihilation of the village.

NOTES

1. As an example of the contraction *-tki* in compound words, the clan name Patki denotes "Cut-off Water," and the place name Wupatki, "Long Cut" or "Long Valley."

2. Fewkes reports that, according to traditionalists at First Mesa, Sikyatki took its name "from the color of the water of the neighboring spring, which still preserves its yellowish appearance" (1895:575). While *sikya-*, indeed, is the combining form for "yellow," *-tki* has no relation to any word referring to water in the Hopi lexicon. Hence, this interpretation has no language-based backing whatsoever.

3. Lyndon L. Hargrave speculates that the tales of gold and wealth that lured the early Spanish *conquistadores* into the Southwest in search of the fabled Seven Cities of Cíbola may have been inspired by pottery vessels of Jeddito Yellow Ware

and the tons of bright yellow potsherds that speckle the ground. He wrote that "to natives without knowledge of metal, gold would only refer to color" (1935:20).

4. For some excellent examples of this collection, now in the Smithsonian Institution, see Fewkes 1898:631–742.

5. One of Courlander's versions also contains a life-and-death race, triggered, however, by a rather trivial dispute over fuel-cutting privileges (1982:43). In the race itself, two birds, a swallow and a chicken hawk, represent the rival factions.

THE LEGEND

Aliksa'i. People were settled at Sikyatki. In addition, there were villages all across the land. In Sikyatki there lived a couple with a beautiful daughter. Their house was somewhere northwest of the plaza.

The girl was a great beauty, so naturally the young men were flocking to her place. Not only from Sikyatki did they come to woo her, but also from Awat'ovi and Qöötsaptuvela. The girl was in the habit of grinding corn in the upper story of the house, so it was here that the clandestine lovers were courting her at night. As a rule, a suitor would talk to the girl from outside the vent hole to her grinding chamber. Whenever the girl did not feel like talking to a suitor, she would tell him to leave. After his departure a new one usually took his place. One after the other they were trying their luck. When the girl finally got tired and felt sleepy, she sent off whoever was still there and closed up the vent hole. Then she went to bed. In this fashion the young men kept wooing the girl there.

As time passed, she did not bother to talk to most of them anymore. At one point, there were only two boys left whom she showed an interest in. When the others heard about this, they no longer sought her out. Now only these two boys, both from Sikyatki, kept calling on her. One of the boys was a member of the Coyote clan. In time, it was this boy that the girl fell in love with. Thus, when the other boy arrived again, she told him not to visit her anymore. She let him know that she loved the other one. To show her interest in the Coyote Boy the girl, therefore, took a stack of piki with some qömi to his family's house. When she arrived with her gift, the boy's mother accepted it, which meant that she approved of the girl as a bride. The girl was filled with joy that she had been accepted into the house of the groom. There she ground corn now. While she was performing this customary grinding, some of the boy's uncles and other male relatives were readying the wedding garments for their new daughter-in-law. They were weaving the bridal robe and the large belt and were making the wedding boots. Thus, Coyote Boy now had a bride at his home and all the required wedding prerequisites were being met.

The boy who had been rejected was jealous. After all, he had lost the girl. "How on earth can I take her away from him?" he kept wondering. This boy was a witch. He was very upset that Coyote Boy had won the girl. His relatives, too, were all witches who were powerful and great troublemakers. As is well known, sorcerers, or witches, have two hearts. By causing the death of their own relatives, they lengthen their own lives. And if they intend to travel somewhere, they do not do so by the strength of their own legs but in the guise of coyotes, wolves, owls, and crows. These sorcerers are contemptuously known as Turds.

This boy's relatives were very powerful, commanding greater-than-human powers. So the witch confided in one of his uncles and told him that he intended to get Coyote Boy's bride for himself. He asked if he and his people would assist him in this endeavor.

The uncle, who was also a witch, agreed at once. After all, the only thing on his mind was how to harm a person. He assembled the other relatives, who discussed the matter. Mulling everything over, they came up with a scheme to deprive the boy of the girl. The day on which Coyote Boy and his bride were supposed to wash their hair, the witch uncle went to the groom's house, where the girl stayed, and declared, "We won't tolerate it if the girl washes her hair with Coyote Boy. At least not before my nephew and he test each other. They will compete against each other for their lives. Whoever survives can marry the girl." This is what he said.

These sorcerers were extremely powerful, so the Coyote members who had the female-in-law did not resist. They had no choice but to comply with the witch's proposal. The plan was for the two rivals to run a race. The course along which they were to run had already been decided. The time of the race too had already been set. After delivering his message, the witch returned home again. There he said to his nephew, "All right, it's all been arranged with them. You'll race with each other, with life or death at stake. The winner will get the girl," he explained. "The Coyote clan people had no choice but to accept the conditions. You, of course, need not worry. We are bound to win with the help of our witchcraft powers."

The two groups were now anticipating the day of the competition. Coyote Boy was not happy about this turn of events, but resigned himself to his fate. Those Turds were very powerful, and if he did not agree with them, they would probably seek to get into a fight with the Coyote clan. For this reason, they all had to comply. If, through some stroke of luck, he should win, he would not lose his life. His relatives were fervently praying for things to turn out favorably for him.

From that day on Coyote Boy practiced running on a regular basis. Just by the time he got to be in good shape, the set date was approaching. The witch boy, who commanded greater than human might, did not even consider getting into shape. Thus, the boy who had the girl going through the wedding prerequisites at his house was the only one to practice running. By this time word of the life-and-death race had spread to the other villages. The people there declared that they would definitely come to watch the event. Who knows, either of the two rivals might win the girl. And so people lived in anticipation of the day on which the race was going to take place. When the morning of the great event was at hand, Coyote Boy was in top running condition. At the crack of dawn the spectators were already arriving. They were gathering at the southeast side of Sikyatki. A huge crowd was assembled by now. One could hear the hum of many voices. Just as the sun rose, the two boys from Sikyatki showed up. Each of them brought his uncles along. Many of their other relatives also came, in order to wish the runners well. By the time of their arrival, hundreds of spectators were already in place.

The uncle of the witch boy drew several lines in the sand. He drew four lines in all, each a different color. Next, he rammed two knives in the ground, one on each side of the lines. Having done that he said, "Well then, from this point I want you to run. Your first goal will be the Little Colorado southeast of here. Then you will continue to the Rio Grande in the northeast. Whoever gets there first must carve his clan symbol on a rock. The one who comes in second is to add his mark underneath the one in the lead. Next you will turn northwest until you reach the Big Colorado River. There you draw your clan symbols again. From the Colorado you are to run this way. Before you do so, however, you must also leave your clan mark at Kawestima. In doing so, we will know where you have been. This is your course. The one who comes in first will pick up his knife and wait for the loser. As soon as he arrives, the winner is to sever his head." This is how the witch instructed the two boys.

At this point, the uncle of the Coyote Boy pulled his nephew aside to a place where they were alone. There he said to him, "All right, you have to run with him now. There is no way out. You probably know that your opponents are witches. Therefore, that boy won't run the entire course on foot. If he had to do that, he would not have agreed to the race. We who have no knowledge of witchcraft, however, won't forsake you. We'll probably meet in the kiva to ponder a solution for you," he said. "So compete with him, but be on your guard. At one point he won't be racing on foot."

After these words from his uncle, Coyote Boy went back to the starting line. The two runners placed themselves side by side. As they stood there, someone started counting for them. He counted up to four, and then the two were off. Sure enough, they headed out in a southeasterly direction. The people all started speaking at the same time, then they were shouting. Some were for the Coyote Boy, others for his opponent. They were wishing them well and exhorting them. Meanwhile, the two boys were running along. True enough, it was not long before the Coyote Boy went into the lead. No wonder, for he was strong and in excellent shape. Soon the two disappeared from the view of the spectators. But even though they were gone from view, the spectators felt no urge to go home. Everybody was curious about the outcome of the race, so they remained at the starting line.

Coyote Boy kept running straight along without stopping anywhere. Already the two were quite far away. At one point when Coyote Boy glanced over his shoulder, the other was nowhere in sight. He scanned the area looking back, but to no avail. Halting his run for a while, he looked about, but nobody came into view. So he decided not to wait any longer and continued on. However, he did not run as fast as he could. Instead, he ran at a relaxing pace, heading toward the first destination they had been instructed to aim for. He was now trotting along slowly.

Coyote Boy was still moving along in this manner when something rushed past him overhead with great velocity. Looking after it, he saw that it was a nighthawk. Since it was a bird, he did not give the matter much thought. After all, nighthawks were living in that area. Without considering the matter further, he ran on. In due time, he reached the first destination of the race. Upon nearing it, he again looked over his shoulder, but the witch boy was nowhere to be seen. So without any further delay he headed straight to his goal. Upon reaching the place where they had been instructed to put their clan symbols, he noticed that the other one had already been there. His clan mark was already incised on the rock. Inspecting it, Coyote Boy muttered to himself, "Gee, when did he get here? No one ever passed me," he thought. Then it hit him. His opponent could not have been on foot. He must have used his witchcraft. That was the explanation. "I remember now," he said. "My uncle warned me that he would do this by means other than on foot."

Without delay he pecked his clan symbol underneath the one left by the witch boy. Then he continued on again. He now headed northeast, running as fast as his feet would carry him. Apparently, the other boy had now used his legs again after changing back into his human form. Before he had not run on foot but had flown over Coyote Boy. When he believed that he was far ahead of him, he had transformed himself back and continued on foot. But he was not as strong as the Coyote Boy and could not run very fast. That did not concern him, however, since he was far in the lead.

Coyote Boy sped along in pursuit of the witch boy. He ran as fast as he was able to. At one point, when he grew tired, he rested for a while. Then he resumed the race. Eventually, he reached the place where the other had again left his human footprints. When Coyote Boy spotted them, he thought, "He's not too far yet, but I bet he's going to use that trick again." Thinking like this, he dashed along in pursuit of the witch boy, his eyes focused in a northeasterly direction. Maybe his opponent would become visible somewhere. The boy in the lead, who was now running in his human shape, did not overexert himself. Finally, Coyote Boy came in sight of him and before long was right behind him. The moment he reached the witch boy, he overtook him. Having passed him without saying a word, he ran on at top speed in a northeasterly direction.

The witch boy tried to keep up with Coyote Boy, but he soon realized that he would not catch up with him. So, when the Coyote Boy was far ahead, the witch boy changed into the nighthawk again and resumed his pursuit. Coyote Boy, who was exceedingly fast, was already far gone. But even though, at some point, witch boy passed him flying over his head. Coyote Boy kept looking over his shoulders. At first, his pursuer was nowhere to be seen, but then somewhere the hawk flew past him. Being a creature with wings, he soon disappeared from view. "There he goes again, not using his legs," he thought, speeding along in pursuit.

The two were supposed to aim for the Eastern pueblos. There was a river there, and their destination was somewhere nearby, northwest of Katistsa. Toward this goal the two runners were now advancing. Here they had been told to incise their clan symbols again and then continue in a northeasterly direction. So they were headed toward this place in pursuit of each other. But since the witch boy had again resorted to the guise of the hawk, he reached the place first and drew his clan mark.

When Coyote Boy arrived after him, he became slightly angry. However, there was nothing he could do. So he too pecked his clan symbol on the rock and then ran on in a northwesterly direction. He had not gotten very far when he encountered a man. The man was from his home village and said, "I'm sure you've noticed that the witch boy is not using his legs. He's far ahead already. But he's bound to use his legs again for a while. When he does that, he'll get tired. You'll be able to pass him again, but when he uses his old trick and overtakes you in the form of a hawk, I want you to shoot him. You can shoot him because he's not on foot. Therefore, watch out for him after passing him. Keep looking back. As soon as he catches up with you and flies overhead, shoot him with this."

This is how the man instructed the Coyote Boy, whereupon he thrust a bundle of arrows in his hand and gave him a bow. "This too is yours," the man added, and handed him something else. It turned out to be a gourd that was split in two halves. Along with it came a piece of sinew. "Well now, if the other does not quit using means other than his legs, you can make use of this device. You'll know what to do and when to use it," he said. "With the help of this gourd you're bound to catch up with him." With these words of advice he said, "Now, run. We won't forsake you. All your uncles are assembled in the kiva. Whenever you need our assistance, speak a prayer, and we'll surely hear you."

With that, Coyote Boy ran off, clasping the arrows and the bow in his hands. He really tore along. However, before he came in view of the other he felt exhausted. He stopped and uttered a prayer to some spirit. True enough, his uncles in their kiva at Sikyatki heard him. They were all gathered there, smoking their pipes. The puffs of smoke they kept exhaling were leaving the kiva and drifting in one direction only, northeast. Upon reaching this direction, they were transformed into clouds. As a result, the sky over the Eastern pueblos became thick with thunderheads. Then they began to release their rain. It really poured. The witch boy, who was still using the guise of the hawk, became drenched. So thoroughly drenched did he become that all his wing and breast feathers were soaked with moisture.

As a result, his feathers became so heavy that he grew exhausted and had to stop. In doing so, he changed back into his human form. When a bird gets dripping wet, it is not strong anymore. The hawk had gotten weak due to the rain, and now the witch boy could not use its disguise any more. Instead, he had to rely on his own legs. Because of the heavy downpour, however, the ground had turned soft, so the poor wretch was now sloshing through nothing but mud. As a result, he did not make much headway.

By now Coyote Boy, his pursuer, had come across his tracks again. Exerting himself, he ran as fast as he was able. Sure enough, it paid off. Before long, he overtook his rival the witch boy. Again, Coyote Boy said nothing to him as he dashed past. Looking back every so often, he saw that he was drawing way ahead. He now turned in a northwesterly direction. No doubt, he had gained a lot of ground and was far in the lead. Eventually, however, the witch boy managed to escape the rain. He took a break to catch his breath. Because he was not as strong as Coyote Boy, he quickly tired and had to pause there. After resting, he changed back into the nighthawk again.

By now, all his wing and breast feathers were dry, so being light-weighted, he could use the hawk guise again. He knew that he would catch up with Coyote Boy, who was far away.

Coyote Boy, who was in the lead, truly was way ahead. For this reason, he would halt in his tracks once in a while and scan the area behind him. He wanted to see whether his rival was approaching. Then he continued on again. He pressed on as fast as he was able to run, always in the same direction.

In due time, the witch boy was closing in on Coyote Boy. He could see where he was running. Seeing him he thought, "He must be aware by now that I'm not using my legs. This time I'll fly high over him so that he can't spot me." With that, he rose way up in the sky, and that's where he flew along.

The boy in the lead was aware of this and placed an arrow on his bow, waiting for his opponent. Waiting where he had stopped, he was looking up when he saw the bird approaching. He fired his arrow, but it failed to reach the bird. Way short of its aim, it fell back to the ground. Coyote Boy shot a second arrow, but it too failed to reach its target. Coyote Boy gave up. "I can't harm him with an arrow. He's flying too high. He's way out of reach." This is what he thought, whereupon he discarded his weapon.

Once again Coyote Boy resumed his pursuit. The witch boy was way out of range as he looked after him. The distance between the two was growing even larger. Farther and farther he flew until he finally disappeared over the horizon. The minute he was out of sight, Coyote Boy halted his run and took out the gourd he had received. He placed one half on the ground. It was not very large, and he did not really know how to get inside. After several attempts he finally managed to fit himself into it. Then he closed the other half over himself. Having done that, he noticed the spot where the gourd has its stem button. From the gourd's center he now stretched sinew in both directions, so that it formed a line from a point at the bottom to the stem of the gourd. Next, he began twisting the sinew between the palms of his hands. Miraculously, the gourd began to lift off. Inside, Coyote Boy kept up the twisting of the sinew cord. The magic gourd was flying quite fast by now. Before long, it had covered a great distance. As the flying contraption zoomed along, it emitted a humming noise.

It did not take long before Coyote Boy passed his rival in the lead. He just whirred past him. Soon he reached the destination in the northwest. There he climbed out of the gourd and incised his clan symbol on a rock. This time he was the first to do so. Thereupon he continued on again. He only flew a short distance before he dismounted. Then he ran on his own strength.

By now his rival had reached the place where Coyote Boy had arrived first to draw his mark. No sooner had he added his own than he continued in his flight. This time, he did not change himself back into his human shape; instead, he flew on in the guise of the hawk. Heading for his home village of Sikyatki, the witch boy was the pursuer now.

Coyote Boy was far away, but as he was coming through the area northwest of Kawestima, the witch boy, who was using the nighthawk, caught up with him. Without paying attention to him, he flew right on in the direction of Sikyatki. He had not vanished out of sight when Coyote Boy, who was running on foot, extracted his gourd a second time. Once more he got inside and resumed the race with his flying machine. It only took a short while before he was abreast of his rival. He passed him, but this time he did not dismount.

Coyote Boy soon neared Sikyatki. He landed at a place where he could not be seen and climbed out of the gourd. After hiding it where it could not be found, he once more started running on foot. He ran off at full speed.

His rival, who was using the hawk, now too had reached a point where he was forced to change himself back. After all, he could not afford being seen arriving in the disguise of the bird. So having completed the transformation, he resumed his pursuit of Coyote Boy. The poor thing ran as fast as his feet would carry him. But he did not gain on the other. It was quite obvious that Coyote Boy had come through here already. So the witch boy just followed his footprints. Meanwhile, Coyote Boy was nearing the village, rejoicing in his heart. One last time he summoned up all his strength, hurtling toward the finish line where the two had started. Before long, he came into view of it. The crowd was still gathered there. Now the spectators had spotted him and exclaimed, "There he comes. One of them can clearly be seen."

Everybody was staring into the direction from which either of the two runners was expected. The boy was getting closer and closer. Suddenly a voice shouted, "It's him!" Others joined in, "Yes, it seems to be Coyote Boy!" Someone else was of a different opinion. "No, it's not him, it's the other boy!"

Ever closer Coyote Boy was approaching. One of the spectators who was sure by now that he had recognized the runner exclaimed, "No way, it's not him. It's the boy who has the girl. He's the winner. He's bound to get the girl. The other is not even visible yet."

This is how the two runners fared. The Coyote Boy had arrived first. Since he was first, he ran over to where the knife was stuck in the ground and grabbed it. Then he waited for the witch to come in. After a good length of time had passed, the witch boy appeared on the horizon. He had no choice but to head straight toward the finish line. The poor thing was trotting slower and slower. Apparently, he was completely worn out.

Eventually, he was in everyone's sight. As he drew nearer, he could be seen stumbling along. The moment he arrived, Coyote Boy ran up to him and grabbed his long hair from behind. Then he thrust the knife into the boy's throat, and cut off his head. The witch boy died instantly. This is how Coyote Boy dispatched his rival. In this way Coyote Boy won.

The relatives of the dead witch boy became unhappy. Regretting what they had done, they were crying. Coyote Boy, who had won the bride and killed the witch boy, now stepped up to the uncle who had delivered the news about the race at his house. "All right," he said to him, "it had to be this way. It was your own wish, and now you have lost your nephew. In helping him, you showed that you did not care for him at all. If it hadn't been for your special powers, there would have been no need for me to kill him," he said. "You caused your own misery, because you are people without compassion. You are so mighty that you could not show any pity. Therefore, for you to live here with us is out of the question. Pack your belongings and leave this village."

But the witches refused, and the witch boy's uncle retorted, "Never. We won't do that." That's all he said. Then he went to his dead nephew and buried him there. Thereupon, he took his relatives and went home with them. Under no circumstances were the witches going to submit to the wish of the Coyote clan people. They had no intention of causing their own ruin by leaving. They were extremely powerful and declined to leave.

After these events the bride was able to continue her stay at the groom's house, and no one challenged the two anymore. As soon as her wedding dress was finished, she had her hair washed and tied with Coyote Boy's, which symbolized their marriage.

Following these events, the people at Sikyatki settled down to their daily routine again, but life was not very peaceful. The sorcerers, or Turds, resented the fact that they had been beaten and were causing every possible trouble for the rest of the villagers. Things kept happening to people, especially those of the Coyote clan, but also to others.

The chief of Sikyatki, therefore, who held all of his children dear, was thinking of seeking someone's help. It was his desire to terminate this corrupted way of life. He wanted the witches wiped out and the village destroyed. With these intentions on his mind he lived there. One day it occurred to him whose help he might seek. He went to the village leader of Qöötsaptuvela. With him he shared his plans and explained that he wanted Sikyatki destroyed.

"Is that so?" the Qöötsaptuvela chief replied. "How are we going to accomplish this? How can I help you in this matter?"

"Yes," the Sikyatki headman said, "I plan to hold a communal harvesting party. On that occasion you can attack the village. As soon as all my capable men have gone down to the field, you can come over and set the houses on fire. And when the men come running from the field, you can kill them."

"Very well, I'll tell my people about it. As soon as you let us know that your people have left for the field, we'll come." This is how the two forged their plans.

The day after the chief returned home from Qöötsaptuvela, he informed his crier chief. He was to announce publicly that there would be a communal harvesting party four days hence. "All right," the crier chief agreed. "I'll make the announcement tomorrow. Once people know, they can think about the coming event and make their preparations."

The night of the announcement, the Sikyatki chief returned to the leader of Qöötsaptuvela to bring him the news. "You can now tell your warriors that they are to make their attack in four days. They can start working on their weapons," he said.

"Very well, we'll surely do that," the other promised.

Early in the morning, on the day of the communal harvest party, the warriors from Qöötsaptuvela set out. Upon reaching the vicinity of Sikyatki, they waited. When everybody who was going to participate in the harvest party had descended to the field, they rushed the village. In no time they were inside. Quickly they pulled the ladders out from the houses where the women and children were. Having accomplished that, they set everything on fire. Some of the warriors had come with pitch they had gathered. This they smeared on the walls of the houses; as a result they quickly caught fire.

The men who were harvesting at the field spotted smoke. They saw that it was coming from the village. Thinking that something had happened, they ran back, one after the other. When the warriors who had set the fire saw them, they fell upon them. As soon as a man reached them, he was dispatched. Since the Sikyatki men had no weapons with which to resist, they died without being able to fight back. They were all killed, poor things.

Only a few Coyote clan members managed to survive by running away. As they were no longer able to live at Sikyatki, they fled to Oraibi. The Coyote clan, therefore, became the last group to be absorbed into the community of Oraibi.

This is how Sikyatki was destroyed. And all the witches, those excrement people, perished. The village chief, who had hatched out the scheme, lost his life with them. And here the story ends.

FIVE

The Abandonment of Huk'ovi

INTRODUCTION

The ruin of Huk'ovi, which translates approximately as "Windy Place-on-High," lies about three miles northwest of Old Oraibi. The site, never excavated or seriously investigated archaeologically, was "occupied in the twelve hundreds," according to Colton and Nequatewa (1932:8). This assumption is based on the occurrence of a number of characteristic ceramic remains, among them Jeddito Black-on-orange and Jeddito Black-on-white, types that do not seem to have been in use after A.D. 1300. Both authors conclude that the pueblo was "abandoned, like so many others in northern Arizona, because of the great drought of 1291–1299" (8).[1]

The mytho-historical events leading up to the ruin of Huk'ovi have been published twice before. Courlander's version, "The Flight from Huckovi" (1971:151–156) closely resembles the narrative presented here. On the other hand, Nequatewa's tale significantly differs from Courlander's and mine in a number of key elements (Colton and Nequatewa 1932:2–12).

Thus, two girls, rather than just one, are interested in the boy protagonist. His overall role in the ritual of the Ladder dance is more prominent. Two Spider Women are featured, one with her grandchildren Pöqangwhoya and Palöngawhoya. The trees employed for the dance grow in height through the magic of the chanting kachina gods. There is a rather unmotivated episode featuring an old man who has survived the kiva debacle. Finally, the avenging woman ghost who expels the Huk'ovi residents drives them westward, rather than eastward or over the cliff, at the request of the protagonist.

Most significantly, however, Nequatewa's story incorporates several more elements of witchcraft. Not only are the two girls vying for the boy witches, but the kachina in charge of the ladder ritual is also a wizard who succumbs to a bribe by the girls "to do crooked work." An additional sorcerer is hired by them to cause the catastrophic collapse of the kiva roof.

As the Hopis of today forgo their native language for English, as the old-time Hopi *homo religiosus* abandons traditional beliefs, the phenomenon of black magic, once a powerful controlling agent in Hopi society, is rapidly losing its grip. Marc Simmons's view "that the Pueblos are obsessively preoccupied with the threat posed by adherents to the black craft and that this fear is endemic" no longer holds for the present (1974:76). Modern Hopis no longer suffer from witch phobia and are not averse to sharing their knowledge of the subject with cultural outsiders. Yet, if the frequency with which the destructive motif of witchcraft is encountered in Hopi oral traditions is any indicator, it must have been extremely pervasive and deeply ingrained in Hopi culture at one time. Of the hundreds of narratives I have recorded in the field, dozens feature the sinister machinations and misdeeds of witches. Of the seven villages presented here, the destruction or ruination of four—Awat'ovi, Qa'ötaqtipu, Sikyatki, and Huk'ovi—is directly or indirectly attributable to the evil uses of sorcery.

As not much ethnographic information is available on Hopi sorcery outside of what can be gleaned from the published body of Hopi oral literature, I would like to present an overview sketched through a series of folk statements volunteered to me by Hopi consultants. Only some of the major aspects of Hopi witchcraft can be highlighted here. A more thorough treatment of this topic would easily fill a book of its own.

The general Hopi term for a sorcerer or witch, male or female, is *powaqa*. While this animate noun pluralizes as *popwaqt*, the same word, when used as an inanimate noun, conceptualizes the abstract notion of "witchcraft" or "sorcery." In this meaning the word occurs in singular form only. Morphologically, the word *powaqa* is composed of the root *powa-* and the element *qa* (one who/that which). Although this analysis ultimately may not be verifiable, the core semantics of *powa-* imply something like "change." Elsewhere I have, therefore, suggested the gloss "transform" for this morpheme (Malotki 1983:461). This meaning can be deduced from such words as *powata* (to make right/cure/exorcise), *powalti* (become purified/healed as from insanity), *powa'iwta* (be purified/be back to normal), and others. The element is likewise manifested in the lunar appellation Powamuya, literally "transform-moon/month" (approximately February), during which the great purification ceremony popularly known as the Bean dance takes place. While the stem *powa-*, which is not attested by itself, embraces positive denotations in these words, predominantly negative ones adhere to it in *powaqa* (sorcerer/witchcraft), *powaqqatsi* (way of life based on sorcery), and the affiliated verb *povowaqa* (to practice witchcraft/exercise black magic).[2] In light of its etymology, the term *powaqa* (witch) can thus be understood as "negative transformer," and *powaqa* (witchcraft), as "practice of negative transformation." As will become evident below, sorcerers attempt to "transform" the world around them for their own personal gain and advantage, usually with negative consequences, including death, for their fellow humans.

Hopi definitions of the *powaqa* (sorcerer) typically employ the label *nukpana*, which denotes "bad, wicked, evil person/evildoer/villain." The special knowledge of black magic that this evildoer commands is characterized as *tuhisa*. It is exploited only for totally selfish purposes.

TEXT 34

They say the sorcerer is really an evil person who can transform into just about anything and then change back again. In addition, the sorcerer is endowed with a great deal of special know-how that is used to harm people. This know-how of the sorcerer is referred to as *tuhisa* (magic power).

TEXT 35

Sorcerers only think of doing something nice for themselves. Therefore, they use their magic powers to benefit themselves. It's not only a man who can be that evil person or sorcerer but also girls, boys, and women.

In the context of a narrative, sorcerers, when operating individually, are often specified according to gender and age. Thus, one encounters *powaqtiyo* (witch boy), *powaqmana* (witch girl), *powaqwuuti* (witch woman), and *powaqtaqa* (witch man), as well as their respective plural forms. When acting as a whole conclave, however, Hopi oral literature frequently refers to them under the derogatory term of *kwitavit* (excrement/feces people/turds).[3] The following text constitutes a Hopi rationalization for the motivation of this supposedly self-imposed cover term on the part of the sorcerers.

TEXT 36

The witches of long ago had their own kiva. But as they did not want to refer to it openly as witch kiva, they covered their ways up by saying, "We're feces. We're nothings." This is how they talked about themselves. They were powerful beings, but to camouflage their activities they said, "We're turds. No one likes excrement. And since people don't like us, we wretched lot have our own kiva here." Feigning humility, they practiced their evil craft. "We poor things have our kiva here at the edge [of the village]. This is our kiva, the excrement kiva," they kept saying, hoping that through this ruse they would not be called outright sorcerers. They did not want people to refer to them as witches. That is why they used the term "turds" for themselves.

According to Hopi mythology, witchcraft previously reigned in the underworld. It and the general chaos of *koyaanisqatsi* were the primary motivation for all remaining good Hopi to seek a new beginning in the upper, surface world. However, evil succeeded in emerging with them from their ancestral home. Interestingly enough, First Witch is a female.[4] She justifies her showing at the emergence place of Sipaapuni with the excuse that she felt obliged to introduce the Hopis to the idea of life after death. Indirectly, she also hints at her responsibility for maintaining the institution of death in the new world.

TEXT 37

The Hopis tried to escape the evil in the underworld by running away from it. Secretly, they emerged into this world, but evidently without noticing, he brought the sorcerer with him. The Hopis had just settled down at the place where they had emerged when a little girl fell ill and died.

The elders cried out, "Oh my, why on earth did this happen to that poor thing? We probably brought a sorcerer out with us into this world. This was not to be. That's why we came here. We were not supposed to encounter death anymore; instead, we were to come to have eternal life. An evil person must have caused the girl's death. He probably wanted to prolong his life with her death. So let's search for this person. Whoever he is, he must be extremely powerful. That's why he is testing us."

The people were unhappy about this event and seriously reflected on the matter. Their leader now took some cornmeal and shaped it into a ball. Having done so he asked all the people to gather in one place. When everybody was assembled there, he said to them, "I'll throw this ball up into the air. The one it falls on will be the sorcerer. We'll put him back down into the underworld or kill him. I don't know yet what it will be."

With that, he hurled the cornmeal ball up in the air. Sure enough, as it came falling down, it landed directly on a beautiful girl. Immediately, they grabbed the girl and said to her, "It's you then. You must have come out with us. You're the witch. Remember, your lot was not supposed to go. Now we'll have to throw you back down again." The girl started crying. "No, don't do that to me. Yes, it's true, I'm a witch, but I came out in order to show you something here. There's life down below. Look, come here," she said to them.

Whereupon she led them back to the location of their emergence. The hole there was still not sealed. "All right," she said, "look down here. That little girl is alive again. She's as healthy as before and is living with all the other people down in the underworld," she explained.

The people went to the hole, and as they looked down, they could see the people walking about. The little girl who had just passed away was in good health and running around playing with the others. She was happy with them. "This is how someone will fare for all the future," the witch explained. "So don't kill me, don't put me back down. There will be life after death. I will see to that. Therefore, when people die, they will enter the underworld and be happy there. For this reason I came out with you."

This was enough to convince the people. They did not cast the witch back down. Thus, it's really true that Hopis who die return to the netherworld from which they emerged. We call this place Maski (Home of the Dead). Once a person returns there, one lives on there with the others.

So now that witchcraft had made its entrance into this world it was not long before the witch began to recruit people for herself. She must have persuaded them with her evil powers and thus brought them on her side. The people, meanwhile, had no desire to stay there [by the Sipaapuni] forever. They started out in many groups and scattered over the land. Not only Hopi departed from there, but others also. Somehow they were not one and the same people when they left. For this reason, evil did not come here only with the Hopi. All the people in the world, therefore, are familiar with witchcraft.

According to Hopi belief, Palangwu is the universal headquarters of all practitioners of black magic. It is located somewhere northeast of Hopi territory. Occasionally, a Hopi will identify it geographically with Canyon de Chelly. The *powaqki* (home of the sorcerers), at Palangwu, is modeled exactly after the Hopi subterranean kiva. As may be gathered from the text below, its division into an upper and a lower floor has hierarchical implications for the double caste system of witches.

TEXT 38

I don't know where Palangwu is, but everybody always says it's far in the northeast somewhere. A huge house is supposed to be there, the *powaqki* (home of the sorcerers). The sorcerers usually invite each other to go there.

For example, if someone has a date with a secret woman or man, they go there in order to be together. If a woman already has a husband, she puts him into a deep sleep and then she gets up. The man does likewise. After putting his wife to sleep, he visits his secret lover at the *powaqki*. After meeting there, the couples have a good time together. This is what I heard. That's how they do it. Sorcerers never want to demonstrate their sexual desire for one another in the open. That is why they go to Palangwu.

TEXT 39

All sorcerers gather there, at Palangwu, in one place. This place is just like a kiva. Actually, they are not all assembled in the same area. Those who meet on the lower floor of the kiva are the really cruel and merciless ones. For this reason, they are referred to as *atkyapopwaqt*, or "lower-floor sorcerers." Those who assemble on the upper platform of the kiva are less cruel and can be somewhat merciful. These are the *tuuwingaqwpopwaqt*, or "upper-floor sorcerers."

Travel to Palangwu is effected by the witches in many different disguises. According to Hopi belief, one frequent mode of flying is as a crow.

TEXT 40

The Hopis claim that the crow is a sorcerer. As is well known, sorcerers travel at night to Palangwu, their witch home, somewhere in the northeast. There, somewhere on the northeast side, are the headquarters of all sorcerers. Some of them transform themselves into crows and travel in this guise to their destination. In this guise they also return home. Early in the morning, when the crows are flying in from their meeting place, people say, "Now the sorcerers are arriving. That's why they're in such a hurry." Occasionally, when one crow is late behind the others, they say, "Oh my, this sorcerer did not make it home before sunrise. He probably didn't wake up in time." That's why people refer to these crows as witch crows.

One important reason for sorcerers to congregate at Palangwu is to induct *powaqwiwimkyam* (witch neophytes) into the *powaqwimi*, their own demoniacal order.

TEXT 41

Whenever people undertake something special, they need a lot of help, especially if it is a ceremony. With many participants during such a ceremonial event, who all focus on doing something with good thoughts in their hearts, things turn out successfully and everyone's most heartfelt longings are realized.

Sorcerers are not different in this respect. Witchcraft is their ritual, so to speak. Since they also need a lot of participants, they are out to recruit people. They engage in evil activities with which they make witchcraft attractive to people or with which they trap them.

As Text 42 explains, people can become sorcerers of their own free will. Or, a practitioner of witchcraft may attempt to persuade a child to join the ranks of evildoers. To protect their children from this danger, parents discourage them from sleeping over at other people's homes.

TEXT 42

Some people are interested in witchcraft on their own in order to acquire precious things. The one who wants to learn this business surely looks around for a sorcerer.

Once in a while, a sorcerer will say to young children, "Don't you want to get initiated into witchcraft? Don't you want to learn about it? Whoever knows witchcraft benefits a great deal from it." One is not to be swayed by this kind of talk. For when the child is old enough to reason and speaks Hopi well, and it has been initiated into witchcraft, it does not profit from it at all. Instead, it dies because of it.

Whenever a boy or girl has a friend whose parents are said to be witches, children are warned not to go there. Especially, they are told, "Don't you ever sleep at their house. When they invite you to spend the night, always say no. Otherwise, they are going to initiate you into witchcraft."

Another method of recruiting novices is by kidnapping infants. To enter the parents' home, the sorcerer is often disguised as a fly.

TEXT 43

People say that sorcerers are evil persons with great magical skills. Thus, when they want to get someone to become their follower, they enter a house at night when its residents are asleep and can't hear. Once in a while, they change into something like a fly first before entering. For even if the people are not asleep yet, they usually won't be concerned about a fly at that time. After all, flies are around at any time of the day. The sorcerer then looks around for a baby. Upon finding one lying next to its mother, the sorcerer picks it up and takes it to the witches' meeting place at Palangwu. In this manner, sorcerers add little children to their ranks. As the household members normally are not aware of a sorcerer making an entrance, they have no way of knowing who among their relatives the evildoer is.

They say that when a baby that is still on its cradleboard is initiated into witchcraft, nothing will happen to it. It will not die.

As Mischa Titiev has pointed out, the initiatory proceedings of sorcerers "are modeled on those of the highly regarded secret societies which conduct Hopi ceremonies. Thus, the novice must be introduced by a ceremonial father chosen from the ranks of the sorcerers, his head is washed in yucca suds, and he is given a new name" (1942:550). Most importantly, through this initiation, candidates acquire the faculty of transforming themselves into the animal familiar of their godfathers and godmothers. By drawing on the supernatural powers inherent or attributed to them, the new witch can now exercise the evil craft.

TEXT 44

They say that it's probably true that one has a godfather when initiated into the business of witchcraft. Therefore, sorcerers probably select a godfather there [at Palangwu]. Also, when one acquires a godfather, the latter names the new initiate. The godfather gives the person a witch name.

TEXT 45

Whenever sorcerers gather at Palangwu, they work there through their animal familiars. It is from their powers that they derive benefits. Of course these animal godfathers are acquired in an evil way. They are not selected by the candidate's parents. Rather, the candidate does it without telling anybody. Therefore, no one knows who the godfather of a sorcerer is. The animals they choose are particularly those that roam at night, such as coyotes, owls, and crows.

By assuming the shape of the godfather beast, a sorcerer is believed to acquire a second heart in addition to the human one. For this reason, the locution *lööq unangwa'ytaqa* (two-hearted one) is commonly applied to him.

TEXT 46

Those sorcerers who know how to make a person go mad are said to possess two hearts. They have coyotes, owls, and eagles for godfathers.

Even a little mouse may qualify for this role. In addition, antelope and mountain lions, bears, elk, and other animals can be godfathers. All of these animals have their own hearts. That is why they say that a sorcerer has two hearts and two sets of practical know-how that can be drawn on during the sorcerer's life.

Nagualism, a phenomenon that involves animal metamorphosis paired with the faculty of deriving powers from it, is not the privilege only of the *powaqa* in Hopi society (Parsons 1939, 1:63). It equally applies to the *tuuhikya* (medicine man) and the *povosqa* or *poosi'ytaqa*, which may be rendered as "seer" or "shaman."[5] Etymologically, the two words incorporate the word *poosi* (eye), which alludes to the fact that these practitioners diagnose a disease by examining the patient through a *ruupi* (quartz crystal).

Obviously, sorcerer, medicine man, and shaman have much in common. All three undergo some sort of initiation. They all seek out tutelary assistants from whom they hope to obtain certain magico-religious powers for their own personal advantage (Eliade 1964:297). But while the medicine man and shaman are essentially curers through the practice of "white magic," the black magic of the *powaqa* achieves the very opposite—sickness and death.

Unfortunately, nearly all knowledge of the ancient Hopi shamanic tradition is lost. One of my consultants, however, had a vague recollection that the Hopi shaman also went into some sort of a trance or ecstasy before he undertook his healing.[6] An additional clue may have been preserved in the word *tuskyavu*. This word, which is frequently applied to the *powaqa*, designates "the crazy, mad person" and may at one time have been associated with the ecstatic experience of the shaman. The fact that it is now used in reference to the sorcerer may therefore be an indication that Hopi sorcery is a version of an ancient shamanic complex.[7] A good portion of this ancient shamanic ensemble could perhaps be reconstructed by integrating all the customary practices of the *tuuhikya* (medicine man), the *povosqa* (shaman), the Yaya' (magician), and the *powaqa* (sorcerer), now scattered and only found in isolation, into one ideological schema.[8]

TEXT 47

Medicine men can also have animal familiars. They receive the aid of game animals or other creatures that roam the land. As a rule, the animal called upon as a godfather is that which one desires to equal in power. With the help of this animal the medicine man then practices healing.

The seer or shaman will sometimes call on a wolf as a godfather and even dress like one when he shamanizes. Others come to have the bear or eagle as a helping spirit. Even the little mouse will qualify, for it is very skillful. However, while medicine men will call on the powers of these animals, they never change into them. Still, they possess their hearts and may dress like them as they treat a patient. They have incorporated the magic skill of these animals.

On the other hand, when sorcerers select animals as their godfathers, they really change into them and go about in their guise. For example, if a sorcerer has a coyote as an animal benefactor, he becomes transformed into a real coyote. No medicine man has ever acquired a coyote as a godfather. I don't really know why, but people say that the coyote is gullible. He believes things right away, and they don't want to be like him. This is also the reason that the coyote was not made into a kachina.

Metamorphosis into the animal familiar by the sorcerer is accomplished by somersaulting over a rolling hoop. It is not clear whether sorcerers each own their own hoops or whether it only exists at Palangwu. Text 48 seems to indicate the former, since the hoop act is carried out in order to reach the home of the sorcerers. Text 49, on the other hand, presents the act as being performed at Palangwu only. Text 50 adds a cannibalistic component to the hoop rite, in that the sorcerer is said to consume part of the familiar's heart. I suggest the term "cardiophagy" for this custom.

TEXT 48
Whenever sorcerers wish to travel somewhere, they somersault over a hoop and then changes into the animal that they have called upon as godfather. In its form, the sorcerer journeys to the *powaqki*, the home of the sorcerers, and returns when the time is close to daybreak. Once more the sorcerer somersaults over the hoop, this time to land on its other side in human shape again.

TEXT 49
When the sorcerers are assembled at Palangwu, they somersault over a hoop. To do that, they all wait in line on the northeast side of the kiva ladder. As soon as it is someone's turn, that person rolls the hoop over toward the northwest, then dashes after it and flips over it. After landing on the other side, the sorcerer becomes transformed into the animal whose powers have been adopted. Now the sorcerer is no longer in human form. One after the other the sorcerers go through

this procedure. Before long, there is a pandemonium of sounds, for all sorts of creatures can be heard uttering their peculiar cries. There are crows, bears, and cougars. Shouting all at the same time, they pay no heed to each other.

TEXT 50

Whenever sorcerers come to the Powaqki and intend to go out and do something, they announce what animal they have for a benefactor. After its heart has been roasted, the witch eats some of it. The sorcerer keeps eating only little bits from it. Later, when they have the meeting in which they transform themselves into their godfather, the sorcerers always take that roasted heart around with them. As they finally assemble then, and one of them is ordered to go on an errand far away, the departing one takes a bite out of the roasted heart. Having done so, the sorcerer somersaults over a hoop to land on the other side, transformed into the chosen animal. Sorcerers draw on the powers of that animal in order to quickly reach their destination. Also, they do this to avoid getting to the village as humans.

Sorcerers, in addition to the animal benefactors mentioned above, are believed to operate in the guise of bats and shiny big flies, also known as skeleton flies. Of the domestic animals, cats and dogs qualify, but only if they are black. The appropriate Hopi terms for the latter are *tu'alangwmosa* (witching cat) and *tu'alangwvooko* (witching dog). Witch dogs are said to attract attention through their odd behavior. Either they bark and whine for no apparent reason or they dig up the ground around the house, which is usually interpreted as a bad omen. Hopis are very suspicious of all of these creatures and either avoid them or destroy them.

TEXT 51

I guess the skeleton fly is truly the pet of the sorcerer. Perhaps because it comes from the graveyard, or perhaps because it only flies around at night. People say that the skeleton fly does not sleep at night. When someone spots a fly at night, one calls it a skeleton fly.

TEXT 52

Once in a while, a sorcerer comes in the form of a bat. When a bat flies into a house, people close it up and quickly kill it. They roast it until it is done, for if the bat was a Hopi, he no longer has a way of getting about.

TEXT 53

People claim sorcerers can change into cats. As a rule, they change into black cats and then roam about at night, practicing witchcraft. That is why they tell us, "Don't have cats as pets, especially not a black one. A black cat is a witch. When sorcerers go witching in its guise, people are generally not aware of it." A cat usually belongs to someone and is together with people in the house. That is why people are unaware that it is a witch.

Then, once in a while, people see a black dog at night. That, they say, is really a witch dog.

One of the prime objectives of the Hopi *popwaqt* is to lengthen their own lives on this earth. This they achieve by causing the death of a relative.

TEXT 54

They say that if sorcerers wish to live long lives, they will sacrifice the life of any one of their relatives. I guess a sorcerer argues like this: "If you die for me, I'll live for a while longer." With that, he chooses one of his nephews, and the latter promptly falls ill. When the witch responsible for this learns of the illness, he goes to his relative and with tears expresses his sympathy. "My poor nephew. You, my younger brother, poor thing," he says, lamenting his illness. But it is only a charade. After all, he caused the illness and only sheds tears hoping that the relative will soon die. This is what people say about sorcerers. They are believed to prolong their lives through the deaths of their relatives. It is for this reason that some sorcerers live to be old men.

To kill a relative, the sorcerer must extract the heart. This is accomplished, symbolically, with an instrument described as a spindle (Text 55). After the heart has been extracted, it is taken to Palangwu and deposited in a special receptacle. Sorcerers who are reluctant to bring a relative's heart and try to cheat by substituting the heart of a domestic animal are found out and fail to extend their lives (Text 56).

TEXT 55

They say that if sorcerers want to lengthen their lives by sacrificing a relative, they will usually extract the victim's heart. The heart is taken to the home of the sorcerers, where something is done to it. People claim that a spindle is employed to extract a person's heart. I have no idea what that spindle looks like. I've never seen one. No one ever told me what it looks like. Who knows what someone has to do to take out the heart? Sorcerers guard this kind of knowledge and, therefore, don't go around talking about it. At the time someone is initiated into witchcraft, that one is informed how to go about this task. I, therefore, have no clue how this heart extraction is carried out.

TEXT 56

It is said that sorcerers will extract a person's heart. This is really true. They do it in a secret way. They have a special tool to accomplish this feat, a spindle. As soon as people are asleep, the sorcerer selects a nephew or niece and visits them. Then he places the spindle on their chest and takes out the heart. With this heart he then travels to Palangwu. Upon his arrival, he places it into a vessel that is kept ready there for this purpose. In this vessel, the human heart can clearly be heard crying.

Even though some persons want to be witches, they are sometimes not willing to extract the heart of their own nephew or niece to sacrifice them. Especially when they're fond of them. Yet, they desire to learn witchcraft; learning that demands a price. They must sacrifice the relative they love. That is the price they have to pay. Still, if one is not willing to go through with it, one will get the heart of an animal and then go to the meeting at Palangwu. Instead of a human heart, the person arrives with the heart of a pig, a sheep, or a chicken.

The minute the person enters with an animal heart, the other sorcerers notice it. For the vessel into which the hearts are placed is not just an ordinary pot. It announces to all those present what kind of a heart is in it. The moment the heart is inside, it produces the characteristic sounds of the being it belongs to. In the case of a chicken, for example, the heart clucks like a chicken.

By killing a relative, the sorcerers add four years to their life expectancy. Titiev's claim that heart extraction must be performed annually was not confirmed by my informants (1942:550). Since many things in Hopi culture occur or exist in sets of four, I would give their statements more credence.

TEXT 57

When a person's heart has been extracted by a sorcerer, the latter can prolong life by four years. When those four years are gone, the sorcerer must sacrifice another life in order to continue living. Sorcerers have been instructed to kill. A human heart is worth a great deal, especially if it belongs to a child, one who is still innocent. A pig's heart or sheep's heart, on the other hand, is not worth anything. In this manner, sorcerers live long lives—that is, as long as they're not recognized and caught in the act.

While death-dealing witchcraft is restricted to the sorcerer's own relatives, disease-causing black magic is not. One method employed involves lodging a pathogenic object in the body of the human target. The Hopi term for this "foreign object charged with malignant power" is *tuukyayni*. According to Titiev, "stiff deerhairs, red or black ants, centipedes, bits of bone or glass, and shreds of graveyard clothes are favorites" (1942:551). Ernest Beaglehole and Pearl Beaglehole add porcupine quills, bones of a dead person, and excrement to this list of injurious objects (1935:6). As Mircea Eliade has pointed out, these injurious objects are not introduced *in concreto* but are created by the mental power of the sorcerer (1964:301). According to Beaglehole and Beaglehole the Hopi *tuukyayni* bullets are symbolically projected from the sorcerer's "left hand by flicking the fingers at the intended victim" (1935:6). Alexander M. Stephen reports that the missile, which was also referred to as *powaqat ho'at* (sorcerer's arrow), was launched by a "magic bow" (1894:212). It was usually sucked out by the shaman, who thereby becomes "the antidemonic champion" (Eliade 1964:508). My text below additionally mentions cowry shells and teeth of the dead as potential disease inflictors.

TEXT 58

It is said that if a sorcerer does not like a particular individual or looks unfavorably upon someone, the sorcerer will magically insert a foreign object into that person. If the sorcerer does it successfully, this person then falls ill. Because sorcerers are very powerful and intend to harm a person, they shoot cowry shells into the body, causing the person to become ill with a disease. In addition, they use the teeth of dead humans as well as all sorts of animal bones. As a result, the person then contracts a disease and even dies. How sorcerers manage to shoot these missiles into people, I have no idea.

When the [ailing] person consults a medicine man, the medicine man always extracts a few items from the person's body. He usually pinches the patient where it hurts and removes something.

A second technique of inflicting misfortune or disease on a victim makes use of a bait object. Generally, it is a person's hair that the sorcerer will try to acquire as the bait.

TEXT 59

A sorcerer will steal anything from a person to do something to it. As a result, harm is done to that person. For example, the sorcerer will pluck a hair from a person and then treat it in such a way that this person meets with bad fortune or falls ill.

One favorite pastime of sorcerers is the pursuit of illicit sex. Both male and female converts to witchcraft are believed to enter clandestinely the homes of people they are lusting after in order to satisfy their sexual desires.

TEXT 60

After changing into their animal forms, sorcerers are believed to roam about in search of a sexual partner. Whenever a sorcerer spots a female he takes a fancy to, he goes after her wherever she may live, even if her home should be far away, such as at Zuni or a Rio Grande village. Of course, he does not travel on foot in order to quickly reach his destination. Then he enters the home of the desired female by means of his magical powers. As a result, the victim is unaware of his coming. Thereupon, he has intercourse with her without her being aware of it. A woman or girl does the same thing. They too enter a boy's or man's home, have intercourse with them, and then return to Palangwu again.

This is the reason that some say they encounter on their travels people who look just like someone from their home village. This is true even when journeying in distant places. The familiar-looking face can also be from another tribe, a Spaniard, or an Anglo. Some people even travel to lands across the ocean and see others who resemble their friends. Which is of course due to the fact that a sorcerer from their own village had intercourse there with a woman who then gave birth to a child.

Within the complex of sexual witchcraft one special form produces what is generally referred to as *tuskyavu* (love craziness) in its victim. To bring about this state of love madness, the love magician renders individuals helpless against their sexual desires by means of a *tuskyaptawi* (charming song).[9]

TEXT 61

It's a fact that [male] sorcerers possess charming songs that they use to bewitch a girl or woman. Once a sorcerer has charmed the female, he gets her to come to him by singing that song. In doing this, witches actually cause a disease in their victim known as love madness. They brainwash the female and mess up her heart. She then goes mad.

TEXT 62

Some sorcerers who know charming songs sing them where they cannot be overheard. With the help of such a song, the sorcerer can gain the affection of the female he desires. She then comes to him without being aware of why. Wherever she happens to be, at home or some place else where she is doing something with other people, once she has been overpowered by the charm, she starts out. Not knowing what is going on, she arrives at the place of the person who has summoned her with the help of the song. No wonder. The poor thing has become love mad.

Charming songs of a different nature also serve to ensure the sorcerer's hunting success. Casting a spell on the game animals, with the song, the sorcerer makes the animals offer themselves freely as prey.

TEXT 63

Sorcerers also go hunting for big game animals with a charming song. The hunter simply sits still somewhere, chanting the song. As a result, an antelope or deer will come running. It's quite obvious that witchcraft is involved because, having been compelled by the song, the animal is foaming at the mouth. Saliva is dripping from it. After flushing out a number of animals like this and killing them all, the sorcerers lug them home. Without bothering to purify them, they bring them in and cook them. Then people eat the meat.

Of course, the antisocial practices a sorcerer engages in are not limited to individuals only. Epidemics and famines are typically blamed on witches. Thus, cloud control, which within the realm of agriculturists and horti-culturists ultimately implies life-sustaining moisture control, is frequently attempted by the sorcerer, because it will impact a large group of people. To this extent, witches either channel clouds exclusively to their own fields and garden plots or they cause rain-laden clouds to withdraw. In the text samples below, offensive odor is used to make the clouds recede.[10]

TEXT 64

Rain that comes from Kiisiwu in the northeast is usually so thick that it obscures the light. I guess the clouds there are very compassionate, because they come to the aid of a person [who needs rain on the fields] without delay. Soon, it looks as if it's really going to pour. But the sorcerers at the refuse and toilet area always interfere in an evil way. Thus, when it is about to rain, they blow through a bone, preferably the bone of a diseased human. This produces a terrible odor. As a result, the rains do not approach the village.

TEXT 65

Sorcerers have extraordinary powers. They can use them, for example, to close in the clouds. Then the clouds cannot reach people, and the rain won't fall.

Once someone related that he observed a man at the mesa edge while there was a really white cumulus cloud up in the sky. It was stacked several layers high and kept moving in the direction of the village. Suddenly, the man who was standing there slid down his pants. Next he bent over, and sticking his buttocks directly toward the cloud, blew at it through his spread legs. As a person's behind stinks a great deal, the cloud did not come nearer because of the odor. It definitely had intended to shed its moisture; that's why it was approaching. However, due to the action of that man, it went somewhere else.

In addition, practitioners of witchcraft are believed to unleash a host of crop-destroying pests. These agents of destruction, combined with the sorcerers' own powers of averting imminent rain, constitute the classic formula for bringing about an ever-dreaded famine.

TEXT 66

People say it's true that sorcerers recruit all sorts of creatures to ruin crops. Certainly, they employ grasshoppers, kangaroo rats, prairie dogs, mice, and cutworms.

Realizing the ever-present danger of witchcraft, Hopi society prescribes a whole array of safeguards and taboos to separate a person from its malevolent influence. These prophylactic measures pertain both to the ceremonial and the secular context of Hopi life. Since the scope of this book does not permit a listing of these, suffice it to say that sorcerers are not immune to discovery. As a rule, when found out they will do their utmost to bribe their way out of what is a potentially fatal predicament. Note that the correct Hopi term for a witch that is seen or heard is *tu'alangw*, not *powaqa*.[11]

TEXT 67

When someone discovers a witch, and it is a woman, she will always offer herself sexually to that person. "If you don't say anything, you may enjoy my body." They say that if one then gives in to her, one spares the witch's life but forfeits one's own.

If the recognized witch is a man, he always offers that person a necklace. If the necklace is accepted, once again the witch's life is spared [and that of the other is forfeited]. Therefore, if one catches a sorcerer, one must say no to whatever he or she has to offer. Then the sorcerer is bound to die.

TEXT 68

People say that if a person actually catches a sorcerer practicing and in human form, that one should walk up and seize the sorcerer. They say any witch caught like this will definitely try to tempt this captor. In the case of a woman she will say, "All right, you've truly recognized me [for what I am]. Don't tell on me. In return, you can enjoy yourself with me. If you want to have sex with me, that's fine. But when you're done, you must not tell anyone. If you do, something bad will happen to you."

If it is a man, he will probably be wearing a beautiful concho belt or a necklace. If he owns lots of sheep or cows, he will say, "All right, you truly found me out. Don't tell on me. If you don't, you can have my sheep or cows. Also, here's a concho belt. And my necklace you can have too."

In case a person has none of the things offered to him and agrees to accept them, he dies for the sorcerer. For this reason, there's an instruction that says to refuse everything a sorcerer offers when caught red-handed. For those who accept the offer will definitely regret it.

As soon as the recognized sorcerer realizes that the discoverer cannot be bribed, the former resorts to pleading for life. As one might expect, however, this plea is loaded with trickery.

TEXT 69

When a sorcerer gets caught red-handed and the discoverer rejects what is offered [in return for not revealing the secret identity], the sorcerer begs for sympathy and says, "If only I could see the sun four more times and then die." A person with brains will reject this plea also and reply, "No. You are completely evil and brought this upon yourself. You must die."

The sorcerer, however, will not give up and will plead to live a little longer, maybe two or three days, and even ask to see the sun just one more time. When a person stands fast, one beats the sorcerer at the game.

Of course, the sorcerer was not just asking for four days. In saying four days, the sorcerer was actually asking for four years. Were someone to grant the request for four days, the sorcerer would actually live another four years. Upon reaching the end of that time, the sorcerer would have to lengthen life again with another person's death. Thus, when the offer of a witch is declined, the sorcerer has four more days to live and then dies.

As Titiev rightly points out, "one of the most telling features of the Hopi attitude toward sorcerers is found in their religious notions. On the whole, Hopi religion is decidedly nonethical, but *poakam* [correctly, *popwaqt*] are severely punished in the other world" (1942:556). Once again, lack of space prohibits any enumeration of the manifold ordeals the sorcerer is subjected to during the journey in the underworld.[12] The example cited below focuses on the last leg of this journey, when the sorcerer reaches the flaming fire pit, the final destination. Here Kwaani'ytaqa, in his role as psychopomp, makes sure that evildoers receive their deserved punishment, while the souls of the pure are permitted to proceed to paradise.

TEXT 70

When sorcerers are dead, they head for the place where we go when we die. But they never reach the location where the pure ones live. Rather, they come to the fire pit that the Kwaani'ytaqa is tending. He has a huge fire going in the pit. As the sorcerers line up at this pit, they are cast into the fire. They line up on all four sides of the hole: the northwest, southwest, southeast, and northeast. As they stand there, the Kwaani'ytaqa who is looking after the fire commands, "All right, throw them in!" Whereupon, all those who died because of these sorcerers cast them in, one after the other. The victimized now exact their revenge. All who murder, once they die, are pushed into this fire pit.

Once in a while, for some peculiar reason, a sorcerer is not easily killed. One simply does not burst into flames and die. Such a sorcerer will return in the shape of a stinkbug. That's what people say.

NOTES

1. Today, due to better paleoclimatological information, based on more accurate dendrochronological data, the "Great Drought" is assigned a much longer period. As a rule, it is said to have lasted from A.D. 1276 to 1299 (Haury 1986:70).

2. *Powaqqatsi* is the movie title adopted by Godfrey Reggio for his sequel to *Koyaanisqatsi*, which has become an international cult movie. Both movie titles, which I had suggested to the films' director, name ancient Hopi concepts. However, while *koyaanisqatsi* (corrupted life) is a static idea that describes social disorder and chaos, *powaqqatsi* is more dynamic in that it portrays an active pursuit of willful, malicious change.

3. The term *kwitavit* (turds) is limited in its linguistic usage to the dialect of the Third Mesa villages. Second Mesa speakers prefer the form *kwitam* for the same meaning.

4. According to Mischa Titiev, "The Hopi believe that all witches are the descendants of a mythological character known as Spider Woman, who plays a prominent part in their stories of the beginning of human life on earth" (1942:549). All of my informants unanimously disagreed with this statement. Spider Woman is considered a powerful, yet benevolent earth goddess who, like a *dea ex machina*, always appears to help those in distress. To quote the rebuttal of one of my consultants: "Kookyangwso'wuuti qa powaqa. Pam pay hiita lolmatsa tuwat wuuwanta, hakimuy sinmuy pa'angwantaniqey." [Old Spider Woman is no sorceress. On the contrary, she constantly thinks of helping people.]

5. *Poosi'ytaqa*, the Third Mesa term, literally means "one who has an eye." Among Second Mesa speakers, the expression *povosqa* (one who [does] seeing/a seer) is more prevalent. *Poovost* and *povosyaqam* are the respective plural forms. In addition to the rendition as "shaman," one also encounters "crystal gazer," "crystal diagnostician," and "eye-seeker" (Stephen 1894). *Poovost* were once organized in *poswimi*, secret societies of their own. An individual initiate into such a *poswimi* was consequently known as a *poswimkya*.

Whether the Yaya' (magician), who practiced white magic, also employed helping spirits in performing his feats of illusion, I have not been able to determine to date. Regardless of this, Mircea Eliade's observations that the terms "shaman," "medicine man," "sorcerer," and "magician" designate certain individuals endowed with magical and religious powers, and that they are found in all "primitive" societies, are certainly true regarding the Hopi (1964:3).

6. Interestingly enough, the ancient Hopi shaman used to employ a special medicine to induce ecstatic behavior reminiscent of his animal familiar, whose form and power he magically assumed. This may be gathered from the following statement: "Poosi'ytaqa aw pitsinanik hiita ngahuy angqw sowangwu. Pu' paasat pam ang pakiqw pu' paasat pam hintsakngwu. Pu' hiita na'ykyangw nuutuupa ma'ynume' pan pam nay an hintsakngwu. Pu' piw pan töqnumngwu." [Whenever a shaman is about to practice, he eats from his medicine. As soon as it has been digested, he acts strangely. As he uses his hands on his patients, he behaves just like his alter animal. He will even utter similar sounds.]

7. That the borderline between shamanism and witchcraft is a narrow one that is easily transgressed is underscored by Frederick Webb Hodge's remarks:

Witchcraft may be defined as the art of controlling the will and well-being of another person by supernatural or occult means, usually to his detriment. If shamans possessed supernatural powers that could be exerted beneficially, it was naturally supposed that they might also be exerted with injurious results, and therefore, where shamanism was most highly developed, the majority of supposed witches, or rather wizards, were shamans. [1969(1910), 2:965]

That a close connection between witchcraft and curing was once also observable in Hopi culture can be gathered from the following statement by Titiev: "On the basis of a widespread belief that the same kind of power which causes an ailment can also cure it, the Hopi tend to equate their shamans with witches." For this reason, "all medicine men are regarded with a mixture of respect and fear" (1956:54).

8. While in Hopi oral literature initiation into the business of curing almost regularly involves death, dismemberment, and resurrection for the *tuuhikya* (medicine man), this seems also to have been the case for the Yaya' (magician). This is evident from a legend of the origin of the Yaya't (members of the Yaya' society) recorded by Henry R. Voth (1905:41–47). Here, the candidates are put to death in fiery pits and then miraculously brought back to life. This ritual death and resurrection scenario, according to Eliade, is typical of a shaman's initiation (1964:38).

9. Beaglehole and Beaglehole also report that a *tuskyaptiiponi* (love sorcerer's medicine bundle) was used in conjunction with the practice of love magic (1935:8).

10. Titiev cites what he calls "a standard technique" for driving off rainstorms:

The two-hearted one takes four reeds, about half an inch in diameter and four inches long and fills them lightly with a mixture of ashes (*qötsvu*) and a vaginal discharge (*hovalangwu*). The ashes represent dust. The other substance is thought to be highly displeasing to the sky gods. When rain appears imminent, the malefactor blows the contents of one of the reeds upward, whereupon the clouds promptly recede. This is done four times, after which, the deities give up and take their rain elsewhere. [1942:551]

11. The following is a Hopi folk definition of *tu'alangw:* "Tu'alangwuy hak tuwangwu hakiy aw hintsanqw sen hinwat hakiy tsatsawinaqw. Pu' powaqat pay hak qa tuwangwu hakiy aw tutu'alangqw. Pam pay qa susmataq tu'alangwningwu." [A *tu'alangw* is visible when practicing. For example, when he is scaring someone. The *powaqa*, however, one cannot see when he is practicing his witchcraft against a person. He is clearly not a *tu'alangw*.]

12. Hopi oral literature contains several Orpheus myths in conjunction with which details of the sorcerer's fate in the underworld are presented. In addition to the ones published by Voth (1905:114–119), Courlander (1971:121–131) and Albert

Yava (1978:100–104), I have recorded four such myths, one of which features Coyote on a visit to the afterworld.

The Legend

Aliksa'i. They say people were living at Pivanhonkyapi. Below this place, at Huk'ovi, was another settlement. Both villages had a lot of people. At Pivanhonkyapi lived a young man who was very handsome. And at Huk'ovi lived a girl who wanted the boy from Pivanhonkyapi. But he did not care for her at all. The girl had tried repeatedly to get him, but he never gave in to her.

More than once, the girl had encountered the boy and spoken to him without being prompted, but he had never answered her. Occasionally, at night she would tell another youth to bring that boy over to her house. When informed of his mission, the Pivanhonkyapi boy refused to go and at times actually became angry. "No way will I go to her place, and yet she has the nerve to ask you to get me there. So tell her not to have anyone else come after me anymore." This is how he used to react to the girl's invitation.

Pivanhonkyapi was a village that frequently staged the Ladder dance. Once again, this event was close at hand. Right at the rim of the mesa where the dance was usually performed were four holes in the bedrock. Into these holes, trunks of pine trees were inserted whenever the ceremony was to be held. As the day for the Ladder dance was drawing near, the participants retreated into their kiva to go through their more esoteric rites. There they would smoke ritually and chant prayers.

The morning after the ceremony got under way, the youth set out to fetch firewood for his parents. By chance that very day the girl from Huk'ovi, too, was going out for wood. The two went at the same time. The boy was already gathering fuel in the area where he intended to prepare his load. He was just going about his business when, all of a sudden, someone spoke to him. "Man," a voice said.

When he looked up to see who it was, he noticed that it was a young woman he did not know. Evidently she was from Huk'ovi. As he had no intention of speaking to her, he wandered off. Again she spoke. "Am I so ugly that you must run away from me?" she inquired. "Do I look so much like an old woman that you're avoiding me?"

At long last the boy replied. "No," he said, "you're a pretty girl."

"Then why do you move away from me? I knew that you were coming here to fetch firewood. That's why I came to wait for your arrival," the girl explained. "Stop gathering wood for a while, and come here to me," the girl invited the youth. "Come over here and enjoy yourself on me. You can have my body."

"Oh no," the boy exclaimed, refusing. "I can't do such a thing. At our village we are nearing an important event. For that reason I can't be doing that," he said, vehemently rejecting the girl's offer. After all, he was going to participate in the Ladder dance. He was one of the men selected to climb on the pole. This he pointed out to the girl as he turned down her offer.

"Don't worry, it'll be all right," the girl assured him. "If we don't tell anyone, no one will know."

"I don't think I'll go along with you," the boy insisted. "Last night the men already had their first assembly. They most certainly included me in their ceremonial plans. Therefore I cannot do what you ask."

Again and again the girl pressed the boy, each time in a different manner. Over and over she urged him to have intercourse with her. But he would not be swayed. Without giving in to her temptations, he picked up his bundle of firewood and departed for home.

The girl also headed home. She was furious that she had been rejected. She was still in this frame of mind when she arrived home. "One way or another I'm going to fix him," she said to herself. "I've come back seething with anger, so I'll do something about it," she vowed.

When the boy returned to Pivanhonkyapi, the pine trees had already been erected. These the kachinas would climb to dance on, so they were all set up. That evening the girl was still fuming. She was determined to do something to that boy. And she would find a way, for she was a witch and a master at her craft. So that night she worked on her plan. By using her magic powers she caused a crack in one of the holes into which the pine poles had been inserted. Yes, she was skilled at her sorcery. Who knows how she accomplished this, but now she was certain the boy would fall. With a crack running though the hole, the pole would give way and crash down over the rim with the boy still on it. This was how she would get her revenge.

The following day was called *suus qa himu*, as nothing special happens on this day, three days prior to the ceremonial climax. The men were gathered within their kiva when quite unexpectedly, Old Spider Woman called on them. She entered their kiva and said, "A girl from Huk'ovi has caused a crack alongside the hole in which your tree is planted. I urge you to go over and fix it. It can't stay the way it is," she warned them. "Here, take this to mend the crack." With that, she handed the men a mushy paste and instructed them, "Pull out the pole and repair the damage."

"Perhaps this is true," some of the men said as they proceeded to the dance site. They removed the pole closest to the mesa rim. Sure enough, they discovered that the hole was cracked. They took the magic medicine Old Spider Woman had given them and plastered it over the crack. They then replaced the tree and made sure that it held fast. That done, they returned to their kiva. Once more that night they carried out their ritual, and then they slept.

The next day, on *piktotokya*, Old Spider Woman showed up again. "The witch has done it again," she informed the men. "Therefore, go over and mend the crack." And as before she handed them something.

The men did as bidden. They went to the ladder hole. Sure enough, there was a new fissure in the rock. After repairing the damage as they had done the previous time, they fastened the pole. Twice more the men had to repeat this routine as they fixed the remaining holes. Apparently, the girl had caused cracks in all of them.

By now the day of the dance was at hand. The people of Pivanhonkyapi and some from Huk'ovi went to see the event. There was a crowd of spectators gathered. And, indeed, the kachinas came out in the morning. They headed to the plaza and began their performance. They danced beautifully and uttered cries that were pleasing to the onlookers. Presently, two of the kachinas proceeded to climb the poles. It was customary for two to do so at the same time and dance on the top of the poles. Next, one would hold on to something at the top and, hanging downward, swing out to the mesa edge to the beat of the chanting. And then he would spin nicely round and round the pole. Up and down the dancers climbed. They performed all sorts of acrobatic acts up there. And in spite of the steep drop-off on the south side, not one of them ever got dizzy.

Now one dancer would jump from one post to another, skillfully grabbing it. There he would repeat this performance, spinning nicely around the pole. At times the kachinas exchanged poles by jumping simultaneously from one to the next, crossing each other in mid-air. When they jumped, it appeared as if they were going to collide. Whenever this happened, the spectators below roared. The screaming from the crowd was deafening. This is what happened there during the Ladder dance. In addition, there were the pleasant sounds of the drum and the grating noise of the bone scapulae as they were scraped across the notched sticks. The kachinas shaking their rattles added to this symphony of sounds.

When the first kachina pair had finished, it was the boy's turn. He, too, climbed the pole with a companion. They performed just as the first two did. None of the dancers were hurt, and the dancing continued until noon, when the men took a break to eat. They returned to their kiva and descended into this underground chamber. Having eaten lunch, they sat around resting. Meanwhile, the leader of the ceremony left for a shrine to deposit prayer feathers and sacred cornmeal. As he went on this mission, the witch girl overheard that the damaged holes had been mended. To find out for sure, she went to see for herself. When she noticed that they had indeed been repaired, she grew angry. "Oh no! Darn it. Someone fixed the cracks. There's got to be another way," she swore. So, by means of her witchcraft, she broke one of the roof beams in the kiva where the kachinas were. They had no inkling that the beam had been broken. Thus, they were still resting there when the roof suddenly caved in. As it broke it crashed down on all those inside.

Everyone tried to get out but soon died of suffocation. The people on top, aware of the disaster, came scrambling and cleared away the debris. But it was to no avail. All the men had already perished. How the people lamented! They were in hysterics about the terrible event. What a day of horror it was! Each of the villagers lost at least one relative or acquaintance in this tragedy.

Now the fun was gone. The dance performance was terminated and the spectators from Huk'ovi returned home. The people of Pivanhonkyapi were all saddened and grieving. This was not so with the Huk'ovis, for they had not lost anyone to this calamity.

This is what took place at Pivanhonkyapi. As night fell no one could be found wandering about, for most of the people had lost a loved one and were sad. It so happened, however, that one man was not in his house but was sitting outside on top of the roof. All of a sudden, from down in the plain a light became visible. It was coming straight toward Pivanhonkyapi. At some point, however, it went back toward the south, then again reversed its course and headed for the village. This is what the flame was doing. The man kept watching. It was really strange to him that it was going back and forth. Finally, it disappeared below the mesa edge. The man was still sitting there when it came up the mesa. It really was a fire. It continued along the outskirts of Pivanhonkyapi and made a complete circuit around it. Then it appeared in the village and entered the plaza. Then it stopped at the shrine. To his amazement, the man now discovered that it was a woman. As she rested there, she muttered something. She was terrifying to look upon. Apparently, she was Tiikuywuuti.

As she sat at the shrine she spotted him. Beckoning to him she said, "Come here to me." She was so ugly, however, that he hesitated to approach her. "Don't be afraid of me. I won't harm you," she assured him.

The man came down from the housetop. When he reached the monstrous woman she said to him, "I've heard what happened here. That's why

I've come. I took pity on you. I know the person who is responsible for the tragedy that took place here. She is a witch girl from Huk'ovi who is full of desire for a young man here. When he remained steadfast and refused to submit to her, she grew so angry that she killed all those men. But if you so wish, I will take revenge for you. If that is your desire, I want some of you to make prayer sticks for me and deposit them here at this shrine. I will then take on this task." This was all the woman said, whereupon she departed, using the fire as a cover. She descended over the mesa rim and, following the same zigzag course, disappeared in a southwesterly direction.

This was what the man experienced in his encounter with the ghastly being. The next morning he went about the village among the survivors, telling them what he had learned and conveying to the others the instructions Tiikuywuuti had left with him. The men agreed with her proposal, and some of them set to making prayer feathers. It was still daylight when the man who had first seen her took them to the shrine on the plaza. But gradually day turned to late evening and then darkness fell. No one was asleep. The people were crowded on the rooftops, waiting for the things to come.

It was late at night when, once again, the flame made its appearance down below. Once more it approached in a zigzag line. Every so often it seemed to head straight for Pivanhonkyapi, but then it turned in the opposite direction again. Finally, it approached Huk'ovi. The fire circled the village and then entered the plaza. There the monster woman went through the motions of grinding corn and singing:

Tutaahe, tutaahe.
Tutaavunaahe, tutaavunaahe.
Heh, heh, heh, heh.

These were the only sounds she uttered. Thereupon she made her way out of the plaza and headed west.

Some of the Huk'ovi people apparently had heard the chanting of the creature, because they came out of their houses to see what all the commotion was about. Some ran in the same direction the creature had taken, but by now she was already moving southwest in the guise of a flame. Those who heard the strange song asked each other, "Who on earth was that creature? It might return, so let's plan an ambush. We can lie in wait tomorrow and then grab it."

The following evening those who had agreed to this plan assembled. Finally, the right time came. It was well into the night when the creature approached. It behaved as on the previous occasion and then entered the plaza. As before, the Tiikuywuuti went through the grinding motions, and once again, she accompanied her grinding with the same eerie song. When she finished and was about to depart, those who lay in hiding rushed upon her. But as the men converged on her, they became terrified and fled in fright, understandably so, for she was a horrifying creature and exceedingly hideous. Her eyes were two hollow pits and her teeth were bared.

The men simply could not get near her. As soon as a person's eyes fell on her, he became frightened and ran. And so she escaped again, taking the same route as before. The people of Pivanhonkyapi watched her from afar. They could easily discern the flame. The Huk'ovi men, at first, did not pay heed to the fire, but then it happened a second time. This occurrence now repeated itself on a regular basis. Each night the creature made its nocturnal visit. It would grind in the plaza and then return where it came from. The people wondered why all this was going on. "She's coming here for a reason," they kept saying. "We must catch her by any means, this ugly demon."

Meanwhile, four days went by, then five days. Still, the creature did not let them be. Seeing this, the leaders of Huk'ovi gathered and said, "This thing that keeps coming here will not leave us alone. Perhaps it has a purpose for doing this. We must be thankful that it hasn't harmed anyone yet. So let's move away from here," they decided. "We're bound to find a place to live somewhere else." And therefore the leaders agreed to abandon the village.

Everyone agreed with the decision. "All right," they said, "we'll go tomorrow." Immediately they began to prepare for the exodus. The next morning, at the crack of dawn, the people started out in a southwesterly direction. When darkness fell, they made camp.

Once more the flame came from the plain. It seemed to be coming straight for them. When it spotted them where they were gathered, it moved past them and on toward their village. There the creature inspected everything. It was looking to see if, perchance, someone had remained behind who needed to be driven out. But not a soul was left, and the fire headed back toward the Huk'ovis.

When the people of Huk'ovi spotted the fire, they got up and trekked on again, even though it was night. By the time the morning came, the creature disappeared. However, the next evening it was back and followed them anew. Wherever the people turned, it prodded them on, usually at night.

So the people had no choice but to move on. Finally, at a certain place the Tiikuywuuti let go of them. Apparently she had her abode there. The

Huk'ovis, however, did not settle there but continued on. Eventually, they reached a site where they established a settlement. There, far away from their previous homes, the people of Huk'ovi were living now. Thus, it was because of a witch girl that the village of Huk'ovi was abandoned and fell into ruin. And here the story ends.

SIX

The End of Hovi'itstuyqa

INTRODUCTION

Hovi'itstuyqa is the Hopi place-name for Mount Elden, a ridge-shaped volcanic dome along the southern flank of the San Francisco Mountains near Flagstaff, Arizona. Distinguished by thick, pasty extrusions of hardened magma, its promontory features a little point that juts skyward. This topographical configuration, which is clearly discernible against the horizon as one approaches the mountain from the northeast, apparently reminded the Hopi of buttocks (*hoovi*) sticking out (*itsta*), for this is what Hovi'itstuyqa implies: "Buttocks Sticking Out Point."

To date, it has been impossible to positively locate the ruin site associated with the place-name. Nequatewa, who published the only other version on the demise of Hovi'itstuyqa (1938:37), believed that it was identical with Elden Pueblo at the foot of Mount Elden in Flagstaff. However, Elden Pueblo, after which the archaeological period between A.D. 1130 and 1200 has been named Elden Phase, is generally known as Pasiwvi to the Hopi (Pilles cited in Malotki and Lomatuway'ma 1987:115). During the Elden Phase, termed the "Golden Age of the Sinagua" culture by Peter Pilles, the Sinagua populated the entire region from Wupatki to the north, Anderson Mesa to the east, and the Verde Valley to the south of the San Francisco Mountains. Malcolm Farmer has consequently suggested (1955:44) that Hovi'itstuyqa could have been one of many sites known to have been occupied in late prehistoric times in the Flagstaff area (Turkey Hill Pueblo, A.D. 1150 to 1200, and Old Caves Pueblo, A.D. 1250 to 1300), along Anderson Mesa (Kinnikinick Pueblo, A.D. 1200 to 1325; Grape Vine Pueblo, A.D. 1300 to 1400; and the Pollock Site, A.D. 1250 to 1325), and in the Verde Valley (Montezuma Castle, which was occupied as late as A.D. 1425).

According to the present legend, Tupats'ovi, the home village of the protagonist, was situated on Nuvakwewtaqa, the Hopi name for the Chavez

Pass area approximately one hundred miles south of the Hopi mesas. On the basis of archaeological evidence indicating that Chavez Pass and Anderson Mesa were inhabited at the same time, Farmer decided on Grape Vine Pueblo as a possible candidate for Hovi'itstuyqa. However, since Grape Vine Pueblo has not been excavated to date, its identification with Hovi'itstuyqa must remain unsubstantiated. As Farmer himself submits, "It will be of some interest some day when this site is excavated to see if there is any evidence of such a destruction" (1955:45).

Nor has Elden Pueblo, initially explored by Jesse W. Fewkes in 1926 and currently being reexcavated by Pilles, yielded any archaeological clues that it was destroyed by enemies from the south, as revealed in the story. Two Hopi sherds of Jeddito Black-on-yellow with the rather late date of A.D. 1300 to 1400, recently discovered by Pilles, in his opinion point to the possible conclusion that Elden Pueblo, first dated to about A.D. 1150 to 1200 on the basis of ceramic finds, was occupied later than originally presumed or underwent "periodic visitation by later inhabitants of the region" (Pilles 1991:10).

While the likelihood is rather high that the present legend garnishes a true historic event, the exact location of Hovi'itstuyqa may never be resolved satisfactorily. As to how the Hopi came to learn of the destruction of the village, one can only speculate. Sinagua people migrating to Hopi country after the final eruption of Sunset Crater in A.D. 1250 may have transmitted word of the extinction of one of their settlements. As I have shown elsewhere (Malotki and Lomatuway'ma 1987:9), Ka'nas, which identifies a Hopi kachina associated with Sunset Crater about ten miles north of Elden Pueblo, may be linguistic proof that some of the Sinaguas were absorbed by the Hopi. Since it is an axiom of Hopi phonological structure that native words only occur with the syllable initial sound sequence *qa, ka* in a word invariably betrays its foreign origin. Thus, nonnative Ka'nas might actually represent the ancient tribal name of the Sinagua immigrants.

Another possible scenario could be, of course, that the destruction of Hovi'itstuyqa has no historic foundation whatsoever. The Hopi's familiarity with the ruin could simply stem from the fact that they discovered it while on pilgrimage to one of the shrines located at Nuvatukya'ovi, the home of their kachina gods. The Hopi must have come across many ruin sites in this way, any one of which could have served as the inspirational departure point for the present legendary account. To satisfy their curiosity as to the possible fate of the ruin's former residents, an "explanation" came about in the form of the present mytho-historical account.

The story itself contains many of the stock ingredients distinguishing

Hopi storytelling and constitutes oral entertainment at its best. Pitsin-sivostiyo, or "Cotton Seed Boy," against the incredible odds of near-outcast social ranking and unattractive physiognomy, wins the girl of his dreams. He does so by meeting the condition the girl has set for accepting one of her suitors as a future mate: he must bring her a live yellow fox. Pitsinsivostiyo accomplishes this challenge with the aid of his grandmother, whose true identity is revealed as Old Spider Woman in the course of the story. When Pitsinsivostiyo's wife, who all along had really been interested in a handsome young man from Hovi'itstuyqa by the name of Sikyaatayo (Yellow Fox) gives in to the adulterous advances of the man and follows him to his home at Hovi'itstuyqa, Pitsinsivostiyo, heartbroken over the loss of his wife, ponders revenge. He realizes his revenge when, at the suggestion of his grandmother, he manages to entice a band of mercenaries living far to the southwest of Tupats'ovi to raid Hovi'itstuyqa and destroy its population. Pitsinsivostiyo personally kills his rival Sikyaatayo and allows his former wife to be carried off by the chief of the enemy party as one of the rewards for the insidious attack.

Although the present tale, in its main points, closely resembles the story told by Nequatewa in 1938, it is nearly four times as long. As is also the case with the other legends of this collection, when compared to previously published accounts, I attribute this difference in length to my method of tape-recording the story in the original Hopi vernacular.

Both stories agree on the proper names of the protagonist and antagonist and their respective home villages. They also concur in the appellation of the Kisispayam, the raider group to the southwest of Chavez Pass. The name, which is etymologically obscure, is assigned by Nequatewa to the Yavapai from the Verde Valley. None of the Hopis I consulted as to the ethnic origin or tribal affiliation of the Kisispayas was able to shed any light on this question. Farmer believes that to identify them with the Yavapai "is of interest and does fit with the present trend of thinking that these groups to the west and southwest of Flagstaff may be the descendants of the people of prehistoric times, in the area, or at least that some element of the past groups is represented in the historic tribes found in the Verde Valley by the first Spanish explorers" (1955:45).

Unlike Nequatewa, who gives the name of the girl as Nagai-si, the girl remains unnamed in the version I recorded.

In addition to the obvious difference in narrative length, the percentage of dialogue is larger in this version. The story is also richer in detail. Thus, the socially inferior standing of Pitsinsivostiyo, as compared to the girl he woos, receives greater emphasis. The episodes in which his grandmother explains to him how to fashion bow and arrows contain lengthy didactic passages. The actual ruse applied in trapping the fox is played out in more elaborate fashion. The scene depicting a woman anxious to satisfy her curiosity as to who might be grinding corn in the old woman's house is psychologically much more convincing than the summary statement in Nequatewa that, incidentally, shows a man in this role. A higher degree of specification also holds for the planning and execution of Pitsinsivostiyo's revenge. In one major deviation from Nequatewa's story line, the fox that is endowed with the faculty of speech and human emotions is not returned to the animal world of his peers after the discovery of the woman's adultery, but only at the very end of the tale. The entire episode, missing in Nequatewa, is highlighted by an explanation of why henceforth the fox pelt will be part of the kachina costume.

Curiously enough, both stories concur in identifying Pitsinsivostiyo's grandmother as Old Spider Woman, although this narrative element is not in conformity with traditional Hopi mythology. As a rule, Old Spider Woman is portrayed as living with her grandsons Pöqangwhoya and Palöngawhoya. Nor is her abode normally confined to the toilet and refuse area of the village, as in the story here. This location may, however, be connected to the standard mode in which the earth goddess contacts a person in need of help. The initial encounter generally takes place at the time when such persons are about to relieve themselves inadvertently in the spot where she has her subterranean house.

THE LEGEND

Aliksa'i. People were living southeast of Homol'ovi. There on the ridge of Nuvakwewtaqa was a village by the name of Tupats'ovi. Way over on the northeast side of Nuvatukya'ovi, the San Francisco Mountains, there was also a settlement. It was known by the name Hovi'itstuyqa. Here in Hopiland there were villages in several locations. Far in the northwest were the two communities of Oraibi and Pivanhonkyapi situated close together. And somewhat northeast of Tupats'ovi was the village of Awat'ovi. The people at home in these villages were all Hopis. Therefore, they were wont to travel into all directions for something or other. Once in a while when a man had a particular trade item, he would come with it and barter for it in the various villages. Then again, if there was a dance somewhere, and a person was not lazy, he would go see the dance. This is how people all had some acquaintances somewhere.

In turn, there were all the other Indian groups living all across the land. Some of them ventured far into Hopi territory to trade their belongings.

Some were enemies and therefore only came to raid. The Hopi, as a rule, did not visit their settlements. Since it was difficult to travel in those areas on one's own, someone would go with several companions if he wanted to go somewhere for a specific purpose. Travelers then usually took some weapon along. This is about the way life was in those days.

At Tupats'ovi lived a boy by the name of Pitsinsivostiyo. The poor lad had only a grandmother, so he lived with her. The two were lower-class people and had their abode somewhere at the southwestern edge of the village, in an area used by the villagers as a dump and to relieve themselves. The grandmother and her grandchild were destitute and had hardly any food. They eked out a bare living. Once in a great while, when a villager had something to eat and felt sorry for them, one would share a portion of food with them. In addition to being poor, Pitsinsivostiyo was quite homely. For this reason, no one of his age group befriended him. He always puttered around alone. Nobody really wanted to get acquainted with the two, which meant that they never had any visitors.

It so happened that a girl was living in the village of Tupats'ovi who was of marriageable age and exceedingly beautiful. She was a member of the influential upper-class people who had their homes on the northwest side of the plaza. She was quite industrious and always did chores for her mother. Also, she was most willing to cook. Therefore she was always busy preparing a meal and her mother never had to cook. Whenever she started grinding corn, she ground long into the night before going to bed. She had just reached young womanhood, which explained why she constantly did the work of her own free will. She was so well versed in all aspects of housekeeping that all the other women were envious of her and wished they had daughters like that.

The girl's facial features were beautiful and the skin of her body light-complected. She was different from anyone else. No one in the entire village was like her. She was known for these qualities, and all the boys and other people had heard of her.

At first it was merely the boys of her home village who came to court her at night. But before long those from the other villages, too, had gotten word of her. They were curious to find out for themselves, so they would go to see her with their own eyes. And it was true. Now they kept flocking to her. There was not one village from which the suitors were not coming.

The girl, however, was still enjoying her girlhood and had no desire yet to take a husband. Each one of the boys, on the other hand, was anxious to make her his girlfriend and wife. They knew they couldn't find anyone else so attractive. The one who married her would be a lucky man.

From all corners of the land the boys kept arriving to woo her. They swarmed to her house. But she did not love any one of them. She would talk to a boy, but when he expressed an interest in marrying her, she simply refused. Eventually, she became tired of all the suitors. Even though she was frank with them and told them how she felt about them they kept coming. She was racking her brain for what she could possibly say to stop them from coming. Whenever she was doing something such as grinding corn or cooking, this was on her mind. Sometimes she was thinking about it when she went to bed so that she could not fall asleep right away. Finally she hit upon an idea.

If any man should ask her to marry him, she would answer him like this: "If you're really serious about living with me, I'd like you to catch me a yellow fox. It's my wish to own one as a pet. Whoever can fulfill my wish will have won me, and I promise to marry him." This was her reply from then on.

The boys were really anxious to win the girl, so they made every effort to be the first to procure the animal for her. The poor things were constantly roaming about in search of a yellow fox. Once in a while one would go after wood, but the fox too was on his mind. They tried all sorts of tricks to capture one. But since a yellow fox is quite skittish, no one ever managed to catch one. Meanwhile, a great deal of time had passed, and still the girl had not taken a husband. The eligible sons of upper-class villagers, too, did not interest her. Material possessions meant nothing to her. These upper-class suitors kept saying they would spoil her with all kinds of valuables if she consented to marry one of them. But the girl remained steadfast. She was not persuaded by any one of them. So, quite a few of the boys lost heart and stopped frequenting her place.

Among those trying their luck was a boy from Hovi'itstuyqa. He was very handsome, but to suitors from villages outside her own the girl showed even less kindness. It so happened that this boy's name was Sikyaatayo (Yellow Fox). The girl did not treat him very kindly, but because he was stubborn, he repeatedly called on her. Still, the girl's reply to him was the same as to the others.

Some six years passed, but still no one had succeeded in catching a yellow fox. The boys, who so far had failed to get the animal, discontinued visiting the girl. They thought she might never get married, because none of them had lucked out with the fox. As it was, some of the boys had even banded together. They had thought that if they went in search of the fox and found one, they could surround him. But each time they did so and sneaked up to him, he somehow became aware of them and managed to escape. They did

not consider throwing their hunting sticks at him, for this would probably
have injured him, and the girl would not want an injured animal. So they
attempted all sorts of approaches in capturing one. Once in a while a boy
tried to extract the fox while he was still in his den, but somehow the animal
managed to slip by him. At other times, a hunter dug into the burrow, but
the fox bit him, and he had to let go of the animal. On one occasion a boy
actually succeeded in stealing a newborn pup from its mother, thinking he
could raise the little thing at home. But it did not take long before the poor
creature got hungry for milk. He had taken a pup that was still suckling.
He knew this when he kidnapped the pup, so when he arrived home, he
tried to have it drink the milk of his dog that had just given birth to a litter.
But the bitch refused to let the little fox suckle. The boy put her tit into
the baby fox's mouth, but each time the dog turned her head and growled
fiercely. When the boy did not remove the fox, the bitch snapped at it, and
after she had bitten it twice, he stopped trying. Soon thereafter the little
fox pup died. So this boy too failed to win the girl as a wife.

Try as they might, not one of the boys, poor things, had ever managed to
catch a yellow fox. They now completely stopped calling on the girl. Only
the boy from Hovi'itstuyqa whose name was Sikyaatayo and who, like the
others, desired the girl was still calling on her. And even though the girl felt
no love for him, he did not give up. Every night he went for a rendezvous
with her.

Pitsinsivostiyo, meanwhile, had grown up and reached an age where he
became interested in the other sex. Without telling his grandmother at
home in Tupats'ovi, he would roam the village, thinking he might make
friends with a girl. Wherever he came across a girl on his nightly excursions,
he would go up to her. When he saw someone else talking to that girl,
however, he did not approach her. Only when he found a girl alone did he
venture up and address her. When the girl was busy grinding and did not
respond, he lost heart and left, going somewhere else. On a rare occasion
a girl, even though busy grinding corn, actually talked to him without
looking up. When she grew tired and stopped to rest and looked up at him,
she would realize that he was homely and totally unattractive. She was then
no longer nice to him. This is how the poor lad fared.

One day when Pitsinsivostiyo strayed over to the house of the beautiful
girl, the boy from Hovi'itstuyqa was at her vent hole, so instead of going
up to her he went home to bed. A few days later he returned and, much
to his surprise, did not see the boy from Hovi'itstuyqa. He stepped up to
the vent, regardless of the consequences. When he got there, he found the
girl grinding corn. He had never seen her before, so he almost swooned

when he saw how beautiful she was. Her facial features were unbelievably beautiful. Not daring to speak a word, he sat outside the vent hole watching her inside the grinding chamber. Finally, without saying a word, he left to go to bed. It was already dark night.

For the time being, Pitsinsivostiyo did not return to the girl's house. In his mind, however, he kept picturing only her, so much so that he was almost in a daze. His grandmother had told him to forget her, but as usual he paid no attention to her. The girl had touched Pitsinsivostiyo to the quick. He became absent-minded and finally was so affected by the experience that he did not eat anymore. Whenever he went to bed, he just lay there, picturing the girl.

At last it seemed that even Pitsinsivostiyo's health was being affected by his encounter with the girl. She was constantly on his mind, so he had the desire to talk to someone about her. But since he had no friend, he could not do so and was really suffering. He became so desperate that he decided to say something to his grandmother, regardless of the consequences. Pitsinsivostiyo was of course fully aware, just like all the others, of the girl's requirement for marriage. He knew that she would only marry in return for a yellow fox. Consequently, he too pondered how best to capture the animal. He tried like all the rest, but since he was all by himself, he had no luck. This was another reason to talk to his grandmother. Since he had no one else to teach him how to hunt this animal, he had no choice but to consult his grandmother.

One morning when the two were having breakfast together, he said to her, "Grandmother, I'd like to ask you something. But first I must tell you something."

"Very well, what is it?" she replied and stopped eating. She was all ears when her grandson began. "Yes," he said, "you've probably heard of this girl who lives in our village on the northwest side of the plaza. She's a ravishing beauty, but shows no love for anyone. Boys flock to her from all over. She chats with them briefly but keeps telling everyone that she's not interested in a husband."

"Sure, I've heard of a girl who's being courted by droves of boys, but has succumbed to none of them."

"Yes, that's the one. She briefly chats with everybody, but she never talked to me. She's not after any material possessions. She's told all those boys whose fathers are rich that she wouldn't marry any one of them for this reason. She's hardworking and self-motivated. She's constantly cooking for her mother, so the latter never needs to worry about fixing meals. It occurred to me that if we put our minds together, we might convince her to marry me. If I could marry her and she would cook for us, you would not need to toil anymore. You could live a pleasant life. I desire her with all my heart." This is what Pitsinsivostiyo told his grandmother. He did not mention the yellow fox yet.

The old woman replied, "My poor grandchild. Is that what has been going through your head? I see, you've gotten old enough to be interested in sex. Dear me, how do you figure we might succeed? Look how homely you are. The people show no concern for us. That's why we live poor and destitute at the edge of the village. We're nothing but dregs, so no one will be willing to become related to us through marriage. Being completely alone, we can't prepare the wedding outfit for a bride. Just forget the whole thing and live your life as you always have." This is what she said to Pitsinsivostiyo. She had no sympathy for him. Her reply made the boy so sad that he could not go on with the conversation.

Thus the matter remained, but Pitsinsivostiyo could not forget the girl. A few days later, when the two were having supper, he spoke to her once more. "Grandmother," he said.

"What is it?" she replied.

"Yes, I'm sure you remember that I talked to you about that girl recently. You told me to stay away from her, but she's always on my mind, so I'd like to ask you a question. I did not tell you everything the last time. I did not mention that she will marry whoever can bring her a yellow fox. The one who accomplishes that will win her hand. It does not matter who he is, she will have to marry him. And because I've made every effort to get her, I tried on several occasions to catch this animal all by myself. This fox, however, is so skittish that it ran away long before I got close to him." His grandmother merely listened and acknowledged what he was saying. Pitsinsivostiyo continued, "You're old, I know, but you've still got a lot of brains. That's why I'm seeking your advice."

"Dear me, is that what she's been saying to her suitors? Maybe she has a special reason. For surely that yellow fox is very shy. He won't be captured by just anyone who's doing this on his own. A fox is much too smart for that, and not gullible like a coyote. He's quite familiar with traps, so he won't allow himself to get caught. But if one goes about it in the proper way, this feat can be achieved. If the girl really speaks the truth, we can give it a try for you. We'll see if she means what she says. If she lied, it'll be her own fault and she'll have to bear the consequences." This is what his grandmother said, whereupon she gave him some instructions.

Pitsinsivostiyo listened carefully to every word. "Well then, my grandson," she started, "tomorrow you get up first thing in the morning and head out to a place northeast of Löhavutsotsmo. There I want you to look for some Apache-plume. When you find a nice good stand, gather a good amount. Be sure not to bring too few. You're new to this and might not pick the sort I want. So cut as much Apache-plume as you can. You should be back home around this time of day. Mind you, it's quite far to that place. You better make your bed now and go to sleep." These were his grandmother's instructions. She also explained to him in great detail what Apache-plume looks like.

Pitsinsivostiyo did as told. He spread out his bedding and lay down. He could not fall asleep right away and kept tossing and turning on his sheepskin. He was looking forward to getting a yellow fox. But as he thought about the matter, he did not know what to think. He was familiar, of course, with the fact that arrows are fashioned from the Apache-plume. He was clearly going to go after arrow-making material. However, how did that relate to the girl? He could not bring her a dead fox. He refrained from further probing why his grandmother wanted him to do this and eventually dozed off.

The following morning Pitsinsivostiyo awoke early. It was not yet even gray dawn when he rose to gather his bedding. His grandmother, who heard him, also woke up now. They quickly had breakfast, whereupon the old woman handed Pitsinsivostiyo an axe. "This you can use to cut the Apache-plume. Be sure to cut a lot. Once in a while a branch is not good and one has to throw it away and take another, so bring a large amount." With that, she also gave him a tumpline to carry the load on his back.

Now Pitsinsivostiyo started out. By the time he passed the area southeast of Wupatki, the sun was up. The boy was an extraordinary runner. His strong lungs allowed him to breathe longer. He had been trotting in a straight line and reached Wupatki without being the least bit tired. He paused for a brief time before he set forth anew, without touching his journey food or taking a drink from his water.

Sure enough, the sun was just a little past its mid-morning point when he ascended the northeast side of Löhavutsotsmo. Upon climbing all the way up, he went in search of the Apache-plume. He found a lot growing there; so convinced that this was the right kind, he chopped off many branches. By the time it was noon, he set down his food belt and, relaxing under a pine tree, ate with great relish. Having stilled his hunger, he lingered a while, taking in the view. He had never been in this area before, so he was very impressed with what he saw. He could hear the constant sounds of all sorts of creatures, for the weather was nice and warm. After Pitsinsivostiyo had stayed for a good length of time, he thought, "I must not waste my time here. If I cut some more, I'll be home soon." So he continued chopping off more Apache-plume. Just as the sun got a little low on the horizon, he stopped. "I guess this is plenty," he thought. With that, he carefully tied the sticks, loaded the bundle on his back, and set out for home.

Eventually, he noticed that he was getting closer to home. He was quite familiar with the area now. He had not been moving very rapidly and so was glad when he realized how quickly he had arrived. The sun had not completely set yet when he arrived from southwest of his house. Upon reaching his house, he deposited his bundle behind the ladder and entered.

As soon as he was inside, his grandmother saw him. Overjoyed, she welcomed him. "Thanks, you have returned. I knew you would be back about this time, so I started making supper ahead of time. The minute I'm done cooking, we can eat." This is what she said, hurrying a little more. She still did not inquire of him whether he had found what she was interested in.

When the old woman was done, she set out the food and said, "All right, come here. Let's eat. You must be starving." Pitsinsivostiyo moved up to the food and as they ate he told his grandmother how he had fared. Again she asked no questions of him but merely listened and nodded to what he had to say. When the two were finally satiated, the old woman cleared the area where they had eaten and Pitsinsivostiyo went outside.

Just when his grandmother had removed everything, he came back in, toting on his back the Apache-plume sticks he had been sent to fetch. No sooner did his grandmother see them than she exclaimed, "Thanks a lot, you brought the right thing. Thank you. Now we can make this for you. We'll need some other things, though. But let's finish this task first before I tell you what to do next," she said. "I'm so glad you brought so much of the arrow-making material. Tomorrow morning we'll start working on it."

The two now went to bed. The next morning they were up early because the boy was anxious to get going. They quickly ate breakfast and then they began. Their first job was to peel the branches. Since Pitsinsivostiyo's grandmother was an old woman, she must have observed at some time in her life how arrows are made. After all, the boy had brought arrow-making material. That's what she had told him to get. Eventually, when all the branches were pared down, she straightened them. Wherever a stick was bent slightly, that part was pulled through the perforated horn of a mountain sheep, a device she used as a shaft-straightener. Next, she handed the shaft to the boy, who rubbed it with a stone to make it nice and smooth. The old granny now trudged to the back room, where she stored all sorts of things, and came back with her feather bundle. Putting a few wing feathers aside, she fletched the arrows. In this manner the two manufactured a great quantity.

"Thanks, this will do," his grandmother finally said. "Remember, I said this would not be all. Well, let me gather our trash and burn it. You go ahead and spread out your bedding and lie down for the time being. You traveled far yesterday and must be tired. When I'm done with this, I'll make my bed too. Then I'll give you some further instructions."

Thereupon the old woman cleaned up the mess on the floor. The boy put out his bedroll and lay there waiting for his grandmother. Soon she was done and made her bed too. After settling down on it she said, "Now, my grandson, tomorrow you must go southwest once more, this time to get bow-making material. But you won't need to go far and stay away so long. What we need is oak. Again you must hack off a good many straight branches. Select the ones about the size of your fist in diameter. When you find any this size, peel off the bark. If the inside is a brown color, then that's the kind you want to get. Anything else does not have the proper strength and is bound to break. So this is what I want you to search for, this bow-making material. We'll make that into a bow for you. An arrow by itself is no use whatsoever. An arrow needs a bow. Just go along the valley here until you come to an oak grove." After giving him these new instructions the two slept.

The following morning the two were up early again. While the boy breakfasted, his grandmother fixed a journey lunch for him. Just when she was done, the boy was satiated. He tied the food to his belt and departed. True enough, it was not yet noontime when he reached an area where young oaks were growing. These were the ones his grandmother had told him to look for. Even if they are small in size, as long as they are alive, they are extremely tough. He had not chopped many branches before it was noon. So he took his lunch and ate in a place that provided some shade. Having satisfied his hunger, he went in search of more oak. By early evening he had a good armload together, so he left for home.

Upon his return, Pitsinsivostiyo placed the oak on the rooftop and entered. His grandmother happily greeted him and thanked him. This time he was back earlier than the day before, so the old woman started cooking and when she was done, they ate.

When the two were full, the old granny cleared the table and said to her grandson, "All right, go get your bow material. If you brought the right kind, we can get under way." Pitsinsivostiyo went outside as bidden and lugged the oak in on his back. He placed the bundle down northwest of the fireplace. Inspecting it closely, his grandmother found the oak branches just right. Glad about this, she said to her grandchild, "Thank you, you brought the right sort. This is what I told you to get."

With that, she disappeared into the room next door and returned with two big knives. One she handed the boy, telling him to watch her for a while and not try himself before she had finished one properly. With that, she picked up an oak branch and trimmed it nicely on both sides where the grip of the bow was going to be. "That's the way it's supposed to be," she said, whereupon she stretched the oak stem across the ladder. She did this by tying the bow down with grass, which held the bow in place to the left and right of the bow grip. Then she encouraged her grandson to start working on one himself. Sure enough, he hacked off all the little twigs, but when he was about to stretch it on the ladder, he bent it too much. As a result, the bow broke.

"Don't worry about it," his grandmother said. "That's why I had you bring more than one piece of oak. Just pick another and try again." So Pitsinsivostiyo tried once more. Finally he got it right. He really finished it nicely. Thereupon, he tied it to the ladder to stretch it.

In this position the wood dried. Next, the boy's grandmother procured some sinew, which she twisted into a cord long enough for the two bows. This bowstring she attached to the bows. They really did a good job. The bow was not very strong, but when the old lady tested it, the arrow zoomed off with great force and flew quite far. Now Pitsinsivostiyo had two nice bows.

Once more the grandmother had instructions for Pitsinsivostiyo. "Well," she said, "now it's time to go after the yellow fox by the rocky hill southwest of here. Be sure to take your weapons along. Once you get there, stop somewhere and collect a large amount of the giant dropseed grass. Then continue until you reach the rock mound. Look for a large, empty place there. When you find one, walk back and forth across it until the earth is really messed up. Be sure to leave many tracks behind. Having done that, shoot your arrows into the ground over all the empty space. Then lie down on the ground so that when someone comes up to you, he will think that you were attacked by enemies and killed. Stick one arrow into your armpit. Break another in half, smear it with pitch at one end, and then glue it to your heart. You must be lying there ready when the sun goes down. Then sprinkle the giant dropseed all over yourself. Be sure to put some also into your mouth. These seeds look just like maggots. With that it will be quite believable that you've been dead for quite some time, and the flies have laid their eggs. Now here are some mice that I trapped for you. Take those with you too. They are pretty much decayed already and stink terribly. Cut their meat into little pieces and stick them on your body. Then you're bound to give off the odor of a rotten corpse. In the early evening creatures such as coyotes, yellow foxes, and wolves roam in search of something to eat. An animal that smells you and finds you will first keep its distance. Then it will come up close and sniff you all over. When it sees the dropseeds and notices your decaying odor, it will be convinced that you are dead. Of course, you can't afford not to breathe for that long. If you get out of breath, just inhale a little bit of air at a time. When the dropseeds start moving then, the animal will think they are live maggots. With a happy heart it will then announce to the other creatures that it has come across some food. Once they hear the call, they will all assemble there." This is how his grandmother laid out her instructions for him.

The next morning Pitsinsivostiyo headed out to the rocky hill. He did exactly as his grandmother had told him. His preparations took until early evening, and then he lay down. What a terrible sight he presented! The whole scene gave the impression that he had been attacked by a large number of enemies.

Not long before the sun went down Pitsinsivostiyo heard something. Opening his eyes, he saw a coyote. The animal kept circling him, inspecting him from all sides. It concluded that the victim evidently had been in a tremendous fight. He must have been attacked by enemies, for there were arrows all over, with one actually sticking in the boy. "What a brave man," the coyote said. "Look at all the arrows that were shot at him and missed. But one of the attackers' shots was well aimed. That's why he is lying there now." This is what went through the animal's mind as it craned its neck toward the boy. "I wonder if he's really dead," it thought as it circled his prostrate body. The coyote came closer and closer until it stood right by Pitsinsivostiyo. No doubt, the victim was dead. He no longer stirred. From the looks of him he had been dead for a long time, because the flies had already laid their eggs. There were fly eggs all over him. "Why don't I call someone," the coyote thought. "I can't devour all of him by myself." So he trotted a little ways northwest and then emitted a series of barking howls.

Stopping its howling, the animal ran southwest and howled once more. After that it went to the northeast. When it had howled into every direction, it returned to the boy and stood by him. It was not long before someone came running from the northwest. The animal stopped and asked, "Well, who's calling here?"

"It's me," the coyote replied. "I found this dead boy here. He must have been brave and fought hard. I called all of you so that we can feed on him."

Before long, all sorts of creatures had gathered. There was still a little bit of daylight, so they came up to the boy and sniffed around him. They were still circling Pitsinsivostiyo when he opened one eye. With this one eye, he had a hard time seeing them properly. With his eyes closed, however, he could not have seen them at all. So he carefully observed them through his eyelashes. Now he could make them out a little bit better. They in turn were not aware of this.

Paying close attention to the animals, Pitsinsivostiyo realized that they clearly intended to eat him. They had quit circling by now and were creeping up closer. Upon reaching his body, one of them licked him with its tongue but did not bite a chunk out of him yet.

When all the creatures were by his side, Pitsinsivostiyo noticed that next to his right hand stood the most beautiful yellow fox. He knew this was the one to get, so he focused his attention on it. The animals were about ready to sink their fangs into him when the handsome fox stepped over the boy's hand. At this moment Pitsinsivostiyo grabbed for the fox and got hold of its leg. He quickly jumped up and, getting hold of its other leg, let out a series of screams. "*Yappahaha, yappahaha,*" he yelled, and the other animals scurried in all directions. The yellow fox fought back as hard as he could, but the boy would not let go of him. The animal became frightened now but showed no intention of biting his captor.

When all the other creatures had disappeared, Pitsinsivostiyo spoke to the fox. "Wait before you do anything. I'm not going to harm you. I don't want to kill you, so you need not be afraid of me," he said. The fox calmed down, whereupon Pitsinsivostiyo told him all about the girl. He explained to him that her heart was set on a yellow fox and that the one who brought her one would win her hand in marriage. "I tried to accomplish this for a long, long time until both my grandmother and I came up with the idea of seeking help from all of you. You consented and came to me, and that's how I managed to catch you," he said. "So don't fuss now. I'm sure that girl will be gentle with you."

The fox replied, "Very well, I'll go with you."

Thereupon Pitsinsivostiyo went home with the fox. When he arrived with the animal, his grandmother was overjoyed. "Thank you, thank you," she kept saying. "You did what I told you perfectly. That's why you caught the fox. Thanks. With this animal you're bound to win the girl. She will have to marry you now. How nice, now I guess you have yourself a wife," the old woman said gratefully. She then disappeared into the back room and came back with a bowl and something in a bundle. Pouring water into the bowl, she crushed something into it and mixed it with the liquid. Then she said to her grandchild, "Now, bring me your animal."

Pitsinsivostiyo obeyed and brought her the fox. He was still resisting his captor. The old granny now dipped her hand into the bowl and rubbed the liquid all over the fox's body. No sooner had she done this than the fox became completely tame. He sat down next to the two and showed no more impulse to flee. The old woman had put some medicine into the water, which produced its magic effect on the fox. For this reason, he became tame. She kept stroking his fur. How soft and beautiful it was! "Thank you," the old woman said to the animal. "We also want to give it a try with this girl. That's why we made you into a pet," she explained.

"Yes," the fox replied, "we were aware of that. That's why we came. And sure enough, this boy had confidence in me and selected me and caught me."

"Of course," Pitsinsivostiyo replied. "Thanks for giving yourself to me."

In this manner the two came into possession of that extremely skittish animal. Pitsinsivostiyo was already looking forward to the following night. And since the yellow fox was tame and showed no sign of trying to escape, the two spread out their bedding in order to sleep. The yellow fox, in turn, lay down next to the boy.

Early in the evening the following day, right after supper, Pitsinsivostiyo told his grandmother that he was ready to go to the girl's house. But his grandmother suggested he wait a little longer. Later, when some of the people were in bed, it would be better to visit the girl with the animal. Poor Pitsinsivostiyo was restless. According to him it was already quite late, but his grandmother did not see it that way. Not much time had passed yet.

Finally, his grandmother said, "All right, this is the moment to go and find out. If the girl did not lie, she will tell you herself that you have won her. However, you're quite homely. She may dislike you for that and not accept you. Even though you bring her the animal she wants, she may but cast a glance at you and change her mind," she said to him.

Pitsinsivostiyo left the house with the fox in his arms and headed over to the girl's place. On the way he set the animal on the ground and let it run after him. The fox trotted after him just like a dog.

Upon reaching the girl's house, the boy picked up the fox and ascended to the upper story. Sure enough, the girl was grinding corn, so he sat down at the vent to her grinding chamber with the fox in his arms. He still did not say anything to her. He watched her first, then he said, "Hey, listen, I brought this for you."

The girl heard him at once and immediately stopped grinding. She looked up at the vent hole. When she spotted the boy squatting there clutching a yellow fox, she got very excited. Quickly she arose from the grinding bin, ran up to the vent, and exclaimed, "How nice, is that your pet? Don't waste your time out there. Step inside. Then you can talk to me." The boy complied and sat down where she had offered him a seat, still embracing the fox.

No sooner had he taken his seat than the girl, not wasting any time, asked him if perhaps he was hungry. Quickly she disappeared into the room next door and returned with a few rolls of piki. These she placed next to Pitsinsivostiyo. "Here, you can eat this while you talk to me. May I hold your pet for you for the time being?"

Pitsinsivostiyo said, "Sure, I brought this fox for you. From what I heard, this is the animal you wanted. I caught it especially for you. The yellow fox is yours."

"How nice, you really brought it for me? Yes, it's true, that's what I used to tell my suitors, but no one ever brought me one. I said that to them because I had no desire to get married," she continued. "But since you came with the animal, you beat me at my game. I will therefore become your wife." She was very pleased with the fox. Without noticing Pitsinsivostiyo's homeliness, the girl had promised to marry him. "Thank you so much," the girl said again. "I will surely live with you. Four days from now I'll come to your house to grind corn as your bride. So tell your relatives to attend the wedding ceremony. The fox, however, I will keep here. For he is what I kept talking about to the boys. I'm glad you were powerful enough to fulfill my wish," she said, stroking the yellow fox and uttering words of delight at the same time. "So take this home with you," she said and wrapped something up for the boy.

Pitsinsivostiyo ran home in happy spirits. When he arrived, his grandmother was still up. "Grandmother," he cried.

"What is it, my grandson?"

"The girl said yes."

"Oh thank you, thanks," the old woman replied.

"Look, this is what she wrapped up for me." He opened the bundle in the presence of his grandmother. There was rolled piki and also *somiviki*. The old woman ladled some water into a bowl for him and then the two ate. They had never tasted anything like this. The food was delicious and they ate with great gusto. "The girl also gave me some instructions. 'Four days from now I will come and get you.' Those were her words."

"Gee, she's really in a rush."

"Yes," said Pitsinsivostiyo.

"Very well. I'll start cleaning up the house," his grandmother said. "We really live very poorly here. I'll dust a bit and whitewash the walls. Then it will look a little more pleasant. By the way, I'm sure she said she will come here to grind as a bride. What on earth are we going to do? We're all alone. Maybe we can get at least some of the things that are part of her wedding outfit before we take her back to her home," she said.

Pitsinsivostiyo now visited the girl on a regular basis. On the fourth day he was a little late, but when he finally arrived, she was all prepared and was waiting for him. In the meantime she had also informed her parents when she was going to the boy's house to grind corn as a bride, so they knew about it. Their joy, however, was tempered by the fact that Pitsinsivostiyo was a low-class person and that he and his grandmother would not be able to provide much for their daughter. Still, they were glad that she had finally found a husband. After all, she was quite old already and still not married. They were concerned she might become a spinster. But now that Pitsinsivostiyo had beaten her at her game, her parents too had to resign themselves to the situation.

So Pitsinsivostiyo came to pick her up, and when he arrived, they gave their daughter to him. The girl gave him a tray filled with corn flour, which he loaded on his back. The two proceeded to his house. Upon arriving he called inside, "Hey! How about some words of welcome. I'm not alone." At once one could hear the old woman's inviting chatter. "Please, come in, whoever is about." Thereupon Pitsinsivostiyo entered with the girl.

The old woman thanked the girl for coming and offered her a seat. The girl sat down. Then the grandmother told her grandson where to place the tray with the flour. After that she fed the girl. "How nice," she cried, "we truly have gotten a beautiful in-law. You are really a gorgeous girl. We must be grateful to have won you, being as destitute as we are. And because you came to grind for us, who are so despised, we'll surely manage somehow to make something for you."

When the girl was finished eating, the old granny announced that it was time for them to go to bed. For Pitsinsivostiyo she made the bed by the door. "You sleep here," she pointed out to him. "We'll sleep over here," she said, as she went into a corner to roll out the bedding for the girl.

Pitsinsivostiyo got quite upset. He thought he had gotten a wife and could sleep with her. Instead, his grandmother was going to sleep with her. The old woman said, "This is how we customarily do this. When a bride comes to grind, one cannot sleep with her during the first four days. Once your hair has been washed and tied together with hers, you can sleep with her," she explained. The boy could not change that, so he slept alone.

The next morning the girl was up early, gathering her bedding. When the old woman heard that, she also got up. Then she asked the girl to accompany her outside to speak the morning prayer. Both of them helped themselves to some cornmeal; then they went out and prayed in the direction of the rising sun. The girl prayed that she would complete her four-day stay without any hardships. Also she hoped that if she cooked some food there would be plenty for everyone. The old woman, on the other hand, was asking how she could provide the wedding outfit for her daughter-in-law.

This is how the two prayed. Then they went back in and ate breakfast. The girl only ate a tiny portion. She was waiting for the old woman, and when the latter was satisfied, she led the girl to the grinding stone. She had already shelled the corn and placed it on the stone for her. Now the bride was grinding there early in the morning.

It so happened that just at that hour a woman passed by the house, on the way to the dump to throw out her trash. She clearly heard the grinding sounds. She went by without giving it much thought. On the way back she heard the noise again. This time she thought, "I wonder who is grinding corn there. That can't be the old woman who lives here. She's far too old for that chore and never seems to be grinding." The woman was at a loss. Back in the village, she told the others about this. They were all racking their brains, but nobody knew who could possibly be grinding corn there.

The women were all dying from curiosity, so they sent one from their group over. She pretended to be coming for some live embers, and when she entered, she said to the old woman, "I wanted to do some cooking a while back when I realized that our fire was out. And when I came by your house earlier this morning to throw out my trash, I saw smoke coming out of your chimney. That's why I came here," she said.

"Sure. Here, I just added wood to the fire, so there's bound to be some good hot coals. Just put your torch in and light it," she encouraged the visitor. While the visitor had her torch in the fireplace, she was biding her time. Standing around, she carefully inspected the house and once more heard grinding noises in the back room. Since the old woman who lived there was still with her, it could not be her.

The visitor could no longer restrain herself and asked, "How nice. Did you ask someone to grind corn for you? Maybe you have a girl back there."

The old woman laughed and replied, "I know you won't believe this, so let me tell you. My grandson came home with a girl last night, who's grinding here as a bride."

"Isn't that nice. So he got himself a wife?"

The old woman replied in the affirmative. The other woman was so surprised that she could not utter a word.

Meanwhile the torch had flamed up. The woman quickly extracted it and excused herself. She was in a great hurry to relate this news to the others. It was an unbelievable story, so she was looking forward to bringing the surprising news. Sure enough, when she told the others, they refused to believe it. She hurried from house to house, telling her story everywhere. The people could not believe what they heard. And thus the news spread throughout the village. But no one took it seriously, so they all went to the girl's house and asked her parents, who confirmed that it was true. It was not even midday yet when all the villagers were informed.

Meanwhile, the girl who was staying at the groom's house had completed her third day grinding corn. The next day was going to be the hair-washing ceremony. That night Pitsinsivostiyo's grandmother went outside and made an announcement. "All of my offspring that live out there, come and gather at this house. Tomorrow we want to wash the hair of my daughter-in-law. We'll be eating her food from this day on." After the announcement she went back in and they slept.

Early the next day the girl's mother arrived with a few of her relatives for the hair-washing ritual. Much to their surprise, upon their arrival they found a large crowd of people gathered inside. They were all related to Pitsinsivostiyo's grandmother. It was incredible how many relatives she had! They were sitting there in great numbers. They all washed the couple's hair. Ahead of time, Pitsinsivostiyo's uncles also had fashioned all of the wedding garments, which they were now bringing in one after the other. The girl in turn was busy preparing the food. There were many guests, but somehow she managed to feed them all. This is how the wedding party came to a close.

The bride's stay really had not been very long. She was now ready to return home. Pitsinsivostiyo took his wife home in person. He had bagged a large amount of venison, six big deer in all. When the girl's parents saw all the meat the bridegroom brought, they were happy.

This is how the old woman and her grandchild assembled their relatives, who helped with the wedding. In no time they finished the wedding outfit, but even though they worked fast, everything was finished beautifully. Never had preparations for a wedding party been completed so soon.

By now the other people had realized that the old woman and her grandson were not just ordinary people but were endowed with greater-than-human powers. No one had been willing to accept them, and they were cast out by the villagers. As it turned out now, Pitsinsivostiyo's grandmother was actually Old Spider Woman. And Pitsinsivostiyo, or "Cotton Seed Boy," owned all the cotton from which the Hopis fashioned all kinds of clothes, kachina costumes, blankets, and everyday garments. To these people the girl had now become an in-law, and she and Pitsinsivostiyo lived together.

The girl, of course, also had the yellow fox as a pet. He had really gotten attached to Pitsinsivostiyo's wife and always stayed on her heels. The girl loved him dearly.

Now this boy from Hovi'itstuyqa, whose name also happened to be Sikyaatayo, or "Yellow Fox," was very handsome. Long ago he had also been at Tupats'ovi and one night had gone to court the girl. But when the girl saw him that night, she had not yet spoken to him. She thought he would surely visit her again. She had taken a liking to him and that is why she kept saying she wanted a yellow fox. But when he failed to return, Pitsinsivostiyo had captured the animal and gained the girl's hand by bringing the fox. There had been no way out but to become his wife, and that's why she went as a bride to grind at his house.

Evidently, Sikyaatayo, who lived in Hovi'itstuyqa, had heard that the girl had taken a husband. He was a powerful lad and also quite aggressive. He therefore decided to take Pitsinsivostiyo's wife away. He was fully determined to do this.

So he went over to Nuvakwewtaqa, where the village of Tupats'ovi was situated. Upon arriving there, he looked up an acquaintance and, while living there, spied on Pitsinsivostiyo's wife to see what she was doing on a daily basis. He soon learned that every morning she went to pray to the sun, accompanied by the yellow fox.

Once Sikyaatayo had found this out, he started scheming where and when to grab her. One day soon thereafter, when Pitsinsivostiyo's wife was going out with her pet to speak the morning prayer, he followed her secretly. He stopped at a hiding place and lay in wait for her there.

Soon Pitsinsivostiyo's wife was on her way back to the house. She had just reached the hiding place of the boy from Hovi'itstuyqa and had taken a couple more steps, when he ran up to her and embraced her from behind. The woman struggled, but he easily overpowered her and forced her to the ground. Revealing himself to her by name he said to her, "Don't resist. It's me." Evidently she recognized the boy, for she held still. The boy now had intercourse with her right there on the ground, and she let it happen without resistance.

As it was, the little fox pet witnessed the scene. He was barking furiously, but apparently no one heard him, because no one came to them. Pitsinsivostiyo had actually heard the barking but did not go see what it was all about. Instead, he waited for his wife to return.

When his wife arrived, she did not feel the same about her husband anymore. She did not respond to him as clearly as before when he talked to her.

Pitsinsivostiyo was at a loss. Thinking about his wife, he felt that she was not her normal self. So he decided to go over to his grandmother's house. The yellow fox jumped up and ran after him.

Back at his grandmother's he sat down. The fox came up and settled down next to him. Lying there with his legs tucked under, it was not long before tears were rolling down his face and he was sniffling. When Pitsinsivostiyo heard that, he looked at him and noticed that he was crying. Stroking his head he said, "Why on earth are you making these noises?"

The fox lifted his head and replied, "Because I feel sorry for you. This morning when I ran along with your wife for the prayer to the sun, I saw something unpleasant." Whereupon he related everything he had witnessed.

When Pitsinsivostiyo heard what the fox had witnessed with his own eyes, he became unhappy.

So now the boy from Hovi'itstuyqa, who was very aggressive and had come all the way to Tupats'ovi because of Pitsinsivostiyo's wife, had gained the upper hand over the woman. He was extremely handsome, and since the girl was not really in love when she married Pitsinsivostiyo, she readily succumbed to him. Pitsinsivostiyo was still with his wife but no longer slept with her.

It was not long thereafter that Sikyaatayo returned home to Hovi'itstuyqa with Pitsinsivostiyo's wife. Pitsinsivostiyo was most disconsolate about this turn of events and told his grandmother about it. He was bent on revenge.

The old woman advised him how to go about this. She fully concurred that he would need to avenge himself. She told him to seek the assistance of the Kisispaya people far in the southwest. This Indian tribe was always about raiding. She was convinced that they would help him if he asked. The next day Pitsinsivostiyo was already on his way.

It was not yet completely dark when he came to a place where he had to descend. Having made the descent, he did not continue on but sat down scanning the area for the dwellings of this tribe. But he could not see anything. Meanwhile it was getting dusk, and the light of fires became visible in the locations where smoke was rising in the air. There were clearly several fires. But Pitsinsivostiyo did not go up to them yet. He just sat there waiting.

Finally, when the night was totally dark and all of the fires had burned down, he left his place and crawled up to the campsite. He halted at the edge and carefully scrutinized the area. Everybody seemed to be asleep.

Right in the center of the camp he saw a roundish hut that was much larger than the rest. Pitsinsivostiyo reasoned that this had to be the living quarters of the chief. Inspecting everything carefully one more time, and seeing that no one was about, he went over to the hut. Seeing the light from a fire, he entered.

Sure enough, there was a man inside. He noticed Pitsinsivostiyo but did not say anything. After a while he merely got up, went to the door, and disappeared. No sooner was he gone through the door than he yelled out a loud war whoop. While he was yelling, he kept slapping his mouth. Following this signal he remained outside.

In a little while Pitsinsivostiyo could hear the noise of many voices outside. Before long the chief spoke. "Are all the men and boys assembled?" he asked, whereupon they all said yes. "A stranger just arrived. That's why I alerted you. I've not yet inquired of him the reason for his coming, but as soon as he tells me, I'll let you know." With that, he reentered the roundish hut.

At first Pitsinsivostiyo had been scared, but when the people outside quieted down, he felt relieved. Surprisingly enough, he understood the language of this group. This was nothing unusual, because the ancient ones used to roam far and wide, encountering all kinds of other people. Enemies would even come to trade at the village once in a while. In this way they learned the languages of other tribes.

For this reason, Pitsinsivostiyo understood when the chief came back in and said, "All right, stranger, have a seat. Having entered my house so purposefully, you must be about for something important."

"Yes, that's true," answered Pitsinsivostiyo, whereupon he narrated how the boy from Hovi'itstuyqa had managed to steal his wife and take her with him. He now wanted to avenge himself on this boy. "It was my grandmother who sent me here. So I came in search of you and to request that you help me in my endeavor. If you're kind enough to comply, I would like you to raid the village of Hovi'itstuyqa in my behalf and destroy it. You can do whatever you want. If you're interested in the women and girls, you can round them up. If you want to kill them along with the rest, that's all right too. The loot such as food and other items of value that you find, you can distribute however you see fit. My only wish is to see that place destroyed." This is what Pitsinsivostiyo said to the chief.

The man did not waste much time and quickly agreed. "Very well. That boy truly committed a wrong. He got himself into this mess through his own doing. By the same token he got all of his people into trouble. It's hard for someone to cope with adultery. We have the same customs. When two people get married, they have to live together. You can rely on us. We'll help you." The chief's reply pleased Pitsinsivostiyo greatly.

Pitsinsivostiyo now set the date for the attack. It was to take place in four days. After arranging where he would wait for them, he departed from the Kisispayas.

Waiting for the appointed date Pitsinsivostiyo became increasingly restless, so on the evening of the third day he left for Hovi'itstuyqa. He stopped before coming in sight of the village. When darkness fell, he ventured inside. He peeked into every house, searching for the one where Sikyaatayo lived. Before long he succeeded and looked in through the opening in the roof. Sure enough, the couple was down there. Sikyaatayo and Pitsinsivostiyo's wife had evidently just lain down and were making love. When he saw the two with his own eyes, he grew furious. The sight really pained him, so he left again and headed to the meeting place arranged with the enemies. Upon his arrival, he found the Kisispayas already encamped there. Full of anticipation, they had come early. There were many fires burning next to each other. But they were camped in a spot out of sight of Hovi'itstuyqa so that they would not be discovered.

Pitsinsivostiyo rejoiced in his heart. They had truly kept their word and were even there ahead of time. Once more he went over everything he had discussed with the chief. Then he added, "I want to kill that boy myself. No one else is to harm him." Thereupon he described where the boy lived. "As soon as I have dealt with him and emitted the war whoop, you can rush the village and fall upon its people. Deal severely with them. I don't want you to spare any man or boy. But that will be tomorrow. So let's catch some sleep this night. Tomorrow we'll attack." These were Pitsinsivostiyo's instructions. The Kisispayas agreed with everything. And since a villager might by chance be about, they slept without any fires that night.

The following morning they built a fire in one spot and then, one after the other, cooked something for themselves. When everybody was satisfied, they began working on their weapons. They did not extinguish the fire but warmed up their arrows over it to straighten them. They also refurbished their bows. By noontime they were finished, and then they waited for the evening. Pitsinsivostiyo was going to issue some final instructions at that time.

Finally, it was dark and Pitsinsivostiyo said to the enemies, "Well, the moment has come. Let's start moving. As soon as we reach the village, I'll enter all by myself and then I'll give you the signal. Some of you can go ahead already and surround the village." With these words, they all set forth toward Hovi'itstuyqa.

Upon getting to the village, those of the enemies who had been ordered were in their hiding places along the village edge. They had Hovi'itstuyqa encircled and were waiting.

Pitsinsivostiyo now ventured forth alone. He ascended the roof of a two-story house and from up there observed the villagers. This was summertime, so the nights were not long. Soon it was midnight. By now the people of Hovi'itstuyqa were in bed and all the lights were out. So Pitsinsivostiyo climbed down from his lookout post and went to his helpers. He reported to their chief, "All right, all the people are asleep. You can enter the village now and wait somewhere in the dark. After I've dispatched that Sikyaatayo, I'll yell a war whoop at the top of my voice. Then pounce on the people and start killing the men and boys. When I'm done, I'll go back to where we spent the night and wait for you." With these words Pitsinsivostiyo reentered the village. This time he did not bother to hide and without any concern for his safety made straight for the house of Sikyaatayo.

When he arrived there, he looked in through the hatch in the roof. The two were not asleep yet. They had unfolded their bedding and were sitting on it clinging to each other.

When Pitsinsivostiyo saw this, his anger flared up again. Without wasting any time, he extracted an arrow from his quiver and placed it on the bow. Since the couple was still up, the fire was still going and it was light inside. Pitsinsivostiyo got ready to shoot and aimed right at the heart of Sikyaatayo. He pulled the bowstring back as hard as he could and let go. With great force the arrow rushed across the bow. It hit Sikyaatayo, who was still sitting there enjoying the girl, right through the heart. He was killed instantly, and his head fell forward. So powerfully had the arrow struck him that it went clear through his back. In the front one could not even see it anymore. Immediately Pitsinsivostiyo let out a war whoop, slapping repeatedly on his mouth. Then he fled the scene of his revenge.

When the enemies heard Pitsinsivostiyo's war whoop, they scattered throughout the village. Rushing from house to house they killed the men and boys. The women and girls were all herded together. The people of Hovi'itstuyqa had of course not suspected anything. They had barely reached for their weapons when the Kisispayas had already cut many of them down. The Kisispayas had an easy time murdering them all. After the slaughter they entered the houses and started plundering the people's valuables. Necklaces, earrings, provisions, and everything of value were plundered.

In the end they took the married and unmarried women, as well as the little girls they had rounded up, to the place where Pitsinsivostiyo had promised to be. When they arrived, Pitsinsivostiyo already had a fire going and was waiting for them. He greeted the arriving Kisispayas, "Sit down a while. Thanks for coming. Did you do as requested?" he asked.

"Yes," replied their chief, "we went by your orders and did not spare any man or boy. All the things we wanted, we bundled up and brought along. We did not lay our hands on the womenfolk, though, and drove them here. This one here I'll take for myself," he said, whereupon he dragged one woman next to the fire. He had chosen Pitsinsivostiyo's wife.

Pitsinsivostiyo replied, "Very well, I promised the women to you. This one here did not want me and followed that boy here. I can't treasure her anymore. It was my desire to have this done, that's why I hired you. So thanks for fulfilling my wish. When you get back home, I hope you will live a long life." After these words of farewell he laid out a road marker in the direction of their homes and they parted.

When Pitsinsivostiyo arrived back at his house, he told his grandmother everything that had happened. The old woman felt sorry for the people of Hovi'itstuyqa but did not say anything. Then she looked to the door and saw the pet fox sitting there. Evidently, Pitsinsivostiyo had brought him along. He had not been killed in the raid. He ran into the house, whereupon the old woman called him over. "Here," she said. She had made a prayer feather for the fox. Next, she turned to her grandson and said, "All right, I want you to take him back where you caught him. Put him down there and send him off to his people. I'm glad that because of him we at least briefly met our in-law. So go and happily join your people again." With this, the old woman handed Pitsinsivostiyo the prayer feather.

Pitsinsivostiyo took the yellow fox and carried him back to the place where he had captured him. There he gave him the prayer feather and said to him, "Take this to your relatives. We made it for them."

"Thanks," the yellow fox replied. "We always desired to have a prayer feather, but no one ever gave us one, until you came along. From this day, whenever you stage a kachina dance, you are to dress with it. And without hesitation you are to wear our pelt as part of the kachina costume." This is what the yellow fox said to Pitsinsivostiyo.

"Very well, we'll do that," Pitsinsivostiyo promised. Happy about this, he returned home.

From that day on life resumed its usual course again, but Pitsinsivostiyo was troubled by what he had done to the people of Hovi'itstuyqa. He repeatedly thought about the events until he became completely preoccupied. He should not have murdered all the people there. After all, not all of them had wronged him. Sikyaatayo alone had hurt him by stealing the love of his wife, yet all of the villagers had perished. Such thoughts kept going through Pitsinsivostiyo's mind. As a result, he was not feeling well. Finally, he blurted it all out to his grandmother.

"My dear grandson," she exclaimed, "I've indeed been aware of your discomfort. I knew when you plotted this wicked scheme that it would be troubling you one day. I did not want to say anything, but sided with you. By failing to talk to you, I am myself at fault too," she said. "I guess if we stay here, we'll never be able to forget. I think we should just get up and go southeast without telling anyone about it. After all, that's where we came from in the first place. Nobody will miss us. We came here not depending on anyone. If we go back to our original place, we'll be able to live there."

Soon thereafter the two started out in the dark of the night. The few belongings they had they did not bother to take along. And since all sorts of edibles were growing along their way, they also went without journey food.

Sure enough, the people along Nuvakwewtaqa soon realized that the old woman and her grandson were gone. Nobody had seen them leave, and now that the two were gone, their cotton was beginning to give out. Since they had neglected to keep some seeds, they were not able to grow it anymore.

It was at this point that the people fully realized that Pitsinsivostiyo, or "Cotton Seed Boy," had actually owned the cotton. When he left, he took it with him. The people now also understood that his name was not just a coincidence. He was named after this plant. Now, too late, they treasured what they had had in him. But now he had left. From that day on they could no longer grow any cotton.

In this way Hovi'itstuyqa was destroyed. Enraged that his wife was taken from him, Pitsinsivostiyo ordered destruction of the village by enemies he took there himself. They did his bidding, and now the village lies in ruin. And here the story ends.

SEVEN

The Annihilation of Awat'ovi

INTRODUCTION

Of the seven pueblos portrayed in the legendary accounts of this collection, Awat'ovi stands apart in that its destruction occurred in historic times and is datable with a high degree of accuracy.[1] Located some nine miles southwest of Keams Canyon, Arizona, along the eastern edge of Antelope Mesa not far from its southernmost point, Awat'ovi was probably the largest and most populous of all the Jeddito villages that once flourished in this part of Hopiland.[2]

The town's name, which literally means "Bow High Place," apparently owed its origin to the Aawatngyam (Bow clan people), who, according to Fewkes, were the most prominent and influential of its founding clans (1893:363).

Perhaps no other ancient Hopi village now in ruins is mentioned with greater frequency in historic documents and in the published literature. For the Spanish *conquistadores* arriving from Mexico, Awat'ovi constituted the gateway to the province of Tusayan, their appellation for the Hopi country. No wonder then that the town became intimately linked with many of the major events precipitated by the Spanish presence in the Southwest. The following synopsis of some of these events, as they were of particular concern to Awat'ovi, is based on information compiled in the writings of Hargrave (1935:17–18), Montgomery et al. (1949:1–43), and Harry C. James (1974:33–64).

Awat'ovi was initially discovered in 1540 by a contingent of the Coronado Expedition under Pedro de Tovar. This first encounter with the white-faced strangers from Spain and their accompanying "man-beasts" (men on horseback) must have been traumatic for the residents of Awat'ovi.[3] That same year the pueblo experienced a second visit by the Kastiilam (Castilians), as the Spaniards came to be referred to by the Hopi. This time, the caller was García López de Cárdenas on his way to the "great river," the Grand Canyon. His assignment was to find the best route from New Mexico to the "South Sea." Disenchanted that none of the rumors about a new El Dorado north of the fabled Seven Cities of Cíbola—the latter had turned out to be the mud-and-stone villages of the Zuni—had proven true, the Spaniards did not return to Tusayan until forty-three years later. In 1583 Aguato, as the pueblo is referred to in the annals of the expedition, played host to Antonio de Espejo, followed by Juan de Oñate in 1598 and 1604.

Contact between Awat'ovi and the Spaniards, who were busy consolidating their power in the Rio Grande region of New Mexico, remained sparse until August 20, 1629, when three Franciscan missionaries—Francisco Porras, Andrés Gutiérrez, and the lay brother Cristóbal de la Concepción, all known for their zeal to convert the Indians—dedicated the mission of San Bernardo de Aguatubi. An architecturally impressive mission complex was erected over the site of a kiva in order to demonstrate the "superiority" of Christianity over the "pagan religion" of the natives. While few details are known about the Mission Period, there are indications that San Bernardo may have served as headquarters for all missionary endeavors by the Franciscans in Hopiland. While a good number of the people of Awat'ovi adopted the Catholic faith, many others remained unconverted, deeply resenting the ideological subversion of their native beliefs and the forced abandonment of their religious ceremonies.

This resentment against the proselytizing missionaries, and general hatred of everything Spanish, was not limited to the Hopi.[4] The cruel inhumanity of the Spaniards toward the Indians of the Southwest, which included their conscription for slave labor, the abuse of women, and the suppression of "idolatrous" practices, was prevalent throughout the Southwest and finally exploded in the great Pueblo Revolt of 1680. This well-organized rebellion was spearheaded by Popé, a religious leader from San Juan Pueblo. Those in Awat'ovi who joined the concerted uprising against the Spanish yoke stoned Father José de Figueroa to death and destroyed the mission church. The resulting period of independence from Spanish domination was soon terminated, however, when Diego de Vargas resubjugated rebellious New Mexico and, in 1692, marched into Tusayan territory. After the resubmission of Awat'ovi was secured for the Spanish Crown, the church was rebuilt and reconsecrated. Apparently, the residents of Awat'ovi were more willing to accept Spanish sovereignty and Catholic Christianity than were the other Hopi villages, for in 1700, they welcomed Father Juan Garaycoechea. He was permitted to visit the town, and he resumed baptizing the natives. John Otis Brew feels that "there must have been strong motivation for their choice to face death and destruction, on the side of the Christian God and the Spaniards, and against their native kachinas and fellow Hopi" (1979:520). According to Adolph F. Bandelier, Awat'ovi "had virtually become again a Christianized pueblo" (1976[1892]:372).[5] The overall Hispanophile attitude and pro-Catholic gestures and overtures so outraged some of the Hopi communities to the west that they conspired to jointly attack the apostate village and burn it to the ground. Awat'ovi, which may have had some eight hundred inhabitants at the time, was successfully sacked late in the fall of 1700. While most of its population was killed, some of the surviving women and children were distributed among the villages of the avengers. Following the massacre, no attempt was ever made to resettle Awat'ovi. The uninhabited site has since lain in ruin.

Harry C. James has called the destruction of Awat'ovi "one of the most significant events in Hopi history" (1974:62). It certainly proved a turning point in Hopi relations with the Spanish. With their relatively strong ally of Awat'ovi gone, the Spaniards were never again able to reestablish the stronghold they had enjoyed in Tusayan.

The earliest contemporary testament to the destruction of Awat'ovi is found in a Spanish document dated 1701. Written by Pedro Rodríguez Cubero, who had replaced Vargas as governor of New Mexico in 1697, it refers to the campaign he waged in the summer of 1701 "in the province of Moqui [i.e., Hopi] against apostate Indians there, following the annihilation which they committed upon the converted Indians of the pueblo of *Aguatubi*" (Wilson 1972:129). However, Cubero's expedition proved a failure. The Hopi, prepared for reprisals by the Spanish, were not intimidated, and their punitive action resulted only in intensifying Hopi "determination to remain free of any Spanish influence, secular or religious" (James 1974:64).

Of the many references to Awat'ovi in the published literature the first one belongs to John G. Bourke, who paid a visit to the ruin in 1881. Interestingly enough, he refers to the site by its Navajo designation of Tolli-Hogandi (1884:109).[6] This term (which translates as "Singing House"), rather than its proper Hopi name, was apparently used also by the First Mesa village chief of Walpi when he remarked on the site to Bourke (Fewkes 1893:363). Bourke himself concludes that Tolli-Hogandi must be identical with the Aguato of Spanish records and that "the singing men" whom the Hopis did not like had been the

> missionaries who, at Tolli-Hogandi, had gathered about them a colony of neophytes, whose rapid increase gave alarm and disquietude

to the old heathen element, and that the latter, upon the first favorable pretext and opportunity, rallied to wipe out at one fell stroke the hated innovation and its adherents. [1884:91]

The first scientific work at the ruin was carried out by Victor Mindeleff, who was involved in a study of Pueblo architecture at the time. He published a brief assessment of the ruin (1891:49–50) and charted the ground plan of its eastern section, which, almost in its entirety, takes up the ancient mission complex (1891: plate IV).

Fewkes was the first to actually undertake its partial excavation. While he drew up a complete ground plan of the pueblo, which also includes the older, western section omitted by Mindeleff, his cursory investigation, which lasted a mere ten days, was primarily designed to verify some of the oral traditions of Awat'ovi's downfall (1893: plate II). The fact that in nearly every excavated chamber remnants of charred wood, ashes, and other evidence of fire were unearthed was ample proof to him that the village had perished in a great conflagration. However, since the number of human bones retrieved was judged too small by him "to answer the requirements of the legend" (1893:373), Fewkes renewed his investigative efforts during a second dig in 1895. This time, many skeletons were found, "evidently thrown promiscuously in a heap, without pious regard or the sympathetic offering of food in mortuary vessels." In his view, this discovery attested to the wholesale slaughter that had taken place and to "one of the most brutal tragedies of the times" (1895:572).

The most extensive archaeological exploration of the ruin to date was that by the Peabody Museum Awatovi Expedition under the direction of John Otis Brew. During five seasons of field research in the Jeddito Valley and on Antelope Mesa, 21 sites were excavated, chronologically ranging from approximately A.D. 500 to 1700 (1935–39). At Awat'ovi alone, 1300 rooms were unearthed, 25 of them kivas (Brew 1941:40). The Franciscan missionary establishment that came to light in the course of the excavation comprised "two churches and foundations for a third; a friary; a suite of offices and schoolrooms; a row of workshops, storerooms, etc.; and the foundations for a barrack-stable" (Montgomery et al. 1949:47).[7] Among the most sensational discoveries by the Awatovi Expedition were the exquisite mural frescoes that adorned many of the kiva walls. Awat'ovi's mural art, which has been presented in an exhaustive monograph by Watson Smith (1952), allows a wealth of ethnographic insights into not only the ritualistic aspects of Hopi culture but also the complete ramifications of the Hopi cultural complex at the time.

Excepting the Hopi emergence myth from the underworld, probably no other tale is attested to more often in the published body of Hopi oral literature than the one relating to the tragic end of Awat'ovi. While Bourke had been the first to briefly comment on the ruin, a slightly more informative account of Awat'ovi's violent demise is found in Bandelier (1976[1892]:371–372). The extended version published by Fewkes was actually obtained for him by Alexander Stephen (Fewkes 1893:364–366). Containing a much greater number of details than the succinct references by Bourke and Bandelier, its summary presentation is not marked, however, by the style that distinguishes traditional Hopi narratives. George Wharton James, who published his account under the title "The Storming of Awatobi," admits that Fewkes was his source (1901:497–500). Retold in the romantic, kitschy fashion so typical of the popular literature of the times, James's version constitutes but an exercise in fictional prose. His story, which he claims he told much as he heard it "from Hopi lips," has nothing in common with Hopi narrative tradition.

Voth recorded two versions of the end of Awat'ovi. The first, told by a Second Mesa man from Shipaulovi, is an abortive sketch of the actual events at Awat'ovi (1905:254–255). The motive given for the destruction—unhappiness on the part of the village chief's son because the marriageable women of the village gave him the cold shoulder—is utterly ludicrous and completely incongruent in light of the bloody consequences that it entailed for the community. Voth's second account was related by an Oraibi man (1905:246–253). That it genuinely reflects the spirit of Hopi storytelling, can, among other things, be deduced from the many dialogue passages it contains. It too, however, is relatively weak in its motivation for the wholesale slaughter of an entire village. This version relates that, during a rabbit hunt in which both sexes participate, one of the mounted hunters accidentally rides down the chief's daughter and kills her. This incident so infuriates the chief that he devises a plan that ultimately leads to the eradication of Awat'ovi.

Unlike Voth's second account, which, in great detail, unfolds the Awat'ovi chief's scheme to gain the support of the Oraibis, Walpis, and Mishongnovis for his planned revenge and devotes a good portion of the narration to the actual attack and ensuing massacre, Edward S. Curtis's account focuses almost exclusively on a string of mythological events prior to the town's fall (1970[1922]:184–188). Nearly all of these events center around the deity of Aaloosaka and his six sons. The town's actual destruction is mentioned in only one sentence, almost like an afterthought: "In the fifth year, they [i.e., the inhabitants of Awat'ovi] became so bad that Tapólo, chief of the

Tobacco clan, secured the aid of the Horn clan at Walpi in destroying most of the people of Awatobi" (1970[1922]:188). However, when the legend is read in conjunction with Curtis's ethnographic section "Migrations of the Tobacco Clan," a more rounded picture emerges regarding Awat'ovi's end (1970[1922]:83–89).

The chapter "The Destruction of Awatovi" in Frank Waters's *Book of the Hopi* contains no narrative passages (1963:258–266). Rather, it is a mixture of historic facts and legends, interspersed with reflective and philosophical observations by its author.

Courlander's first published version of the demise of Awat'ovi also does not reflect the true flavor of Hopi storytelling (1971:209–220). It constitutes, in fact, a composite based on input from six different informants, as is admitted by the author himself (1971:268). Several of its passages read like summary statements from sources in the literature. Often, they are analytical and quite specific, a style that runs completely counter to that of Hopi narrative tradition.

These observations do not hold, however, for Courlander's second version (1982:55–60). Its authenticity is easily recognized. It features one detailed episode of wife-stealing as an example of the lifestyle bordering on *koyaanisqatsi* brought on by the Awat'ovi *kwitavit* (turds). The immoral behavior displayed between men and women in the kivas moves the *tsa'akmongwi* (crier chief), rather than the *kikmongwi* (village chief), to initiate the doom of the village.

Finally, Albert Yava's remarks, edited by Courlander, once more constitute a mixture of analytic comments and narrative sections (Yava 1978:88–97). Among other things, he suggests that the sacking of Awat'ovi had a great impact on how the Hopi came to regard themselves: "They had always been the Peaceful People, but, after the destruction, they had to live with guilt feelings for violating their principles" (1978:88). He claims that the Hopi are ashamed of what happened and that nowadays they "want to forget the whole Awatovi affair" (1978:95).

The present Third Mesa version is the most comprehensive narrative available to date on Awat'ovi's destruction. Obviously, it mirrors or is reminiscent of a good number of plot elements in the other accounts. On the other hand, it introduces a host of details missing in the previous versions. Of course, this is not surprising in a situation where traditions are passed on orally. Good storytellers are frequently familiar with more than one variant of the same tale. In addition, they may inadvertently drift into the context of another story. They will even freely borrow anecdotal events from another tale to enhance the impact of their narrative. Occasionally, a certain subplot may be fleshed out to such an extent by a skilled narrator that it will turn into an independent tale. Due to the fallibility of human memory, as Fewkes reminds us, "errors too must be expected, and the personal equation should always be considered. These folk-tales are not mathematically exact, although capable of scientific treatment, and versions vary" (1893:366). My narrator's version reflects all of the above techniques, whether intentional or unintentional and, therefore, constitutes a typical product of the Hopi narrative tradition.

Thematically, the legend, as presented in this book, is divided into two major parts. The first part, rich in mythological content, is foremost the story of Pavayoykyasi, a moisture deity who is said to command the rainbow.[8] The second part, which exudes a much stronger historical flavor, relates to Ta'palo, the Awat'ovi village chief, and his involvement in the fate of the pueblo.[9] Pavayoykyasi, the protagonist of the first part, is said to reside at Tuutukwi, the (Hopi) Buttes south of First and Second Mesa. When the girl he falls in love with is abducted by the evil Lepenangwtiyo (Icicle Boy), who lives in an ice cave at Nuvatukya'ovi (San Francisco Mountains), Pavayoykyasi sets out to rescue her. In the process, he defeats the abductor, who embodies polar weather, and banishes him, in culture-heroic fashion, to a region in the north, where snow and ice are naturally at home.

While in many ways reminiscent of Curtis's version, the plot in the first half here nevertheless shows more differences than similarities (see Curtis 1970[1922]:184–188).[10] The protagonist in the account Curtis has preserved is Aaloosaka, a two-horned germinator god. He resides at Alosaktûqi (Aaloosaktukwi), which is also located in the San Francisco Mountains.[11] After Aaloosaka ferries the girl, who accompanies him of her own free will, from Awat'ovi to his home aboard a flying shield, Hahay'iwuuti, the mother of all the kachinas, imposes a number of grinding ordeals upon her. Successfully passing these tests with the assistance of Spider Woman, the girl is found worthy of an alliance with the god.

Owing to their supernatural powers, both Pavayoykyasi and Aaloosaka prove immensely beneficial to Awat'ovi, where, in accordance with Hopi matrilocal marriage customs, they take up their residence. Aaloosaka, in addition to providing bountiful harvests and plentiful rains, is portrayed as the heroic savior of Awat'ovi in an episode related by Curtis outside the legendary account. When the village was threatened by a firestorm burning across the plain, he "ran forth from the village and met the wall of fire. He ran his horn into the ground in the path of the flames and tore up the earth in a narrow furrow. There the fire stopped: it could not cross the furrow" (1970[1922]:84).[12]

Both my version and Curtis's share the fact that six sons are born to their protagonists Pavayoykyasi and Aaloosaka.[13] The children's names, Sakwyeva, Moomo'a, Hoyniwa, Siisivu, Wuktima, and Patösqasa, which are also the same in the two accounts, may symbolically emphasize the good life that reigned under their fathers' tutelary influence at Awat'ovi. Thus, according to Curtis, Sakwyeva, the name bestowed on the first born, denotes "the greenness of the fields covered with flourishing crops" (1970[1922]:186). The Hopi will generally concur with this interpretation. *Sakw-*, the combining form of *sakwa* (blue/green), is the color typically used to describe plants. Moomo'a (mouths), according to Curtis, is supposed to signify "that the mouths of the people would be full" (186). My informants were not able to confirm this interpretation because the regular plural form of *mo'a* (mouth) is *mom'a*, not *moomo'a*, in the Third Mesa dialect. Hoyniwa, the name of the third child, which is glossed as "winnowing" by Curtis (186), is instead associated by a consultant of mine with ritual smoking. Although the simplex *hoyna* may indeed mean "winnow," an unrelated, homophonous form refers to the "releasing of smoke out of one's mouth, after retaining it momentarily, while in prayerful thought." This definition would make the name symbolic, in a religious sense. Siisivu, explained as the plural of *siivu* (pottery vessel), according to the view of Curtis, implies "the desire that everybody have full cooking-pots" (186). My informants rejected this interpretation, suggesting instead that it referred to *siivu*, the black soot left on the pot from the burning wood. Wuktima, defined simply as "stepping" by Curtis (186), is explained by one of my informants to be a description of the gait of a bear. Since the bear is one of the animal familiars customarily selected by medicine men, the name may have magico-religious implications regarding healing. Finally, Patösqasa, the name of the youngest son, cannot be satisfactorily unlocked as to its etymological meaning. Curtis's suggestion that it refers to "the sound made by thumping a watermelon to determine if it is ripe" (186) is rejected by the people I consulted. While there exists a verb *patöqsamti* (to pop), which comes close to the name, this term cannot be used with regard to a watermelon. The noun *patöqsasa*, defined as a legume of the *Astragalus* genus with inflated pods that children pop, may be a more likely source for the name, although its phonetic shape does not accurately match that of the name (Whiting 1939:79–80).

A story song, which enumerates the children's names in the version presented here, is still familiar to many elderly Hopi and is held to be an ancient Wuwtsim song. Linguistically no longer transparent in every aspect—several words are already obsolete—it poetically condenses the bad life at Awat'ovi, precipitated by the Catholic church and its Hopi converts.

While the presence of a moisture and fertility deity in Awat'ovi turns out to be a tremendous boon to its residents, it eventually also becomes the catalyst for disaster. Extraordinary powers and greater-than-average achievements are generally perceived with great suspicion by Hopis and arouse their jealousy and envy. People who excel in certain ways or distinguish themselves from their fellow humans by their unconventional attitudes and nonconformist ways are typically vulnerable to a charge of witchcraft. The act of accusing someone in this way has been conceptualized in the Hopi language by the verb *powaqsasvi*, literally, "strike someone as witch." This way of mind and action control, which is easily achieved in a small society, has left a long-lasting impact on the Hopi psyche, and the dread of being accused of sorcery explains many behavioral traits of the Hopi. As Elsie Clews Parsons points out, "In such a social code or theory of conduct innovation is discouraged, and any show of individualism is condemned" (1939, 1:107). Titiev confirms this observation:

> The constant terror of witchcraft under which the Hopi labor has had a marked effect on their characters. Brought up in an atmosphere of dread and helplessness in the face of evil attacks, they quickly learn to avoid all appearance of having exceptional ability, and to emphasize moderation in all things. They constantly decry their powers, make frequent professions of humility, and, through fear of arousing the envy or jealousy of the two-hearted, prefer not to seek great honors or to hold high offices. [1942:556]

That jealousy is indeed responsible for a great deal of factionalism, dissension, and overall social disruption in Hopi society, is easily observed in the body of Hopi oral literature, where this detrimental sentiment occurs as a motif that wreaks havoc time and time again. Jealousy also pollutes the dealings of the inhabitants of Awat'ovi with their benefactors Pavayoykyasi and Aaloosaka. According to Curtis, a faction of sorcerers and witches "believed that the children of Alosaka had had nothing to do with the prosperity the people had been enjoying. They were jealous, and desired to kill the Crier Chief, his wife, his daughter, his grandchildren, and Alosaka" (1970[1922]:187). The Hopi term for the emotion of jealousy or strong resentment toward others is *qa naani*, literally "not laugh/not be amused," for the one-time manifestation, and *qa nanani* for an ongoing or repeated experience of this feeling. This latter term, though in pluralized form, is also the expression used by the narrator in the Hopi original, here, to characterize the sorcerer faction of Awat'ovi.

Although modern Hopi are no longer as vulnerable to an accusation of witchcraft as in former times, they are nonetheless painfully aware that actions and decisions in their daily lives are still governed occasionally by this deep-seated fear. Since it is central to understanding the Hopi character, the following three testimonials, which analyze this phenomenon from a Hopi point of view, are cited in full.

TEXT 71

They say that the Hopi are evil. We're always bothering one another and have no love for each other. There are all sorts of things that arouse our envy of others. When people achieve something good, others criticize them. "That guy is a sorcerer," they say. Or if they don't want to say that, they say, "He must have sold a corpse in order to get that precious thing."

Therefore, when a Hopi acquires something nice, that person is not supposed to boast about it. Or if a man does something outstanding, he must not brag. We are afraid of talk; therefore we do not speak about our accomplishments. Since we all long for material possessions, everybody wants to have beautiful things. But no sooner does one get something by working hard than there are persons who are jealous and calling the hard worker a sorcerer. As a result, one loses heart.

The old people used to labor during hot weather and on burning sand in order to grow their crops. But if one of them succeeded, someone else was envious and branded that person a sorcerer. Or, when a man has some nice plants, someone else will get jealous. Looking unfavorably upon that, he will do something to them to bewitch them. Then they won't grow well anymore.

TEXT 72

Whenever a man, by his own hard work, assembles a few things for himself or his children, he will be called a sorcerer by someone. One who is envious of him is bound to speak against him. The old people and the elders also used to say that the Hopis are evil. They say the Hopis simply use their name [which means "civilized"] to hide behind, in order to cover their evil ways. There is no good person. We're all like that. We all have evil in us. Nobody is innocent. For this reason, we constantly talk against each other. Even though no one actually lays hands on another person, one will hurt the other with words, especially with lies.

This problem will not go away. Not until we come to the judgment day, when our creator will purify us. Therefore, our elders used to say

long ago, "One must not live with a mean heart. A traveler is always
to be welcomed. The person who enters someone's house must be
fed some food." They were talking about a life of mutual respect and
caring, but no one lives like that.

TEXT 73

If a man has extraordinary powers and has special knowledge in things,
he usually causes trouble for other people. A sorcerer is just like that.
For example, if a person is successful, the sorcerer becomes jealous
and then does some harm to that person. Maybe the sorcerer plans
something against the successful one. Or he spreads a rumor. The
other people then believe the bad things the sorcerer said and talk
about the successful one in the same manner. As a result, persons
treated this way get so disheartened that they no longer succeed in
their affairs.

While the version recorded by Curtis lists jealousy as the single factor
that prompts the murder of five of Aaloosaka's children—he himself, with
his youngest son, escapes to his home at the San Francisco Mountains—
additional reasons are introduced to motivate the massacre in the account
recorded here. As a consequence of the crime, drought and famine befall
the inhabitants of Awat'ovi. When Pavayoykyasi eventually returns and
miraculously saves the remaining survivors from starvation, they elect his
son Patösqasa as their new leader. Thereafter the people's lives return to
normal. Before long, however, this state of happiness and harmony is
shattered by a new inroad of evil. By now, the chief of the village of Awat'ovi
is Ta'palo, who, according to Curtis, invites the neighboring inhabitants of
Walpi to destroy the town.

The whole scenario of the violent end of Awat'ovi, which Curtis sums
up in a couple of lines, takes almost the entire second part of this version
(see Curtis 1970[1922]:188). While in many instances this version confirms
the general unfolding of happenings depicted in the materials recorded
by Fewkes, Voth, and Courlander, it builds a much more dramatic case
for the state of *koyaanisqatsi*, the social disease of turmoil and corruption
that affects the community. Ultimately, three major events induce Chief
Ta'palo to seek the annihilation of the pueblo. First, his daughter is killed
during a communal rabbit hunt, as a result of reckless riding by one of the
hunters. Next, the pueblo succumbs to a gambling craze. This craze reaches
its culmination when the crier chief, one of the most respected officials in
a Hopi community, is publicly compromised by the participation of his
wife. Finally, the residents of Awat'ovi engage in social dancing. After the

people's decision to stage a Butterfly dance, the nightly practice sessions soon degenerate to a level of unabashed sexual promiscuity. The general atmosphere of *koyaanisqatsi* comes to a climactic crisis for Ta'palo when he witnesses an act of adultery between his wife and her dance partner.

The subsequent events leading to the conflagration of the town and the fratricidal butchery of its population more or less parallel those in the versions recorded by Fewkes, Voth, and Courlander. Overall, however, the present version is more graphic in detail, which is probably due to the fact that it was recorded in the Hopi vernacular.

To be sure, there are a number of differences between the various versions, some of which may be worth pointing out. Thus, the murderous scheme with the Wawarkatsinam (Runner kachinas), in which Ta'palo attempts to entrap the village leader of Shungopavi into sacking Awat'ovi, also occurs in Voth's version (1905:247–250).[14] While his four Runner kachinas are identified as Hömsona, Angwusngöntaqa, Tsilitosmoktaqa, and Sikyapku, the latter two are replaced in this account by Leetotovi and Sikyaatayo. Voth's version has the Awat'ovi chief, whose name we never learn, offer two small clay figures to the village head of Oraibi: one symbolizing the males and the other representing the females of his village. The Oraibi chief is thereby given the option to select whatever group he fancies as a reward for this assistance in the mission of revenge. The same anecdote is alluded to by Curtis (1970[1922]:86). In this version, Ta'palo, the night before the raid, hands over his *tiiponi* (chief's medicine bundle and status emblem) to the joint war chiefs of the enemy forces as a gesture of forfeiting his "children."

In Cosmos Mindeleff's version, the signal for the attack is given when the Walpi war chief utters his war cry (1891:34). In Voth, it is conveyed by the chief's son, who is supposed to leave the roof on which he is sitting when the right moment for the attack has arrived (1905:252). According to Voth's narrator, the son had been bewitched by his father, who is characterized as a *powaqa* (sorcerer). In Courlander 1971:217, the Awat'ovi chief waves a firebrand as a signal. In Courlander 1982:59, it is the crier chief who uses a blanket for this purpose. In this version, Ta'palo himself gives the signal with the blanket.

In the aftermath of the storming of the town, many of the villagers are tortured and slaughtered at various locations. Fewkes identifies one place by the name of Maski (Home of the Dead), another as Mastsomo (Death Mound) (1893:366). Voth refers only to Mastsomo (1905:253). Curtis also gives Mastsomo (1970[1922]:88), as does Waters (1963:264). Courlander mentions three places: Masqötö (Skull), Mastukwi (Death Butte), and Mastsomo (1971:218). The same is true for his 1982 version. Yava speaks of

"Skull Ridge" or "Skull Mound" (1978:93), which I assume to be translations of Masqötö. The account given here mentions Masqötö and Mastsomo.

Of course, information on the geographic location of these torture and execution sites varies from version to version. Fewkes claims that Mastsomo was pointed out to him by the Hopi but that he did not excavate it "to try and find the bones of the unfortunates" (1893:369). Voth puts Mastsomo "at a place between Walpi and Mishongnovi" (1905:253). Masqötö, where a number of female prisoners were decapitated, according to Courlander, lies not far from a site called "Five Houses." Mastukwi is placed at "the wash just a little to the east of where the village of Polacca now stands," and Mastsomo "near Wepo Wash, on the west side of Walpi" by his narrator (Courlander 1971:218). In my account, Masqötö remains unspecified as to its location, and Mastsomo is rather vaguely placed somewhere "on the west side of Walpi."

Christy G. Turner and Nancy T. Morris, after analyzing the fragmented human bones excavated at a multiple burial site "on the left bank of Polacca Wash ten miles south of the Hopi villages," found that "thirty Hopi Indians of both sexes and all ages were killed, crudely dismembered, violently mutilated, and probably cannibalized some 370 years ago" (1970:320). According to the two researchers, "the location of, dismemberment of bodies in, and radiocarbon age of this mass burial" indicate the bodies were indeed those of the captive Awat'ovis slain following their departure from the razed village. Both agree that "southwestern archaeological evidence fitting legendary events has seldom been better" (1970:330).

There are various explanations as to what happened to Ta'palo, the Awat'ovi village leader. Whereas Fewkes makes no mention of his fate, Voth indicates that both he and his son were destroyed in the kivas with the others (1905:258). According to Curtis, he went into hiding before the raid, only to return after the event and contribute to the general slaughter by single-handedly suffocating a survivor he finds in one of the kivas (1970[1922]:87–88). Waters claims that, according to Oraibi tradition, Ta'palo went to live in a Rio Grande pueblo (1963:265). In Courlander's version, he chooses to die with the rest of his people (1971:219). Yava reports that he, together with several clan relatives, is supposed to have escaped from the village before the raid (1978:94). The legend here simply states that Ta'palo perished in the inferno.

Survivors of the massacre, who were transplanted to Oraibi, Mishongnovi, and Walpi, contributed a number of significant new cults to the ceremonialism of these villages. There is consensus in the narratives that among the Awat'ovi rituals perpetuated in this fashion were two women's ceremonies: the Maraw (Fewkes 1893:366; Curtis 1970[1922]:89; my account) and the Owaqöl (Voth 1905:253; Curtis 1970[1922]:89; Courlander 1982:60). There is further agreement that the Wuwtsim, Al (Horn), and Taw (Singer) societies continued in the Hopi villages to the west (Curtis 1970[1922]:89; Courlander 1971:219; Yava 1978:95). The version presented here is the only one that also includes the Lakon, the third of the three women's ceremonies that are part of the Hopi ceremonial year. Since none of the other accounts corroborates this fact, my narrator may have been in error.[15]

Generally, 1700 is the year now accepted as the one that marked the end of Awat'ovi. Both the ample evidence from Spanish chronicles and other sources gathered by Brew (Montgomery et al. 1949:20–24), as well as the Spanish document from 1701 recovered by John P. Wilson (1972:125–130), strongly suggest this date. As to when in 1700 the actual attack took place, several of the legendary references point to the month of November. Cosmos Mindeleff mentions the annual "feast of the Kwakwanti [Kwaakwant]," always held in November (1891:34). Fewkes confirms this statement (1893:369). He gives the "Na-ac'-nai-ya [naa'asnaya]" or "New Fire" ceremony, regularly celebrated in November, as the time of the tragic event. Curtis simply says that it was the "season of the New Fire ceremony" (1970[1922]:87). Waters specifies that the attack was planned for "the first night of Wuwuchim [Wuwtsim], when all the men would be meeting in the kiva" (1963:264). My narrator gives *suuwuwtsimtotokpe*, which translates "exactly on Wuwtsim eve."

Wuwtsim was once one of the most important ceremonials in the course of the Hopi ceremonial year. Now extinct save in the Second Mesa village of Shungopavi, it is generally characterized as a manhood initiation rite. Jointly performed by the Wuwtsimt, Taatawkyam, Kwaakwant, and Aa'alt initiates into the Wuwtsim, Singer, Agave, and Horn societies, it usually lasted eight days. When staged in the form of a *wuwtsimnatnga* (Wuwtsim initiation), it was announced sixteen days in advance. This is the form to which Fewkes's locution refers. *Naa'asnaya* simply describes the initiatory act during the sacred night of *astotokya*. However, it is not the idiomatically established term for this ritual. Its culturally appropriate name is Wuwtsim. Since *totokya* (eve) always refers to the day prior to the ceremonial climax, *wuwtsimtotokya* (Wuwtsim eve) in my account designates the seventh day within the eight-day ceremonial span. If one assumes that the ideal period for the Wuwtsim ceremony is November 20–28 and that the narrator did not err—in the course of nearly three centuries that the legend has been handed down orally, mistakes must naturally be expected—Awat'ovi would have been destroyed sometime during the last week of November 1700 (Malotki 1983:372).

Overall, the account of the destruction of Awat'ovi follows the rules governing Hopi storytelling tradition. This adherence to that tradition is particularly evident in the first half, the story of Pavayoykyasi. If any historical events underlie this part, they are camouflaged beyond recognition. Many of its episodes are the stock material of a good storyteller and could easily be exchanged for anecdotes from other tales. The second half, on the other hand, which presents the story of Ta'palo, violates several of the established narrative rules. What was clearly mytho-historical in the first part assumes in the second part much more the flavor of a historical account. To be sure, the general camouflage of factual information continues. However, it is pierced by historical fact in several instances. Thus, we not only learn the name of the village chief but it is also revealed that the *popwaqt* (sorcerers) responsible for much of the social turmoil in the town are identical to the Spaniards. The term *popwaqt* here is not used in its narrow definition of "witchcraft practitioners" but in the broader sense of ideological troublemakers. Characterized as an evil, uncivilized lot, they are reported to be baptizing the residents of Awat'ovi, thereby confusing minds and dividing the population into two factions.

By adding this explanatory note to the tale, the narrator indirectly also exposes the function of the same cover term of *popwaqt* (sorcerers) in the first part. I believe that it there, too, denotes the Spaniards and the missionized Hopi of Awat'ovi. Based on this interpretation, which must remain speculative of course, the narrative segment featuring Pavayoykyasi would represent the historic events leading up to the Pueblo Revolt of 1680. The killing of five of Pavayoykyasi's six sons could then symbolize the deadly blow Hopi religion at Awat'ovi suffered under the missionary onslaught of Catholicism. The return of Pavayoykyasi and his remaining son Patösqasa, on the other hand, would signify the recovery of the ancient religion during post-Revolt times. Free of the Spanish priests and their proselytes, indicated by the perishing of the sorcerers during the famine, the town can once again enjoy harmony and peace. However, as soon as Awat'ovi submits to Vargas and welcomes the padres anew, the Hopi devotees of the Christian faith, previously branded as evil sorcerers, once more make life untenable for the traditionalists. *Koyaanisqatsi*, with all its social aberrations, having reigned prior to the Pueblo rebellion, reasserts itself. This reassertion of *koyaanisqatsi* (read Catholicism) prompts Ta'palo into action.

Whether the attack on Awat'ovi was indeed masterminded by its leader or the other Hopi villages simply took matters into their own hands, we will never know. Ta'palo's initiative certainly runs to type with Hopi narrative traditions.[16] Parsons has advanced the hypothesis that Awat'ovi was not destroyed by the Hopi at all. She believes that the motivation for Awat'ovi's destruction "is given in such fictitious terms of personal revenge or outrage or of desire to capture young women and children" that it seems more probable that the town was destroyed by nomadic tribesmen, such as the Utes (1939:12). One of the arguments she proposes in support of her theory is the fact that Walpi, fearing it might be next on the hit list of the nomadic raiders, invited the Tewas from the Rio Grande area to establish a colony on First Mesa. While Parsons's point has some merit, it seems to me, on the basis of both the documentary and legendary evidence, that Awat'ovi was destroyed by Hopi from other mesas.

Waters thinks that the tragedy that took place at Awat'ovi dealt a devastating blow to the Hopi intrinsic commitment to peace, a notion supposedly anchored in their very tribal name:

> Their complete destruction of one of their own villages, and their ruthless massacre of their own people for betraying a human tolerance toward a new faith, was an act of religious bigotry that equaled if it did not surpass the cruelty of the hated 'slave church' itself. For the Hopis were a People of Peace, dedicated since their Emergence to a universal plan of Creation which ever sought to maintain in unbroken harmony the lives of every entity—mineral, plant, animal, and man. Now, in the one act of unrestrained hate and violence, they had committed a fratricidal crime of mass murder that nullified their own faith and stamped forever an ineradicable guilt upon the heart of every Hopi. [1963:266]

I believe that Waters greatly exaggerates his case when he states that the Hopi have been guilt-ridden ever since the atrocities of Awat'ovi. At least, none of the Hopi I consulted in matters of Awat'ovi showed signs of guilt nor were they in any way reluctant to discuss the events surrounding the downfall of the village. The argument Waters submits critically hinges of course on the meaning he assigns to the word *hopi*. In interpreting the tribal name as "People of Peace," he unjustifiably characterizes the Hopis as elitist pacifists. Such pacifists the Hopis have never been.

As I have shown elsewhere, *hopi* does not signify "peaceful" (Malotki 1991:45). Rather, it denotes "good" in the sense of "well-behaved." Considering that the sedentary Hopi compared themselves favorably with their predominantly nomadic neighbors, the term is perhaps best defined as "civilized." The Hopi achievements in agriculture, architecture, and ceremonialism must have induced a feeling of ethnic superiority in them, which is reflected in the onomastic label they gave themselves.

The fantasy that *hopi* means "peaceful" is both erroneous and misleading. It has not only created "the unreal Hopi" but also contributed to the widely held view that the Hopi constitute an Edenic society living in tranquility and harmony on the high plateau (Shorris 1971:148). This falsehood about the Hopi has led people from around the world to expect something of them that is impossible.

As it turns out, there is not a single word in the entire Hopi lexicon that captures our idea of peace. On the other hand, the Hopi language contains an extensive vocabulary that relates to the business of war. Thus, in addition to the term *naaqöyiw* (the killing of one another), which approximates our concept of war, the language provides two verbs for the notion "to kill." While *niina* refers to the killing of one or two persons (or animals), *qöya* implies the killing of three or more. Based on this observation, one could easily turn the tables on the mistaken peace-exegetes and claim that Hopi are obsessed with killing. After all, their language operates with terms for single as well as mass murder.

Obviously, nothing could be further from the truth. Conclusions of this sort are fallacious, if not ludicrous, because the lexical differentiation into *niina* and *qöya* is entirely a grammatical one. The Hopi language has a number of verbs that behave this way, in other words, that lexicalize differently according to whether the object or target they act upon is singular/dual or plural. Thus, *tavi* means "to place one thing or two things," and *oya*, "to place many things." Normally, native speakers are not even aware of such suppletive stem packages in their respective languages. How many speakers of English pay attention to the fact that the present tense form of "go" changes to "went" when it is used in a past-time context? Grammatical irregularities of this kind do not affect the mind, nor do they sum up the psychological makeup of a people or determine the worldview of their speakers.

Hence, one noun for "war" and two verbs for "killing" do not make the Hopi a warlike people. Neither does the fact that the domain of warlore was quite extensive in Hopi culture (Malotki 1991:47). Also the fact that Hopi oral history is brimming with violence, feuding, and death, on an individual as well as a communal scale, as is evident from the stories in this book, must not be taken too literally. After all, even the Hopi kachina gods, whom one would expect to be spiritual role models, are portrayed in Hopi mythology as death-dealing avengers when they are wronged.

None of these observations precludes the Hopi from striving for peace and harmony within religious or philosophical parameters. They only make the Hopi appear more like the rest of humankind. Both Hopi and Christian theology aim high at such ideals as brotherly love and peace, being fully aware that the most hideous crimes have been perpetrated in the name of their respective gods.

NOTES

1. For the village name Awat'ovi a list of twenty-seven spellings of Spanish and Anglo provenience has been compiled in Montgomery et al. 1949:xxii. They range from such renditions as Abattobi and Ahwat-tenna to Waterby and Zuguato. In accordance with the principles of Hopi standardized orthography, the correct transcription of the town's name is Awat'ovi.

2. Other well-known villages on Antelope Mesa, which lie in ruin today, were Mösiptanga (wild gourd), Kookopngyam (Kookop clan members), Tsaaqpahu (small spring), Lölöqangwtukwi (bull snake butte), and Kawayka'a. The last place-name is of non-Hopi origin.

3. The Hopi belief in the return of a white elder brother—he is commonly referred to as *itaapava* (our elder brother) or *itaaqötsapava* (our white elder brother)—who would establish peace and justice throughout the land may have helped the Spaniards in their initial confrontation with the Hopi. The belief, which is probably traceable to the widespread pre-Columbian myth of the return of Quetzalcoatl or Kukulcan, the Toltecs' and Mayas' bearded white god in the form of a plumed snake, was quickly shattered, however, when this white brother, in the person of Pedro de Tovar, demonstrated aggression and brutality against the Indians.

4. The Hopi term for the Catholic priests during the time of the Spanish occupation was *tota'tsi* (dictator, demanding person). Still applied today to a particularly bossy person, the word turns out to be a Nahuatl loan (Kenneth Hill, personal communication 1991). Pronounced *totahtzin* in the Valley of Mexico accent, it originally meant "our honored father." The fact that this word found its way into the Hopi vocabulary, though with a radically different denotation, indicates that Nahuatl speakers not only accompanied the Spanish missionaries to the Hopi but also resided among them.

5. Yava reports that the Spanish padres were so successful at converting the people of Awat'ovi that "eventually more than half the population allowed itself to be baptized, and the ones that resisted were a minority" (1978:89). Waters claims that, early in the spring of 1700, Garaycoechea "persuaded seventy-three Hopi to be baptized" (1963:259).

6. The Navajo name is additionally encountered in such spellings as Tolla-Hogan, Talla-Hogandi, Tally-Hogan, and the Navajo-Hopi hybrid Atabi-hogandi.

7. For a conjectural restoration of Mission San Bernardo de Aguatubi see Montgomery et al. 1949: figs. 35 and 36.

8. As the god of the rainbow, Pavayoykyasi is linked with moisture and fertility. He is occasionally impersonated as a kachina. When several of them dance, they are referred to as Pavayoykyasim. Etymologically, the initial segment of the god's name seems to relate *pava-* to *paavahu*, the plural form of *paahu* (water/spring). The element *yoy-* is the combining form for *yooyangw* (rain).

Pavayoykyasi also designates the rectangularly shaped frame carried on the back of the Kwaakatsina (Eagle kachina) and Leenangwkatsina (Flute kachina.) As a rule, this board is called a moisture tablet or rainwater shield in the Hopi ethnographic literature. Horst Hartmann, in an extensive comparison between the two germinator gods Muy'ingwa and Aaloosaka, shows that Aaloosaka was closely linked with the Alwimi ([Two] Horn society) at Walpi (1975:293–346). Fewkes's collection of Hopi kachina renditions depicts Aaloosaka with a *pavayoykyasi* on his back and a rainbow forming over his head and shoulders (1903:180). This shared attribute of the moisture tablet seems to explain the substitution of Aaloosaka in Curtis's First Mesa legend for Pavayoykyasi in our Third Mesa version.

9. The name of the Awat'ovi village chief, Ta'palo, which has a foreign ring to it, occurs in a variety of different spellings, for example, as Ta-po'-lo in Fewkes (1893:364), Tapólo in Curtis (1970[1922]:84), and Tapolou in Waters (1963:263). Two of my informants who were familiar with the name pronounced it Ta'palo.

10. For a considerable length of the narrative, Curtis's account, "The Origin of the Awatobi Fraternities and the Alosaka Cult," runs closely parallel to the Hopi legend of the eruption of Sunset Crater recorded in *Earth Fire* (Malotki and Lomatuway'ma 1987a). The same is true for "The Hisanavaiya Myth," collected by Titiev (1948:32–37).

11. The place-name commonly heard for the home of Aaloosaka at Third Mesa is Aaloosakvi. It is either identified with one of the peaks of the San Francisco Mountains or situated at a point west of the mountain range.

12. Without mentioning the heroics of Aaloosaka, Alexander M. Stephen also reports the occurrence of a great fire during the Spanish period: "The valleys around all the mesas were burned up, excepting the valley around Awat'tobi" (1936:388).

13. In his version, Courlander speaks of "a priest of the One Horn Society who had three sons—Sakieva [Sakwyeva], the eldest, Momo'a [Moomo'a], the second, and Pakushkasha [Patösqasa], the youngest" (1971:209). Since the two-horned Aaloosaka is considered the patron deity of the Al ([Two] Horn) society, the statement that the priest is associated with the One Horn society is obviously in

error. The proper Hopi term for what is often referred to as the One Horn society is Kwanwimi, which translates "Agave society."

Yava also mentions only three sons (1978:94). His reference to "a Two Horn priest dressed up in an Alosaka costume" correctly reflects the cultural reality. Curtis introduces Sákuyeva [Sakwyeva] as "chief of the Al-wimi fraternity," and Sísivu [Siisivu] as the "Kachina chief" (1922:84).

14. My corpus of hitherto unpublished Hopi stories contains one that expands this incident into a fully fledged, independent tale. It was entitled "Awat'ove Neyangmakiwta" (Mixed Hunt at Awat'ovi) by its Second Mesa narrator.

15. Parsons, who refers to Awat'ovi as a "treasure town of ceremonies" because of all the rituals reputed to be derived from it, assigns the Lakon to Walpi (1939:869).

16. Communities embroiled in *koyaanisqatsi*, a life marked by social chaos of irredeemable proportions, are typically "cleansed" through some scheme of catastrophic punishment devised and orchestrated by their own chiefs. As a rule, the chief perishes in the course of the disaster. The pattern encountered in the present legend also applies to the ones relating the destruction of Sikyatki and Pivanhonkyapi in this book.

The Legend

Aliksa'i. They say they were living at Awat'ovi. Great numbers of people were at home there, so many in fact, that some people did not know each other. In addition, there were settlements all across the land. The residents of Awat'ovi were wont to do all sorts of things. In particular they would perform various kachina and social dances.

Among the residents of the village was an elderly couple. The man held the rank of crier chief. The couple had a beautiful daughter who was desired by all the unmarried men. They courted her, but in vain, for she gave in to no one. She felt no love for any of her wooers, nor was her heart set on finding a husband.

This is how things were when it turned early summer and people everywhere were in their fields planting crops. Day in and day out, they trekked to their plants. The crier chief, too, had sown and, like the others, constantly went to and from his field. But since he was already quite old, he was no longer as strong as he used to be and once in a while barely managed to return home. Each time he grew more exhausted as he returned to the mesa top. Whenever this happened his daughter felt sorry for him. One day as her father had returned tired again, they were eating their supper when suddenly the girl said to him, "Why don't I go check on your plants tomorrow, and for once, you can stay here and rest without worrying about them."

When her father heard her say this, he became happy in his heart. "Thank you so much, I'm glad you're suggesting this. I'll wake you up early in the morning and you can go in my place," he said. "As soon as you get there, build a fire for yourself. I have wood by the field hut set aside for this purpose. Warm yourself first by the fire before you take care of the plants." This is how the crier chief instructed his daughter.

After sitting there for a while talking, the family finally went to bed. At daybreak the following morning the man woke up his daughter. She fixed a lunch for herself, descended the northwest side of the village, and, upon reaching the plain below, headed straight to her father's field. It was not yet the time of yellow dawn when she reached her destination. She went directly to the field hut where she found the pile of wood, selected a few pieces, and built a fire for herself. As it flamed up a little stronger, she settled down by it to warm herself.

The girl had only been sitting there a short while when she spotted a person coming from the southeast. Since it was not yet full daylight, she was not quite able to determine who it was. She simply followed the person with her eyes. As he moved along, he traversed the field, heading straight toward the girl. He held two prayer feathers in his hand and, as he strode through the planted field, kept motioning to and fro, seemingly throwing something. As the stranger got closer, she saw that he was a very handsome young man wearing beautiful clothes. He wore an embroidered kilt with a colorful kachina sash and carried something on his back. He had eagle down in his hair, and in his hand he held a sort of wand.

Without the slightest trace of fear the girl addressed the stranger. "Have a seat, whoever you are," she said, whereupon the boy sat down northwest of the fire. Without delay the girl opened her lunch and bade him eat. "Here, eat this. You must be hungry," she said, offering him her piki. Then, she poured some water into a bowl and put some *kwiptosi* in it.

The boy began to eat, while the girl wondered who he might be. At the village she knew nearly all the young men, and this one was definitely not from there. After a while he stopped eating. "Are you full?" inquired the girl.

"Yes, thank you for the food," the young man replied. "I'm somewhat in a hurry, so I have to move on," he said. "But there's something I'd like you to do. When you get home tonight and you and your parents eat supper, ask them if they'd permit us to get married. If they will, have your father bring you back to this place four days from now. I will then take you home from here."

Having proposed to the girl like this the boy got ready to leave. Before he set out, however, the girl handed him the rest of her lunch. With that he started out in a southeasterly direction. The girl looked after him until he disappeared from sight. After warming herself for a while by the fire it finally became yellow dawn. Now it was time for her to go and work in her father's field. All day she hoed weeds, thinned out the plants, and hunted for worms, and when early evening came she headed for home. On the way back all her thoughts were of the boy and getting married to him.

When she arrived back at her house her parents were happy to see her. Her father exclaimed, "I'm glad you're back. Thank you, you really caused me a lot of joy. I rested nicely while you worked on my plants." He was full of gratitude.

"You too rest a little now," the girl's mother added. "We'll eat shortly."

Soon her mother set out the food on the floor and the family sat down to eat. During the meal the girl told her parents how she had fared at the field. She also mentioned the visitor and his marriage proposal. "I know everybody here, so he must be from another village. He was dressed in beautiful clothes. He wore an embroidered kilt, had a kachina sash around his waist, and carried something on his back. In his hair was tied eagle down and he held some kind of wand in his hand," she explained to her parents.

Right away the girl's father recognized who the stranger had been. It must have been Pavayoykyasi. It is he who at that time in the morning asperses all the plants. For that reason he probably carried the aspergill in his hand. "It could not have been anybody else," he said. No question, the parents approved of the match. They told their daughter that they had already been thinking of getting her a husband. Her father had grown quite old and was always exhausted when he returned from the field. If Pavayoykyasi should marry her, he would have a helper for his farming chores. This is what the girl's father had to say, and her mother concurred.

The three of them sat together for a little while, then lay down for the night. The next day the girl built a fire under the piki griddle to make piki with her mother. The two wanted to prepare all kinds of things for the set date in four days. They were baking piki and grinding corn, and to better cope with these chores they both took turns. When the agreed day arrived, the girl got everything ready that she planned to take with her. The father, doing the young man's bidding, took his daughter out to the field. It was still early when the two arrived there. The girl's father built a little fire with the wood he kept stored below the field hut, and he and his daughter warmed themselves while waiting for the stranger.

Before long a man came into sight from the southeast. Just as the first time, he strode toward the middle of the plants, doing something amidst them as he came, and then headed straight toward them. She recognized him at once as the boy who had come before and, after bidding him sit down, took some piki out of her bundle. Once more she poured water into a vessel, added the *kwiptosi*, and invited him to eat. Then she told her father that he was the boy who had recently approached her. Her father was elated. The boy began to eat, but he seemed to be pressed for time. He only tasted the food a few times and then said, "All right, we'll have to go now. I'm somewhat in a hurry."

"Very well, you two be on your way then," replied the girl's father. With that he loaded his daughter's corn bag on the boy's shoulders, and as he looked after them, they set out in a southeasterly direction. Before long, the two had disappeared behind a ridge.

Now the girl's father began to tend his plants. They had gotten there so early that only now was it turning gray dawn. A short time later, the crier chief was hoeing weeds among his plants when a second stranger arrived. The chief had not noticed his arrival and it was only after the stranger addressed him that he looked up. "You're all alone. Didn't you bring your daughter with you?" said the stranger.

"Sure I did. We were both here quite early. A young man just took off with her in a southeasterly direction."

"Is that so? Oh my, why did you give her to that man? He's evil. He lives at Nuvatukya'ovi, the San Francisco Mountains, where he abducts these girls and freezes them to death. He's called Icicle Boy. It's too bad that you handed your child over to him."

The crier chief and the stranger talked there for a while, feeling quite depressed. At one point the newcomer confessed that he was Pavayoykyasi. "Well, I must go. It was I who first talked to the girl. I therefore gained her, but Icicle Boy has made off with her, and I can't tolerate that. I must follow them," said Pavayoykyasi, heading off in a southeasterly direction.

The girl's father no longer felt like caring for his plants and decided to go home. Pavayoykyasi, meanwhile, had walked a little ways southeast where he had left his pet, a magic flying shield. The shield had two parts, with the lower one spinning and the upper one remaining still. Climbing aboard, Pavayoykyasi rose up into the air and flew off. He was traveling to his home, in the Hopi Buttes area, where he lived with his grandmother at a place called Siipa. Upon his arrival he told his grandmother how he had fared and why he had come without the girl. "When I got there, only her father was working in his field. He did not notice me until I spoke to him. Then he explained to me that someone had already led the girl away.

Evidently it was that evil boy from Nuvatukya'ovi who got there first and took her away from me. I'll have to go after the two. After all, it was I who spoke first to the girl and therefore I should be entitled to her." This is what Pavayoykyasi said, all bent on following the evil one and his victim.

In vain his grandmother tried to talk him out of this intention. "That Icicle Boy won't give her up. He's full of extraordinary powers." But Pavayoykyasi did not worry what might happen to him. Fully aware that the other might destroy him, he left his house, went to his magic vehicle, and climbed aboard.

Meanwhile, his evil rival also had put the girl aboard a flying shield and was on his way to Nuvatukya'ovi. The two of them were nearing the base of the mountain range when the girl told him that she needed to relieve herself. "Why don't you land your pet for a while? I have to relieve myself. Then we can continue."

Icicle Boy complied and landed his flying shield. The girl climbed out and walked away for a short distance, where she squatted down. She was straining to defecate when suddenly she heard a voice. "Phew! Go farther away. Move a little farther over there to do your business. When you're done, I want you to enter my abode here." The girl obeyed the instructions of the voice and stepped aside to relieve herself. When she was finished, she came back. At the spot where she had stood before there was a tiny hole in the ground. Into this she spoke, saying, "How on earth can I get in there? The entrance is much too small."

"All you need to do is rotate your heel into the hole and you'll be able to enter," the voice replied.

The girl did as she was told and rotated her heel into the little opening in the ground. Sure enough, the circumference of the hole widened, and a ladder protruded from it. By means of this ladder the girl climbed down the kiva opening. Inside she found an old woman sitting all by herself, who bade her take a seat. The girl obeyed and sat down to the northwest of the fireplace. Thereupon the old woman said, "Dear me, my grandchild, you will never return from where you are going. The man taking you with him is evil, yet you fell for him. He's the Icicle Boy, and he freezes young maidens to death at his house. When you get there, you'll see that the rungs of his entrance ladder are extremely sharp. For this reason I'll give you this medicine. When you land, chew it, and as soon as you step on the ladder, spray the medicine on it. The rungs will change back into the ordinary kind." This is how the old woman instructed the girl. Handing her the medicine, she added, "Well, you'll have to go on and accompany this boy to his home. But I'll come with you for the time being. I'm Old

Spider Woman and I'll ride along behind your ear. Be sure, therefore, that you don't scratch there when you itch. I'll watch over you at Icicle Boy's place and then I'll come back again. Don't worry, I won't abandon you," she assured the girl.

The girl was most unhappy about these revelations, but she had no choice. She would have to go to the evil boy's house. Once again she climbed aboard his flying pet, and it rose into the air and transported them both directly to Nuvatukya'ovi. There they flew to a village located high up in the mountain range. At the edge of that village the magic shield landed, and after disembarking, the two walked toward the boy's house. Immediately, the girl put the medicine in her mouth and, chewing it, followed the boy. Soon after entering the village they reached the plaza, from where they continued in a northwesterly direction. Icicle Boy had his home at a point northwest of the plaza, where a gigantic ladder stood. True enough, when they reached the ladder, the girl could see quite clearly that its rungs were as sharp as knife blades. The boy climbed up first with the girl right behind. But first she sprayed her medicine on the ladder. As a result, the rungs became quite normal and did not cause her any harm as she stepped on them. At the top was an entrance similar to the one a kiva has. Through this entrance Icicle Boy led the girl inside.

Apparently, the evil boy had two younger sisters who were living there. They welcomed the pair. "Thanks for coming," they exclaimed. They had evidently been grinding corn, for the older of the two came out of her grinding bin to receive the bag of ground corn from her brother. After storing it away somewhere, she had the girl sit down northeast of the ladder. The boy, in turn, disappeared into the inner room. There he took off his clothes, and after he came back out he announced that he was going to the kiva. Before long it was late afternoon, and upon Icicle Boy's return they all ate supper.

Now Old Spider Woman said to the girl, "Eat your fill. It's still a long time till daybreak." The girl obeyed and only after she had really satiated her hunger did she leave the area where the food was set out. After supper all of them sat around for a while until they were ready to go to bed, at which time one of the evil boy's sisters asked the girl to move to the northwest side. "Come here. You can sleep in the inner room," she said as she opened the northwest door. She urged the girl to go in and, without leaving any bedding for her, was gone again.

The chamber was a veritable ice cave. It was extremely cold. "I anticipated this," said Old Spider Woman. "I knew they would do this to you when they brought you here. But don't worry, I came prepared for this." With that she made a bed for the girl out of two down feathers. They were the softest turkey down. The girl lay down on them, and the old woman covered her up with two more feathers. It was not long before she was nice and warm. Soon the girl fell asleep, and she made it to the following day without freezing to death.

In the morning she could clearly hear the others eating in the front room, yet no one bothered to invite her to breakfast. After a while, when they were full, one of the sisters came in and served her the leftovers. Now she ate too, and as soon as she was full, the two sisters took her to the grinding bin. Next they hauled something in from the inner room. It was ice, which the girl was told to grind on the metate.

The poor girl's heart sank. But Old Spider Woman was still with her and said, "Chew what I give you and spray your saliva on the ice while you grind. I assure you, the ice will melt quickly. Also, spit into the palms of your hands and rub your body with the saliva. You'll see, you won't get cold." With that she handed her some medicine and departed again. The girl chewed it as told and kept spurting it onto the grinding stone. Lo and behold, the ice was thawing. Also, when she rubbed herself, she did not suffer from the cold anymore.

The two sisters of the evil boy could hardly believe their eyes when they saw that the girl was unharmed. Pouring the melted ice water into pottery vessels, they kept storing them on top of a wooden shelf. By late afternoon the girl had crushed all the ice. Both Icicle Boy and his sisters were at a loss to comprehend this.

That night after supper they placed the girl into a chamber in the southwest. This, like the one to the northwest, was also an ice cave. Again she was compelled to sleep there. As soon as the one who had put her in there had left, she made her own bed with the turkey plumes and lay down. After covering herself in the same fashion, she fell asleep and slept through the night without suffering from the cold.

This time the girl received no breakfast whatsoever. Instead, they simply dragged her out of her chamber and put her to work at the grinding bin. Again, one of the boy's sisters brought something in. This time it was icicles on a flat tray. Once more the girl was forced to grind. However, she still had some of the medicine, which, mixed with her saliva, she kept spurting on the icicles, causing them to melt right away. As before, the two sisters poured the water into pots that they stored on a shelf.

That night the girl was closed into another chamber facing southeast. Knowing full well that nothing would harm her, she fell asleep without worry and, indeed, woke up in the morning safe and sound.

Meanwhile, Pavayoykyasi, who had been following the two, arrived at exactly the same spot where his girlfriend had felt the urge to relieve herself. He, too, felt the need to defecate, so he landed his flying pet and climbed out. Having walked a little ways off he had just squatted down when a voice cried, "Phew! Go farther away. And when you're done with your business, come back and enter my abode."

Pavayoykyasi did as bidden and moved aside, where he relieved himself. When he was finished, he returned to where the voice had spoken to him. Scanning the area, he discovered a tiny hole in the ground. "There's no way I can enter this hole here," he protested. "The opening is much too small."

The voice replied "Just rotate your heel in the hole. That will make it larger."

Pavayoykyasi obeyed and rotated his heel. Lo and behold, the hole widened into a big opening with a ladder standing there. On climbing down it, he found an old woman sitting there all alone. She welcomed him, bidding him sit northwest of the fireplace. Of course, she was Old Spider Woman. Thereupon Pavayoykyasi told her why he was about. He explained that the evil Icicle Boy had abducted his girlfriend and that he was following him with the intention of getting the girl back somehow.

"Oh dear," said Old Spider Woman, "I know he keeps taking girls there to freeze them to death. Your sweetheart actually stopped here, so let me give you the same advice that I gave her. When you land at the edge of the village where Icicle Boy lives, chew this medicine. Only then go to the northwest side of the place where he and his two sisters live. His big entrance ladder, as you will see, has rungs that are as sharp as knives. Onto those you must spray your medicine, whereupon they will be transformed and be unable to harm you any longer. Also, I will personally check on you to see how you're faring on your venture." This is how the old woman spoke. With that Pavayoykyasi left, once more climbed aboard his magic pet, and continued his journey.

No sooner had he departed than the Old Spider Woman also left. She went to the place where the gophers were living. Upon her arrival she told them all about Pavayoykyasi and the girl. She said she was helping them both so that the evil Icicle Boy would not win the girl. "It occurred to me that you could be of some assistance. That's why I came."

"Very well, we'll certainly go with you. Let us know what you expect of us, and we will do it."

Old Spider Woman was pleased with the gophers' reply, so she instructed them, "Thank you for agreeing so kindly to my request. Now I can ask you without hesitation what I want you to do. Go to the base of the mountain range of Nuvatukya'ovi. There I want you to tunnel your way to the top. If you surface, just continue until you arrive directly below the house of the evil boy. That's as far as I want you to burrow."

"Agreed, we will do that. You can rely on us," the gophers replied. Old Spider Woman was elated with this response. She now started out after Pavayoykyasi, who was already bound for Nuvatukya'ovi.

Pavayoykyasi, meanwhile, had advanced to the top of the mountain, where he found the village he was looking for. He sat down his flying shield right by its edge, climbed out, and after chewing his medicine headed for the village. Entering its confines, he searched for the plaza. When he found it, he looked around. Sure enough, there was the house with the gigantic ladder, and, no doubt, its rungs were sharp as knives. He stepped up to them and spurted on them the medicine he had been given. Then he climbed up, and since the sharp edges of the rungs had been dulled, he reached the top unharmed. He entered the kiva opening and without delay stepped inside. The three girls were still busy grinding, but when they spotted the newcomer they abruptly halted. Pavayoykyasi recognized his girlfriend right away. Of course he did not know the two other females, so he asked them, "Where is the owner of this house?" There was no reply. Once more he asked but more forcefully. This time one of Icicle Boy's younger sisters answered. She said that her brother had gone to the kiva. "I've come to see him. Go get him," Pavayoykyasi commanded. Quickly one of the girls ran out to fetch her older brother.

As soon as she arrived in her brother's kiva, she begged him, "You must come over to our place. There's a stranger there who wants you right away. It seems he's not around without a purpose. He talked to us in a somewhat agitated voice."

"Who on earth would be doing a thing like that?" the evil boy exclaimed, quite angry. "Well, I'll follow you," he said to his younger sister.

It was not long after her return that Icicle Boy came in. "Why are you entering our home like this?" he asked reproachfully. "No one dares do that here."

"Yes, but you took off with my girl. I was the one who first talked to her, and I was going to marry her. That's why I came after you," Pavayoykyasi retorted. "And I won't go home without her."

"I won't give her up under any circumstances," the evil boy shot back. "I'm the one who brought her here, so she's mine." But then he changed his tune somewhat. "At least for the time being. Let's first test each other's power. We'll compete for her. If you beat me in this contest, I may give her back to you. So let's go to my kiva."

Both men left the house and headed over to the kiva. The very moment they entered the subterranean abode, the gophers arrived, digging directly underneath. The two sat down on the northwest side of the fire pit, and the evil boy announced, "Well, I'll fill a pipe for you that I want you to smoke. However, no smoke must escape from it. If you smoke up all the tobacco without exhaling any smoke, you'll be the winner."

Just then Old Spider Woman caught up with Pavayoykyasi. Perching behind his ear she whispered, "Don't you worry. You'll survive this test. Just make sure you sit still when something tickles your behind. That will be the ones who came to help you. You simply keep swallowing the smoke." These were the old lady's instructions.

Icicle Boy now went to the southwest area of the kiva. From a niche there he removed his tobacco bag and his pipe and brought them over. The pipe was enormous. Icicle Boy sat down next to Pavayoykyasi and started filling it. When it was filled to the brim, he held it out to Pavayoykyasi and said, "Well, now you can find out how good you are. I told you what to do, so you'll be on your own." With that he lit the pipe.

Pavayoykyasi was about to grab it when he felt an itching at his behind. Heeding the old woman's advice, he sat still and did not move when he accepted the pipe. It was, of course, the gophers that had pierced the ground right under his behind. As they were coming through now, they kept touching his buttocks, which tickled him. Pavayoykyasi started smoking. Each time he drew on the pipe, he swallowed the smoke. Each time he swallowed the smoke he would fart. Each time he farted, the smoke inside of him escaped and came out from his behind. As it did it entered the tunnel the gophers had dug and eventually exited above ground quite a distance away. For this reason the old woman had asked the gophers to burrow the tunnel. In this fashion Pavayoykyasi did not have to suffer. Soon he had finished all of the tobacco and handed the pipe back to the evil one.

Icicle Boy was surprised when he inspected the pipe. "My, my, you are no ordinary man," he had to admit. "But this won't be all. Now we'll compete with crops. We'll plant all our seeds, and whoever gets them to mature first will win the girl."

With that Icicle Boy left, only to return a short while later with a load on his back. Evidently he had bagged some sand, which he piled up northwest of the fireplace. He disappeared again but before long reentered with another bundle, also containing sand. This he repeated several times. When he had spread out as much sand as he wanted, he drew a line with cornmeal across its middle, from a point in the northwest to the fireplace, dividing the area into two sections. That done he said to Pavayoykyasi, "You can plant on this portion here that extends to the northeast. I, in turn, will sow on the part that extends to the southwest." Fortunately, Old Spider Woman had gathered up some sweet corn seeds that she had brought along. These she now gave to Pavayoykyasi. "You use these when you plant. These are very fast and grow without complication."

Thereupon both contestants began sowing on their sandy lots. On both sides they planted all the crops they had. Pavayoykyasi, of course, also included sweet corn. As soon as the owner of the kiva was finished, he opened a chamber to the northwest. All of a sudden clouds emerged from this chamber in large quantities. They shed their moisture on the two men's fields. After soaking them thoroughly they retreated again. No sooner had they disappeared than fog followed them out of the chamber. It kept billowing out until the entire kiva was filled. So thick was it that it became dark inside. Old Spider Woman also had brought along a cicada that she had kept hidden. But now that the light was gone, she sat the insect down in the dark. No sooner had she done so than the cicada started singing, squatting comfortably on the ground. As it sang, the air was filled with nice sounds.

The evil boy, meanwhile, kept leaving and reentering the kiva, all the while engaged in some mysterious activity. Again and again he would go out. Since it was dark, there was no telling what he was up to. It was impossible for the others to see. As it turned out, he was making icicles, which he tied into bundles. Then he hung them from the ceiling with the result that the air was turning colder. Now the cicada began to freeze. As it shivered from the cold, its singing grew fainter and fainter.

At this point Old Spider Woman recalled something, for she turned to Pavayoykyasi and cried, "Darn it, why didn't I think of this? Now our pet is growing weaker. Go outside quickly and bring back a whole saltbush."

Pavayoykyasi did as bidden and ran outside. There he searched for a saltbush until he found one. Having uprooted it he came back inside the kiva with it. The old woman was overjoyed. "Thanks, that will do it," she exclaimed, whereupon she ordered him to insert the bush in the pit of the fireplace. That accomplished, she placed the cicada on top of the saltbush twigs. Immediately, the cicada gained its strength back and started singing quite loudly again. As a result, the air was rapidly warming up, and before long it was like summer. Now everything began to grow—squash, watermelon, muskmelon, and corn. Things were really growing. It was incredible how fast the crops came along. Maturing as quickly as they did, Pavayoykyasi's crops were winning the upper hand over those of the evil boy. When it was evident that his sweet corn was ready for harvesting, Old

Spider Woman said to Pavayoykyasi, "Well now, your corn is mature. Go over and pick an ear. Then husk it and roast it in this fireplace. When it's done, taste it once or twice and then throw it over to the evil one." Pavayoykyasi obeyed her instructions. He stepped up to the plants and broke off an ear of fresh corn. Then he husked it and roasted it. When the corn was done, he took two bites out of it and threw the rest at the feet of Icicle Boy. Pavayoykyasi had beaten his opponent in the contest.

"You're a formidable man," the evil boy conceded. "You were the first to grow all sorts of things. I admit, you've won."

Now it became light again in the kiva. The fog disappeared into the chamber from which it had first emerged. Once more one could see clearly. From the ceiling bundles of wild grass, which had been icicles before, could be seen hanging. When the evil boy began to lose, they had started melting so that once again only bundled grass was dangling here. At this moment the old woman said to Pavayoykyasi, "Go to him and command him to go outside and make an announcement from the rooftop. Tell him to have his relatives come and harvest these crops and do with them whatever they please."

Pavayoykyasi approached Icicle Boy and explained to him what the old lady wanted him to do. Obediently he went outside and cried out the public announcement. Then he came in again and said to the winner, "Well, there's nothing I can do. You beat me. Remember I said that the better one should have the girl. Since you defeated me, she is yours. So let's go to my house. There you can take her with you." With that he led Pavayoykyasi to his house.

Upon arriving there Icicle Boy said to the girl, "Well, this was my decision. He beat me in the contest, so he can take you with him now." The girl got up from the grinding bin and went to Pavayoykyasi.

However, the evil boy spoke once more. "Wait a minute! Don't go just yet. Look in here first and then you can be on your way." With that he opened a door leading into a room on the northwest side. Pavayoykyasi and the girl followed him inside. There was a big slope there and all the way down girls were stacked against each other. Some of them had died only recently. They were still in good shape and had not completely turned into ice yet. Icicle Boy said, "This is what I intended to do with her. After freezing her to death, I would have thrown her down here with the others, but you came after me. At that point I decided that we would measure our powers. I said the stronger one would get the girl. As it turned out, you won. So you have her now." With that he gave Pavayoykyasi the girl.

"Yes," Pavayoykyasi replied, "all of you who live here are evil, but you can no longer remain here. Instead, you will go as far northwest as you can. There you will live as remote from people as possible. And this is how it will be from this day on: People will first harvest their crops and gather them into their houses before you can have your turn with the cold weather." This is what Pavayoykyasi said to the evil boy.

Thereupon he loaded the girl's corn bag on his shoulders and went out to the girl. They headed to their flying shield and stepped aboard. Soon it rose up into the air and with both of them riding in it, it flew along. Evidently the flying shield was familiar with the boy's home, for it took them straight to the Hopi Buttes area. Pavayoykyasi had finally brought his bride home. The craft landed right atop the boy's house. After climbing out, the boy shouted inside from the roof, "*Haw!* Say some words of welcome. I'm not alone."

Pavayoykyasi's grandmother asked them to enter, and the two went in. The old woman cried from joy. She was really glad. "Thank you, you've brought her! I was worried about you being that far away and quite unhappy for a while. I'm glad you succeeded, for now we have a bride," she exclaimed, airing her joy again and again.

"Yes, but I did not conquer that evil one by myself. It was an old woman and other beings who helped me to get her back. I'm most grateful to them," Pavayoykyasi explained. With that he told his grandmother in detail how they both had fared.

When Pavayoykyasi ended his account, his grandmother said, "Yes, indeed. The old woman who lives there is the grandmother of all people. Whenever people are in need, she takes pity on them and helps them. I'm so glad she came to your rescue, for this is how you survived," she said, expressing her gratitude to Old Spider Woman. She then took out some corn for the new in-law, shelled it for her, and had her kneel by the grinding bin, this time grinding real corn. Finally, she got some cotton, twisted it into a string, and tied it into the earlobe of the bride.

For three whole days the girl ground corn. Early in the morning of the fourth day, the old woman took her by the hand and led her outside. There she cried out, "You, my offspring, who live out there! Come here and wash our bride's hair with me!"

Before long clouds began to gather from all directions, moving toward the two. Right above them they merged and then released their rain. They had come to wash the bride's hair. Having accomplished this they disappeared again to where they had come from.

The following morning the old woman rose early. Once again she went outside and made an announcement. "You, my offspring, who live out there! Come and gather here! We have a new bride here!" Then she went back in again.

It did not take long, and some beings began to enter. This time it was the spiders that kept arriving. There were lots of them. They came in droves and soon filled the entire house. When it appeared that all had arrived, Pavayoykyasi's grandmother vanished into the back room and started bringing out cotton. She brought out large quantities of it. Immediately, some of the spiders set to carding the cotton. This they kept doing, always putting the clean cotton to one side. Other spiders now fell upon the cotton and began to devour it. Whenever one of them had gobbled up a good portion, it crawled up to the ceiling. There it would stick its rear end up in the air and extrude from its behind a little cotton, which became attached to the ceiling. Then the spider would lower itself back down, spinning around and around as it descended. In this fashion they twisted the cotton and made it into thread. By the time they were all down, long cotton strings were dangling from the ceiling. Next, a few of the spiders ran the threads back up, rolling them up into balls. When they had made several balls, they began to set up the loom. Now the big spiders got their turn. They each swallowed an entire ball of yarn and defecated it as they ran over to the other side of the loom. Back and forth they ran and in this way completed the warp. Then they set the loom upright and, scuttling to and fro between the warp threads, began the actual weaving. Since there were multitudes of spiders the work was finished in no time.

Now a man entered carrying someone on his back—a lame man who himself carried a big buckskin on his shoulders. The man put the lame one down on the floor northwest of the fireplace. No sooner had the lame man been put down on the floor than he began to fashion wedding boots for the bride from the buckskin he carried. He was extremely quick and soon finished the footwear.

It was not yet noontime and he was already done. He handed the boots to the bride, who tried them on. They were exactly her size. She had no problem putting them on, and they did not hurt her anywhere. In this way they were all busy making the wedding garments for the bride. Everything was finished in no time.

Meanwhile, Pavayoykyasi went hunting. He was an expert hunter and had not advanced very far when he killed two big elk. The weavers were not even finished when he returned with his prey on his back. He had already taken out the innards and only brought back the meat. His grandmother thanked him profusely and immediately set to making stew from one of the animals.

It was still not yet the noon hour when everything was ready. The bride had finished baking piki and was grinding corn for the somiviki. When that chore was done, she prepared lunch. By the time she was ready, the others also had finished their work. Everybody settled down to her food and ate, gorging themselves. There was so much, however, that they could not eat it all. Whenever someone felt satiated, that person moved away from the place where the food was set out and lay down by the edge. The guests were lying all over, relaxed, with full stomachs. Later, as their fullness passed, one after the other got up and went outside.

Pavayoykyasi and his family thanked those who were leaving. The old woman kept saying, "Help yourselves to the bride's food and save some for later. It's not getting less."

So, as the guests filed out, they put some food aside for later. As they did, the old woman urged them, "Toward early evening I want you to come back and have some stew. I'm so glad my nephew was lucky enough to bag some meat."

People were leaving with large quantities of food. As it turned evening, they returned, looking forward to the feast with great anticipation. When everybody appeared to have arrived, the old woman and the bride set out the supper. That done, they once more invited everyone to eat. All the guests sat down and ate to their hearts' content. Pavayoykyasi had killed a large buck, so the stew was mostly meat. As soon as guests were full, they moved to the edge and lay down. People did just as they did during the midday meal. When all were satiated, the old woman and her in-law cleared the table and joined the others.

By now it had turned black night. The whole group had not been sitting there long when some newcomers could be heard on the rooftop. Soon a rattle sounded from above, and the old woman welcomed them in. "Come on down, we're waiting for you!" she shouted, whereupon they entered.

The new arrivals were kachinas who had come to entertain the bride. With them they had brought loads of gifts, especially crops. The ears of baked sweet corn were big and long in size. In addition, they had muskmelon, squash, and all the other field fruits in great quantities. There were several Hehey'a kachinas who kept coming and going, hauling these things on their backs. As soon as they had brought everything in, they departed. The other kachinas, however, remained and staged a dance for the bride and her guests. The kachinas were very good, and the spectators all watched in silence. After ending their dance they distributed their presents to the people inside. And since the bride received more than one gift from each of them, she accumulated a large pile.

Thereafter the kachinas filed out. No sooner had they left than a new group arrived that did exactly what the first had done. In this manner the kachina groups kept coming, one after another. Each group only danced once. To the departing kachinas the bride handed somiviki, which they were to take along on their journey home. Fortunately she had had the foresight to prepare a lot of it. She now distributed all of it to the succeeding dance groups. For the Hehey'as she also bundled up some somiviki, which she gave to one of the kachinas to take along for the group. No doubt the Hehey'as had raised all sorts of crops, for they were really good farmers.

Eventually the night became still. Now the old woman said, "Well, I suppose that's that. I'm grateful the kachinas came to visit us and provided us with a good time. And I'd like to thank you for helping us make the wedding outfit for the bride. Now go back to your homes with happy hearts." This is how she kept expressing her thankfulness to everyone.

Thereupon the guests started leaving for home. Everybody had some food wrapped in a bag, even the children. This is how the bride was entertained at the wedding. Now the old woman said to her grandson, "All right, tomorrow you must return to your wife's home. I'm sure her relatives are already waiting. It's been quite some time since your bride left. Her parents must be missing her. So let's go to bed now. In the morning I'll have some more to say to you." With that they all went to bed.

The next day the old woman woke up the couple early. First she wove the bride's hair into a braid, then she dressed her the way a bride is supposed to be dressed when she returns home after the wedding. That accomplished, all three of them went outside, where the old woman laid down a road marker for the couple. Along that Pavayoykyasi and his wife started out. On his back he carried a bag full of meat that had not been used for the stew. Along with his wife, he was taking this meat to the home of his in-laws. Once again the two boarded the flying shield, which soon rose up in the air. They were going to fly with it all the way to their fields at Awat'ovi. After landing at a field hut there, they climbed out of their pet and walked the remainder of the way to the village. The girl was finally bringing home her husband.

In those days young boys used to be up on the roofs early. No wonder they noticed a whitish speck in the distance. As the speck approached the base of the mesa, they realized that it was a woman in her bridal outfit and that she was bringing a young man with her. Now prior to the couple's departure, the old woman had instructed her grandson as follows: "When you arrive at your bride's home, say this to her father: 'I want you to cut up all this meat and cook it. In the evening then you can invite all the villagers to come and feast.'" When the couple arrived at the girl's house, her parents were elated. And Pavayoykyasi said to his wife's father, "Let's boil all of this meat. Then, in the evening you can invite all the people to join us and eat with us." This is what his son-in-law said.

When all the meat was cooked, the new husband and wife set out the food for the feast. The girl's mother left and went from house to house inviting everybody to come and eat with them. Soon those people who cared to eat started arriving. Whenever anyone had eaten, that person was happy. This went on until everybody was satiated. Soon they had all departed again, and the girl cleared everything away.

From that day on Pavayoykyasi, the new son-in-law, would rise early at dawn to head out to the village crier's fields and sprinkle the plants with dew. Every morning he would do this to all the plants. He was a most industrious man. And when summer came and the girl's father had sown, Pavayoykyasi hoed weeds and cared for the plants. As soon as he was done with this, he would assist whoever was not finished. As a rule, it did not take him long to complete the work. In this manner Pavayoykyasi spent his days. From that time on it always rained a lot and the Awat'ovis harvested a great abundance of crops.

As the days went by with Pavayoykyasi living there, his wife became pregnant and gave birth to a boy. His grandmother washed his hair and named him Sakwyeva. He quickly grew bigger, a year passed, and the woman was again with child. Once more she gave birth to a boy. His name was Moomo'a. A third time she became pregnant. This child too was born a boy and was called Hoyniwa. Each year Pavayoykyasi's wife bore another boy. The fourth one was named Siisivu, the one after him Wuktima, and the last Patösqasa. Six sons in all she bore for Pavayoykyasi, and all of them were endowed with greater-than-human powers. All were extremely intelligent. Sakwyeva, the oldest, was barely six years old when he was made village leader of Awat'ovi in charge of all the villagers. This happened because he did so much for the welfare of the people. Each year they planted, they had big harvests. It always rained, and in winter there was plenty of snow. Life in Awat'ovi was pleasant. The people were always happy and kind to each other. All of this was due to Pavayoykyasi. His sons, too, were endowed with special powers. Since they were never lazy, the villagers profited from them in many ways. Because of them they lived a most agreeable life.

However, there was one group of people in Awat'ovi that could not stand Pavayoykyasi. Also, the fact that Sakwyeva had become the village leader did not please them at all. This group consisted of sorcerers and witches. They had their kiva at Kwitavi, the "Excrement Place," and for this reason they were known as the Turds. They were constantly racking their minds, thinking how they could change things for the worse and how one of them might succeed in becoming village chief. However, they were not able to do much because of Pavayoykyasi's powers.

Meanwhile, Sakwyeva's brothers were getting older. They reached an age where they wanted to go around shooting with bows and arrows like the other boys, so they spoke to their father about it. "Please," they asked, "make us some arrows. We're envious of the other kids who have them. We would like to shoot around with arrows too." So their father fashioned bows and arrows for them.

Now Pavayoykyasi's sons were able to play bows and arrows with the village children. But since their father was Pavayoykyasi, the arrows he had made for them were actually lightning bolts. As his sons were now shooting around with the other kids, if they so much as touched one of them, as a result the child would die. As time went by, a great number of children perished for this reason.

When so many children died because they came in contact with the boys' arrows, the sorcerers and witches were filled with joy. After all, they now had some reason to confront Pavayoykyasi. Now they would be able to plan some detrimental things for the people. They therefore decided to make the villagers crazy. This they would accomplish by bewitching them. If, indeed, they should succeed in driving the people mad, they could blame this on Pavayoykyasi's sons. This is what the sorcerers thought.

And this is exactly what happened. People began to change in their ways. There was no mutual respect anymore. They were constantly arguing and fighting with one another. People were robbed of their food. A woman would be taking piki somewhere, only to have others snatch it away from her. No one had any concern for others. For all kinds of reasons people would get angry at each other. Men and boys would reach under the dresses of women and girls and rape them. People seemed to be blind to what they were doing. They got worse and worse. For example, if children encountered an old man relieving himself, they would smear excrement all over him. They showed no compassion for anyone. The leaders of the religious societies, too, grew increasingly negligent in their ceremonial duties. Everything was completely insane. The life the inhabitants of Awat'ovi were living was one of utter chaos. They were all pitted against each other. No one displayed any fondness for anyone else.

The Turds insisted that this life of turmoil and corruption was all the fault of Pavayoykyasi's son, who was the village leader. As a result, they planned in their kiva how to kill the entire family. It so happened that one of the

Turds was a friend of Pavayoykyasi's. That night they decided to assemble in their kiva, so their headman said, "When you've eaten supper, come back. We need to decide what to do with Pavayoykyasi and his lot." The sorcerers did as told, and after they had finished eating in their houses, they met in their kiva again. When everyone had gathered, their chief declared, "Life here in Awat'ovi is not good anymore. Obviously, this is the fault of our leader. We must therefore kill him. It is my wish that we do away with the entire family." The kiva members consented. "Well, in that case let us kill them four days from now," their leader declared. This was the goal they were pursuing now.

Pavayoykyasi's friend left the kiva and went over to his friend's house to reveal the intentions of the sorcerers. Upon entering Pavayoykyasi's house he said, "They've hatched out some evil plans against you. They've decided to kill you four days from now. They claim life in the village is so bad because your son is in charge. They put all the blame on him."

"Is that so?" exclaimed Pavayoykyasi.

"Yes, that's why I came to let you know." With that his friend departed again.

Not long after, someone else arrived at Pavayoykyasi's house. It was the chief of the sorcerers in person. Pavayoykyasi said nothing. He did not inquire why he was about. He simply welcomed him in, whereupon they smoked, exchanging the pipe between them. Only then did he speak. "Well, you must have come for a specific reason."

"Yes, indeed," the head sorcerer replied. "Ever since your son became village leader four years ago, we've been thrown into turmoil. Because of you and your family, the rains have ceased, and our crops have failed. It's because of you that we've not come to our senses," he accused him. "We must therefore kill you."

"Well, I suppose so," answered Pavayoykyasi, who did not try to contradict him. "If that's your intention, go ahead and do it."

In four days the sorcerers planned to perpetrate the deed. Pavayoykyasi conveyed this news to his wife. "They want to kill our family," he said. "I did not object. 'Do to us what you want,' I said. Anyway, that's what they've been thinking about."

With this terrible news Pavayoykyasi went to his grandmother. He related to her what had happened. "The sorcerers have instigated an evil scheme against us. Four days hence they want to kill us. My friend confirmed this. Maybe you can come up with a plan for us. That's the purpose of my visit."

Pavayoykyasi's grandmother exclaimed, "Dear me, why on earth do they want to do that? It used to be because of you and your family that life was flourishing at Awat'ovi. So why would they wish to do this to you? Come back tomorrow. At that time I should be able to advise you," she said.

With that Pavayoykyasi returned home again to his children. He spent the night there and in the morning once more visited his grandmother. Upon his arrival she instructed him as follows: "First I want you to take your youngest son Patösqasa to a shelter at Nuvatukya'ovi. Next, after your return to Awat'ovi, have your family remove ears representing all the different kinds of corn from your corn stock. Have them shell the ears and place the kernels into a shallow receptacle. Also add seeds from all the other crops. Then you must dig a hole in the floor of your house and store everything there. Mix ashes in with the seeds so they don't get wet. They will not spoil that way."

With these instructions Pavayoykyasi returned home again. He and his family did exactly as he had been told. They buried large amounts of seeds, and after the hole had been covered with dirt, they sealed it with plaster. "This should do it," Pavayoykyasi remarked.

On the third day Pavayoykyasi decided to take Patösqasa, his youngest child, to Nuvatukya'ovi. "He's the only one I'm taking to safety," he said. "The rest of you will have to suffer what they're going to do with you. I'll be on my way now." With that he vigorously stoked the fire. When it really flamed up, he poured a liquid medicine on it. As a result, clouds of mist billowed up and drifted out through the vent hole. Outside the mist changed into fog. It enshrouded the entire village of Awat'ovi. Now a rainbow began to arch from Pavayoykyasi's house all the way to Nuvatukya'ovi. "Let's go!" he shouted, whereupon he and his son climbed atop the rainbow. Once more the rainbow arched up and, carrying the two on its back, delivered them at the foot of the mountain range.

After the departure of Pavayoykyasi and his youngest son, the rest of the family bathed and washed their hair. Then they dressed, putting on their beautifully embroidered kilts and belts. Finally, they decorated their bodies with paint and tied eagle plumes in their hair. Prepared like this they awaited the morning. The Turds, in turn, were busy readying their weapons, gloating with anticipation. "With this I'll kill Sakwyeva," one of them would declare. Another would say, "With this I'll kill Siisivu." This is how they were boasting and laughing with malicious glee.

Then the new day arrived. The moment the sun was in its mid-morning position, Pavayoykyasi's family filed out to the village plaza. Sakwyeva led the group, with his younger brothers following. No sooner had they entered the plaza than the Turds pounced on them. The brothers, who offered no resistance, were clubbed down, and every one of them was killed. After this deed the Turds hauled their victims, one after the other, to the southeast side of the mesa. Pavayoykyasi and his sons had a ground oven there to roast corn. Into this ground oven the sorcerers hurled the dead bodies and closed it up with dirt. Having disposed of the brothers, they displayed their joy by staging dances.

The summer following this atrocity it did not rain. The winter passed without snow. As a consequence, people's crops were smaller than usual. In addition, the wind blew fiercely and unearthed their plants. When they planted anew the subsequent year, the same thing happened. People were still planting, and already it was the middle of summer. This time they harvested even less. By now, two years had passed without rain. It was the same during the third year, and by the end of the fourth year, nearly all of the food reserves were depleted. Some people had used up everything. By the fifth year no one had anything left. People would go out in search of cactus and plants of that sort. That's all they were eating. At this point when people were dying from starvation, they would say, "We used to get plenty of rain because of Pavayoykyasi and his sons. But we had nothing better to do than to destroy them. We committed a great crime," they kept saying with deep regret.

By the beginning of the sixth year only a few villagers were left. The poor wretches were all dried up and nothing but skin and bones. Their knees were swollen and their eyes were like empty sockets. The members of the sorcerer kiva who had attacked the brothers perished in great numbers. The sorcerers were dying, but in the mornings when they came across a man who was taking his spun yarn to the kiva to make prayer feathers, they snatched it away from him. "Why are you doing that? We are the ones who are praying for rain, not you. It's none of your business to carry this yarn around." And they would rip the ball of yarn away from him. Just about anywhere, in a corner or behind the ladder, people were trying to make prayer sticks, but it was not going to rain. As a result, many of the Awat'ovi residents lost their lives.

At this point Pavayoykyasi returned to Awat'ovi with his son. When the two arrived, they found no one walking about. Upon entering the house where they once had lived, they dug up the floor where their big seed cache was. Father and son had arrived on the morning of the day when the members of the Soyal society were in ceremonial session. Pavayoykyasi therefore decided to enter the kiva with the initiates on the night of the second day of their ritual gathering. He made this decision while he was uncovering the seeds with the help of his son. When this task was finished, they filled bags with the seeds.

It so happened that Pavayoykyasi's friend from the sorcerers' kiva was still alive. After hearing the news that Pavayoykyasi was back, he hastened to call on him. Pavayoykyasi was filled with joy to see him, and the two began to talk about all sorts of things. Pavayoykyasi learned from his friend how people had fared at the village. They talked for a long time. Finally, his friend said that he had to return to his kiva. He was already on his way out when Pavayoykyasi called him back, "Wait a minute, don't leave just yet. There's something I need to tell you. I want you to come back again at midnight. I'll have some instructions for you then." With this information his friend left.

That evening, shortly after darkness had fallen, Pavayoykyasi painted his body in the fashion of the Al society initiates. He dotted his arms and legs with white clay and tied a tortoise shell rattle to each of his legs. He dressed his son in the same way. For both of them he also made something to lean on, sticks that were curved at the upper end. Below the curved handle all kinds of corn were tied to the shaft. In this guise father and son were waiting for their friend.

Before long Pavayoykyasi's friend arrived, and Pavayoykyasi welcomed him politely, saying, "Thanks for coming. This is what I had hoped you would do. I'm grateful you consented. You remember, I told you I'd have something to say to you. I'd like us to leave now and go from kiva to kiva, first the Excrement kiva and then the rest. While I and my son enter, I want you to listen from the rooftop. When we're done inside and have come out, the people down below will surely comment on us. Pay careful attention to what they have to say. After we've visited every kiva, follow us back here again. You can then reveal to me what you heard." This is how he instructed his friend.

As the three of them were leaving now, both father and son each slung a bag full of seeds over his shoulder. Then they headed to the Excrement Place, the kiva of the sorcerers. Since it had been they who had instigated all the evil plans for Pavayoykyasi's family, they went to this location first. As they arrived on top of the subterranean chamber, Pavayoykyasi took a large handful of seeds and threw them inside. The men down below were squatting there in deep silence, tightly wrapped in their blankets. When they noticed the seeds scattered across the floor, they vied for them. Some of them were too weak to do so. They were at the end of their strength. A few managed to pick up a seed here and there and began to chew them. Others who still had some stamina left carefully tucked the seeds away as they picked them up. Four times Pavayoykyasi dispersed the seeds, then he and his son made their entry. When the two reached the floor below, they glanced around among the men. They looked terrible. The men, in turn, with their hair all messed up, were staring at Pavayoykyasi. They were mere skeletons, with their teeth bared and eyes hollowed. Pavayoykyasi and his son positioned themselves at the northwest end of the fireplace and started dancing. The song that accompanied their steps went as follows:

Meeheheyeye heyewloohoo'o'o
Meeheheyeye heyewloohoo'o'o
Haa'o'o haa'o haa'a'a'oo'oha'a'o'o'o'o
Haa'o'o haa'o ohaa'o'ohaa'a oo Sakwyeva, Moomo'a
Haa'o'o haa'o ohaa'o'ohaa'a oo Hoyniwa, Siisivu
Your words came true.
Your plans for the killing came true.
Many people came to be in Awat'ovi.
Meeheheyeye heyewloohoo'o'o
Meeheheyeye heyewloohoo'o'o
Haa'o'o haa'o ohaa'o'ohaa'a oo Sakwyeva, Moomo'a
Haa'o'o haa'o ohaa'o'ohaa'a oo Wuktima, Patösqasa.
Your words came true.
Your plans for the killing came true.
Many people came to be in Awat'ovi.
For no good reason at all you are waking people.
Wrongfully you are taking the piki away from people.
Wrongfully you are taking the yarn away from people.
Wrongfully you are making prayer sticks by the ladder.
Wrongfully you are making prayer sticks in the corner.
Your hearts being this way are painful.
Blaming one another.

Hya'aw, hya'aw a'a'a'aw
Hya'aw, hya'aw here somewhere.
Even if the heart gets pure,
Even if the words get clear,
People just live in their houses without caring.
This way, this way, remember,
Spoke Sakwyeva from the earth oven.
His rain power he let steam up in the fire.
From yellow corn, from blue corn,
Our mother, he took the embryos out,
Smearing his body with them.[1]

Let us go, all of us, to the spirit world.
No one shall remain here.
Remember, this is how Sakwyeva spoke.
Mee'ee'yeeye aa'a'ahayaw
Ayayaw yeehay
Uu'i, uu'i, uu'u'u'iy.
For sure,
Haa'o' haa'o haa'o'o'oo'oha'a'o'o'o'o
Haa'o'o haa'o ohaa'o'ohaa'a oo Sakwyeva, Moomo'a
Haa'o'o haa'o ohaa'o'ohaa'a oo Hoyniwa, Siisivu.
Because of you we have been hidden,
Because of you our hearts have been destroyed.
For sure,
Yo'o'hoy uu'u'u'u'iy
Oh my poor child crying from hunger
Thick piki, white and blue piki you are asking for.
Wrongfully she does not feed her child chewed food.
Wrongfully she lets her child drink in the corner.
For this evidently,
For this kind of thing,
They have been gathering at Pövöngvi, the sorcerers' kiva.[2]

This was the song Pavayoykyasi and his son sang. Finishing their dance performance, they once more scattered some corn in front of the men and exited from the kiva. Together with their friend they moved on to the next kiva. There they staged the same dance and sang the same song. This performance they repeated in every single kiva. Only then did they return home. Their friend followed them, listening carefully to what the men had to say.

And indeed, after they finished at the Excrement Place, the friend listened while someone remarked, "I guess it was really because of Pavayoykyasi and his sons that once we enjoyed a great life here. But we committed a heinous crime against them. For this reason we brought this awful situation upon ourselves, and people here have died by the hundreds."

This is what he overheard. Then he followed the two to their next destination and finally to Pavayoykyasi's house. Father and son entered, so he went in after them. "Sit down," Pavayoykyasi greeted his friend, and then he inquired, "Well, what did you hear?" His friend repeated the various comments he had listened to. "In all the kivas they were saying the same," he explained.

The first time Pavayoykyasi and his son toured the kivas was in the early morning hours. They did the same thing at noon. By early evening they had repeated their rounds for the fourth time. Each time they danced, they threw away a larger amount of corn kernels. The men inside, poor wretches, were scrambling for the food. No sooner had a man picked up a seed than he stuffed it in his mouth, for every one of them was famished. The corn kernels handed out by Pavayoykyasi were magical in their effect. The corn revived them and their strength grew a little. This is what happened to the men. They stilled their hunger a little.

When father and son were through, they returned to their house. Arriving there, they took off their costumes, and Pavayoykyasi said to his son, "I want you to remain here. I'll go back alone." And so he left his son in Awat'ovi while he returned to the Hopi Buttes area.

After Pavayoykyasi had departed, the boy went from house to house distributing corn kernels. As he did so, he would say, "I don't want you to eat these for the time being. Instead, put them where you usually keep your corn stacks. But you must not look at them before the next morning."

Some of the people, however, were so weakened from starvation that they could not refrain from eating a few of the seeds. Others devoured them all. But those who did not eat them placed them in the empty spaces of their corn stacks. The following day when they checked on them they found, to their great amazement, that the formerly depleted spaces were bursting with corn. Due to this miracle, not all of the villagers perished. They were not all wiped out. Pavayoykyasi's youngest child gave them their strength back.

As a result, the Awat'ovis made Patösqasa their new village leader, and from that day on he was the chief there. The first winter after this event it snowed a great deal. Also, it began to rain again. By the time the people reached summer, they resumed their planting activities and, just as in the olden days, harvested great amounts of crops.

In this fashion the Awat'ovis recovered and everything came back to life again. Living was pleasant once more. No one was starving, for the crops were bountiful. The suffering was over and the population of Awat'ovi was increasing again. Those who had nice fields worked hard in them and reaped large harvests. They were rich. As time passed, some of the villagers even acquired horses. By raising horses they were able to use them for their farming chores. They also went hunting with them. This is how the inhabitants of Awat'ovi were living.

A number of years went by. Then, ever so slowly, people began to drift into the same corrupt lifestyle they had experienced before. Once

again it was the sorcerers and witches that neither showed respect for their
fellow villagers nor thought them worthy of anything. Their minds were
focused on bad things only. Wasting and undoing things was what they
paid attention to. If a man was working on his field somewhere, they
would go up to him, take his tools away, and rough him up. All kinds of
nasty things they did to people and then left them in their misery, only to
continue somewhere else. Once in a while they actually committed murder.
Prime targets were women, of course. Wherever they encountered a single
woman, they ripped off her clothes and raped her one after the other. They
also pursued the girls, for they had no respect for anyone. For this reason a
girl or woman dared not go after water or leave her house unattended. They
accompanied each other and helped each other in this way. The behavior of
the sorcerers was disgusting. The hunters, too, they molested. They would
take from them the game they had stalked. They stripped them of their
other belongings, too, beat them up, and then abandoned them. This is
the kind of life that was going on.

Before long the rainfall became sparser and sparser. Although crops were
still growing, they did not grow as lushly anymore. The harvests, too, were
not as large as in prior years. The sorcerers who were responsible for these
changes did not listen to anyone, neither to their fathers nor their uncles.
They also paid no attention to their religious beliefs. The words of their
kachina godfathers and Powamuy godfathers meant nothing to them. They
only had contempt for people in leadership positions, no matter what their
rank—village leader, warrior chiefs, or those in charge of religious societies.
They neglected their old beliefs and kept criticizing and ridiculing their
religion. For this reason all kinds of evil things took place in the village.
People were even bewitching each other. The situation was as grave as it had
been long ago in the underworld. People were on their own. They became
more and more scared of the sorcerers and preferred to stay inside their
homes.

Meanwhile years had passed and Patösqasa had gotten old. And since
village chiefs are successively put into their position, a certain Ta'palo was
now in charge. He was worried about the situation, for it was not good.
There was no happiness among people. Strife and turmoil were returning
to the village.

One day there was going to be a mixed hunt. On such an occasion girls
participate in the hunt. And this is exactly what happened. The girls were
going to join the men. They would go on foot, of course. A few of the boys,
however, those who owned horses, would ride them. On the morning of
the event people were leaving for the hunt. Upon reaching their destination

they turned around to head back. Long ago it was customary during such a mixed hunt that if a boy or man killed a jackrabbit or cottontail, it was placed on the ground somewhere and the girls competed for it by running. The one who reached the prey first was entitled to keep it. She then handed her prize to a brother, father, or uncle of hers, who carried it for his clan woman. This is what typically took place during such a mixed hunt.

At the occasion of this hunt, the daughter of the village chief, a beautiful girl, decided to go along as well. The group was already homeward bound when one of the young men flushed out a jackrabbit. Immediately, he set to pursuing it on his horse. But alas, during his pursuit he rode over the daughter of the village chief, and the poor girl was killed on the spot. Ta'palo, her father, who was also a member of the hunting party, cried out, "My, why did you do that to her? Perhaps you did not see her. Well, it can't be helped now. Let's not be angry with each other about this." In his heart, however, Ta'palo was furious. "I'm sure that was no accident. He did that intentionally. That was all planned." This is what he said in his heart even though he had assured the boy that he was not upset. But he had only said that with his mouth. To himself, he swore that somehow he would avenge his daughter's death.

This tragedy, of course, took the enjoyment out of the event, and the hunt was terminated. It was no longer fun, and with subdued spirits the group headed back. In this frame of mind the hunters and girls arrived at home. Ta'palo, however, said, "My children have turned bad. Things are out of hand. They're not listening to anyone anymore." He was full of rage and he knew he would have to seek revenge for his daughter's death.

While all this was going on someone suggested, "Why don't we play *sosotukwpi?* With this gambling game we can cheer each other up again." Sure enough, all of the boys and men in his company agreed with him. "Yes, that's a great idea," one of them replied. "We're here in the kiva to be happy. We don't know what to do in our homes. Only here do we truly have a good time." The others shouted their consent. "All right, let's indeed try this game." So all the menfolk, young and old, began playing *sosotukwpi.*

Each time the players returned home after the game, they were raving about it. After all, *sosotukwpi* is great entertainment. "Maybe some of the girls would enjoy joining us when we're having so much fun." This is how the players kept talking, so those who had younger or older sisters said to them, "Why don't you come over? *Sosotukwpi* is great fun."

Others, in turn, suggested, "We'll take you over to the kiva and you can watch from the rooftop. You can then make up your minds. If it really is fun, you can join us later." Soon they were taking their younger and older sisters to the kivas where they gambled. Then they observed the players from the rooftop. There was laughing and shouting. The boys and men were merrily singing along as they competed with one another. Returning from the kivas the girls agreed, "Yes, that game is fun. Why don't we participate?" The girls who had witnessed the game told friends about it. "We're going to play with the boys because that game is a great deal of fun." First they asked their parents for permission. "Can we go with them if we don't go inside the kiva? The boys and men shouldn't be the only ones having fun. Just watching them would be really enjoyable." It was the month of Paamuya, the time of year when *sosotukwpi* was normally played. So the parents replied, "Sure, you may even go inside. We're glad they are playing there and are having a good time. During the winter month of Paamuya a Hopi is supposed to be happy, so there's nothing wrong with you going there. Enjoy yourselves with the boys." The girls were elated about this reply.

The next day the players all brought their younger and older sisters along to the kiva. Whenever one of them arrived accompanied by a younger or older sister, he shouted down from the roof just before entering, "*Haw!* How about some words of welcome. I'm not coming alone."

Right away one could hear boisterous shouting from below. "Come on in!" they yelled.

Every boy arriving with a sister received a great welcome upon entering. "All right, do come in! Be careful as you climb down the ladder! Have a seat here!" The girls who accompanied their brothers replied merrily, "There can't be any harm in participating."

The boys and men explained to the girls, "Watch carefully how we play. Once you learn the rules, you can join us." That's what they said to them down in the kiva there.

Before long the game got under way. They took out the cottonwood cups from where they usually kept them and began to play. Everybody was enjoying it. There was a great deal of laughter and boisterous shouting. The girls who were only watching also had a good time. Then they went home. The following night they returned, and when the game resumed, the men urged the girls, "All right, now you can try. But first we'll divide you into two groups. Then you can play mixed in with the boys against each other."

And this is what they did. They divided the girls into two groups. Then the game got under way. Both sides were competing with each other. This went on day after day. Meanwhile, the players began to bring some of their possessions to the kiva. These were the stakes they gambled for.

On one occasion the group on the southwest side was about to win, when all of a sudden a beautiful girl sat down close by the players. The boy who was supposed to guess moved up to the game. As he held his hand over the gaming cups, he looked at the girl who had squatted down beside him. That instant the girl pulled up her dress and revealed her knee. The girl was exceedingly beautiful and had light-complected knees. The boy's eyes were riveted on the girl's knee as his hand moved along the gaming cups. He was searching for the hidden object under one of the cups. He knocked all of them over and still did not find it, so the other side won. This happened, of course, because the girl had teased him with her exposed knee. Now all of them started using this trick, and when one group came close to winning, a girl from the opposing group would bare her knee.

This went on and on until they became so wrapped up in the game that they would not hear of going home on time. As a next step, a girl would now pull her dress all the way up so that her big thighs became bared. With the view of an exposed white thigh the boys or men could not help but get all aroused. Excited that a girl had revealed herself, they would feel compelled to touch the girl's thigh, and their side would lose. Finally, the boys made it a practice to offer their older or younger sisters as prizes. One player would challenge another and say, "All right, let's play each other. If I beat you, I can sleep with your sister. If you beat me, you can have mine." This is what they agreed to; so that's what they did from then on.

Things started getting more and more out of hand. Without letting up, the gambling continued until the early morning hours. Upon coming home all the girls told their parents how much fun the game had been. Some of the married women shared this news with each other. "Upon coming home our daughter was raving how much she enjoyed herself. She thought that maybe we should also give it a try. Anyway, that's what she said."

Thereupon another woman replied, "Sure enough, my daughter came home with the same news and also suggested that we go there. It's supposed to be a lot of fun. I think we should therefore ask our husbands if they will allow us to participate."

This is what the women decided to do. Indeed, they asked their husbands for permission. The latter were anxious to please their wives and answered, "Sure, why don't you go there. That game must really make everybody happy, for that is what our daughters are reporting. Go there and enjoy yourselves with the rest."

Some of these women's husbands had already been at the kiva, so they were able to confirm this. "Yes, it's true. It's great fun. Come on over and join us."

Now the women also came to the kiva. So engrossed did everybody become in the game that no one considered going to bed. When the players finally tired of *sosotukwpi*, they began dancing. They danced and danced until daylight came. Meanwhile, the wives of some of the priests also became involved in this gambling craze. They, too, would not return home on time. It got so bad that the women even took their food to the kiva. They would cook something and take it along, with the result that the priests and the other men who did not participate would go hungry. So busy were the women getting to the kiva that they did not feed their husbands. The men tried fixing various things, but alas, a man does not know how to cook, so they did not eat properly anymore. Some of the women also had little children, whom they began to neglect. Thus, the poor wretches were starving. The men finally had to pick up the children and take them to the kiva. Looking inside, they could see the mothers of the children all engrossed in the game. They called their wives by name, but to no avail. The noise of the players was so deafening that they did not hear. The men just stood there with children in their arms calling down, but there was no response. The gambling craze finally reached a climax when the wife of the crier chief became involved. The gambling did not stop at daybreak anymore, and the dancing continued until the sun was up in the sky.

The crier chief was very upset when they got his wife to join. Because of this he sought out the village leader. He said to him, "You know, I feel as if my wife has been taken from me. They have caused me great pain. I'm so angry, I wish we could all die. At least, this is how I feel, so I came to let you know about it. But don't tell anybody else."

In this manner things continued at Awat'ovi. One day, a couple of young men were making plans in their kiva to stage a social dance. They told their kiva partners about it and asked if there were any objections. The kiva mates were delighted about their plan. "Sure, that's fine with us," they replied. "If that's your intention, we'll see to it that you complete it successfully." Immediately they selected two men to be in charge of the female dancers. Then they chose an elderly man who would do the ritual smoking for them.

Now that permission for the dance had been obtained, the organizers broadcast it publicly from the rooftop the following night. After the announcement they had supper, whereupon they repeated the announcement. Next they recruited the menfolk into the kiva. During their first nightly gathering they memorized their songs. The next morning the leader said to them, "All right, I want you to bring in the girls tonight." Once more an announcement to this effect was made in the evening: "All right, come to the kiva. Come early!"

The announcement was repeated twice, whereupon the man in charge said, "Well, it's time to assemble the girls." They left the kiva and went from house to house, inviting the girls as follows: "All right, you girls, go to the kiva!"

Slowly but surely they picked up the girls and took them to the kiva. As they arrived on top of the roof, they hollered in, "*Haw!* How about some words of welcome!"

The boys and men down below were delighted to comply and many voices could be heard shouting, "Well, come on in. Be careful as you enter. Sit down here on the benches." When all the girls were seated, the leader commanded, "All right, I want you boys and men to sing. The girls must hear the songs so they can learn how to make their dance gestures." No sooner had he spoken than the drummer picked up the drum. He started the song, and they began to sing. The two men in charge of the girls now said to them, "Listen carefully to the song and make your dance gestures." The girls complied and started moving their arms.

They were still listening to the song when the leader said, "All right, now you practice this. If we keep practicing, we're bound to be able to dance to the song by the time we reach the eve of our event."

The girls rose from their seats and each picked a boy. Soon the dancing got under way. They had decided to do the Butterfly dance in which the female dancers wore no bangs but had their foreheads exposed. This had been the boys' request. And so they kept practicing. The dancers were really good. When the practice session was over, everybody went home. Early in the morning of the next day, people were talking about nothing else but the Butterfly dancers and how good they had been. That was the talk in every house. That night the procedure of the night before was repeated. Thereafter they practiced every night. Evidently, there were no plans to stage a dance during daytime. They continued doing this because they greatly enjoyed themselves.

Eventually, word of the nightly dancing also reached the wife of Ta'palo, the village leader. By now it already occurred once in a while that the dancers failed to go to bed, or if they went to bed, it was very late. Soon this habit got so bad that nobody returned home before daybreak. Just when this started happening, the wife of the village chief heard of it. On several occasions she mentioned to her husband that the dancers practicing in the kiva were really good. "I've been thinking," she said to her husband.

"What have you been thinking about?" he replied.

"Well, I might participate. I hear they are really enjoyable. Quite a few women are already there. They don't just need girls. Those women who went told me that it was a great deal of fun. 'You should come with us,' they've been urging me. That's what I wanted to ask you about. Maybe I should go too. What do you think?" she asked her husband.

The village leader replied, "If you want to be with the others, go ahead and join them. It's up to you. You all can be happy. I have you as my children so that all of you can be happy. Since they are having a good time practicing for a dance, you should be happy. By all means, join the dancers if that's what you want."

From that time on Ta'palo's wife never missed a dance practice. As a rule, she returned late. Eventually, she did not come home at all, or rather not before it became daylight. And always there was laughing and shouting in the kiva where they were practicing. Her husband, on the other hand, stayed at home smoking and pondering the ways of the villagers, his children. Meanwhile, the boisterous noise at the kiva went on and on. Once again Ta'palo's wife did not come home before daybreak. The village leader grew concerned. Maybe something was not right. "Why on earth would my wife remain so long? I have to go over there and see for myself when they practice tonight. Who knows why those boys and men are making so much noise." This is what he thought.

Once more Ta'palo's wife was looking forward to the evening. She spent a lot of time putting on some fine clothes. Next she combed her hair and powdered her face with a lot of cornmeal. That done, she nicely fixed her hair and brushed off her dress. By the time the ones in charge of the female dancers came around to pick her up, she had meticulously prepared herself. She left right away, saying to her husband, "I'm going to the kiva again."

"All right, enjoy yourselves. Go on, take part," he replied. And so his wife went to the kiva and the dancers lined up. Ta'palo could hear how they started dancing and singing. He kept listening. Sure enough, there it was again, the roaring laughter and the shouts of merriment. The dancers were clearly having a great time. When it seemed that things would not calm down, he rose from his seat. He was curious about what was going on in the kiva. Picking up a tanned hide he usually kept draped over a beam, he slung it across his shoulders and headed over to the kiva where the practicing was taking place.

Upon arriving there Ta'palo climbed up to the roof, with the laughing and shouting as loud as ever. People were yelling at the top of their voices. Now he had reached the edge of the hatch in the roof and looked in. Sure enough, there they were dancing, and his wife very much part of it. Dancing with great enthusiasm, she was smiling broadly as she motioned with her hands. No doubt, she was really enjoying herself. As she neared the men in the chorus, the shouting increased markedly. The village leader who noticed all of this said to himself, "So this is the reason for this merriment." It really hurt him. Each time his wife was approaching the chorus, the shouting and laughing increased. That caused the village leader a great deal of anguish. It was no laughing matter for him. Still, he thought, "Why don't I watch a little more? I'd like to see what really goes on." With that he squatted by the kiva opening and looked down.

It was obvious to him that the noise level was not as high when some of the other women neared the chorus. The shouting occurred when his wife came closer. Each time they did that, Ta'palo's heart ached. All kinds of thoughts crossed his mind, but outwardly he remained calm. Now the dancing stopped. Since the dancers were hot, they were filing out of the kiva to cool themselves off. His wife, too, emerged accompanied by her dance partner. It was so dark, however, that the two did not recognize the village leader. No sooner had his wife exited than she said to her partner, "Why don't you come with me to the latrine area?"

"Sure, why not," replied the man. "Let's go." With that they headed away from the kiva in a southeasterly direction. Then they continued on down the northeast side.

The village leader looked after them. When quite a bit of time had passed and still the two were not back, he decided to go after them. Following the path they had taken, he finally caught sight of them. The instant he did, he saw that the man was having intercourse with his wife in the corner of a house. This sight broke his heart. He became furious. He was outraged, yet he did not lay hands on the lovers. Instead, he went home. Upon entering his house he grabbed his tobacco pouch, filled his pipe, and smoked. He was beside himself and was hardly able to think straight while he smoked. He felt terrible, but he smoked on and on. All sorts of thoughts kept crossing his mind. The thoughts he had for his children, however, were not good. He should have been thinking of good things, but none came to mind. The fact that he had caught his wife in the act of adultery caused him great pain. Life was out of joint. Awat'ovi was living *koyaanisqatsi*. This is what Ta'palo thought.

Only recently, at the occasion of the mixed hunt, a horse had run over his daughter and killed her. The loss of his child had grieved him a lot. But now they had gotten to his wife, and he was full of rage. Not knowing what to do, he considered all kinds of options. Finally, he said, "Well, what's done is done. We'll all have to be wiped out here." This is the conclusion the village leader reached as he was smoking there.

So Ta'palo set to work. There was no other way: he would seek revenge on his children. The village of Awat'ovi was not to exist there any longer.

Nothing good was going to be forthcoming from it. Where the village site was now, only weeds would be sprouting in the future. Things of this nature Ta'palo was pondering. It was as if the people there, his children, had actually decided upon this fate when they had turned bad and become sorcerers and witches.

The people of Awat'ovi continued living in this corrupt fashion. Ta'palo, however, kept nursing his plan. Quite a bit of time had gone by, when one day he said to his wife, "Things really have come to a head here. We've been living immorally for too long. I can't think of anything else. There's nothing good left that could save us. I will therefore go to Walpi," he told his wife.

His wife did not object. "All right, you do that," she replied.

So Ta'palo headed over to Walpi. Upon his arrival he sought out the house of the village leader and entered. The latter welcomed him in, realizing at once that the headman of a village does not call on a peer merely to gossip. The two of them repaired to a kiva, probably the one the Walpi leader was associated with. Upon entering, the first order of business was a ritual smoke. The two passed the pipe back and forth between them. After a while the Walpi leader said to the headman of Awat'ovi, "Well then, you must be about for a purpose. You can't just have dropped in for nothing. What is it?" he asked.

Thereupon the Awat'ovi leader said, "Yes, I did not know whom to turn to. Then I thought of you and came," he replied. "I've been mulling over a terrible plan in my mind, for I've been unhappy for quite some time. In our village the sorcerers, those creatures of evil, do not let anyone go free anymore. Their influence is devastating. They are destroying people whenever they can. They are seducing the unmarried girls and having intercourse with them wherever they can. It's a lot worse than it ever was before. I'm at my wits' end. I don't know what to do anymore. That's why I came."

"Yes, I see," replied the Walpi leader. "So what do you intend to do? Tell me."

"Well, you can see that once again we're leading a life of corruption, just as we did in the underworld. That's why we emerged to this upper world. But the Spaniard, this evil, uncivilized person, also came up with us. He's baptizing people here. In doing so he's encouraging them not to respect anyone or anything, neither the elders nor our ceremonial dancers. The same thing we once experienced in the underworld. It was total chaos, and we lived any old way."

The Walpi headman asked, "So what is it you want from me?"

Thereupon the leader from Awat'ovi replied, "I'm asking you to do something big. I want you to come from Walpi to raid our village at Awat'ovi. That's the place I want you to attack. Send over your strong fighters. Have them prepare weapons such as bows, arrows, and stone axes. Whatever the weapon, get it ready for the raid. Then lead your men over, instructing them to this end: 'Wipe out the Awat'ovi people, finish them off. Kill each and every one of them. No one is to live there anymore.' This is what I'm asking of you. If you do this, I'll pay you with all the crops that grow near Awat'ovi. If you fulfill my wish, that shall be your reward."

The Walpi leader just sat there in silence, bent forward, thinking and thinking. After a lengthy pause he said, "So this is the reason for your coming?"

"Yes," answered Ta'palo, "that's why I came. What do you have to say to that? What's your opinion?"

"Well, the population of your village is large. Your people outnumber us by far. If they offer resistance and fight back, they're bound to overpower us," he said. "To be sure, we are brave men here. We are courageous and know how to fight. When the Paiutes attack us, we fight them. The same is true for the Apaches. When they raid us, we fight them. But when they attack us, we fight back in our own interest. We fight because we don't want to die. But you just told me that you want me to destroy all of your people. Awat'ovi is a Hopi village, and so is Walpi. We would be fighting against Hopis there, and that is not right," he said. "That would be bad. That's impossible." Arguing like this the village leader of Walpi refused Ta'palo's request.

"Very well," the Awat'ovi leader replied. "I guess I'll have to look for somebody else, some other place."

With that Ta'palo rose and departed. He had not received a favorable response. Heading southwest he came to Shungopavi. After climbing up to the village he made straight for the house of its leader. Arriving there, he entered. He found the village leader asleep, so he shook his head and he tapped on his forehead until he awoke. Right away he got up and threw some wood on the fire. Then the two men sat down by the fireplace, facing each other. Ta'palo took out his tobacco pouch, filled his pipe, and lit it. He puffed a few times, then passed the pipe to the headman of Shungopavi. When the headman had smoked it empty, he handed it back to the Awat'ovi leader. The latter carefully cleaned the bowl and put the pipe away. Now the Shungopavi leader said, "All right, tell me why you are about at this time of night."

"Well yes," he replied, "I'm not a happy man. These children of mine

at Awat'ovi are out of control. They have no respect for anyone, nor do
they listen to my words. Recently we had a mixed hunt. They rode over my
daughter and killed her. Of course, I took care of her in the proper way, but
I'm still furious inside. I'm very depressed. I want the village erased from
the earth. Awat'ovi is to disappear completely. Let it turn into a mound of
dirt with nothing but grass growing over it. This is the reason I came," he
explained.

"Is that so?"

"Yes. That's why I want you to tell your young men, your best runners,
to practice running and get in shape. Four days from now I'll come back
again." With that he got up.

Thereupon the Awat'ovi leader returned home. Upon arrival he ordered
his own young men, relatives of his, to practice running too. They did as
bidden and from that day on ran to make themselves strong. The people
in both villages did not give it any thought. Neither in Awat'ovi nor in
Shungopavi did anyone know what the two headmen were after. No one
paid any attention to the runners. On the fourth day, at night, Ta'palo
once again went to Shungopavi. The leader there had already gone to bed,
but since he was expecting his friend from Awat'ovi, he was not asleep yet.
When he heard that his visitor had arrived, he got up and stoked the fire.
"You've come," he said as Ta'palo entered.

"Yes. Remember I instructed you to ask your strongmen to practice
running. Did you do that? Were they willing to do so?" he asked.

"Sure," he replied. "They are racing and they are doing it willingly."

"Very good. Now this is what I had in mind when I told you to do this,"
said the Awat'ovi leader. "Send your best runners over to my village. Have
them come in the guise of Runner kachinas, just four of them. Upon their
arrival at my village, we'll race each other."

"So this is what you were thinking?" the Shungopavi leader exclaimed.

"Yes, that's what I want. Three days hence have your men put on their
costumes and on the fourth I want you to come to my village." With that
Ta'palo departed again.

So the date had been set four days hence. For the next three days the
Shungopavi runners practiced again and raced each other. At the end of the
third day, four of the men were getting ready. Their mothers had prepared
the customary gifts of boiled corn and roasted sweet corn for them. One
of the young men dressed as Hömsona, another as Angwusngöntaqa. The
third costumed himself as Leetotovi and the last one as Sikyaatayo. On the
fourth day the four kachinas went to Awat'ovi with their presents. As soon
as they arrived, they headed to the plaza. The Awat'ovi plaza is similar to

the one in Shungopavi. They laid down their gifts at the shrine located in the plaza. Right away the crier chief of Awat'ovi made an announcement from the rooftop. He was calling all the boys: "You boys out there, gather at the plaza. These Runner kachinas have arrived to compete with you. Don't tarry, but come at once." This is what he announced publicly.

Obviously, boys and young men who were able runners had heard the announcement, for they assembled in large numbers at the plaza. Soon the races got under way. And so they competed there, running against each other. Once in a while the kachinas were first, then the other side, the boys from Awat'ovi. As this continued the kachinas' presents, which were bestowed on the winners, were getting fewer and fewer. Finally, only one bunch of baked sweet corn remained. A boy from Awat'ovi picked it up and put it aside. "I'm going to win this," he proclaimed. "I'll race anyone for it. But I know it will be mine," he boasted.

The Hömsona kachina stepped forward, ready to meet the challenge. The race was on. The boy from Awat'ovi ran extremely fast, and the Hömsona was not about to catch up with him. Or rather, he pretended that he was not able to catch up. He just ran after him. When the kachina had fallen way behind, he simply waited somewhere for the boy to return. By now the latter had reached the turning point all alone and was dashing back. The instant he came upon the Hömsona, the latter grabbed him and threw him on the ground. Having the boy down, he jumped on top of him and drew his knife. A Hömsona always carries a knife, which he uses to cut off a loser's hair, usually the knot that is tied behind the head. But instead of cutting off the boy's hair, he thrust his knife into his throat. The blood just spurted out. This is what Hömsona did, and for this reason he had raced this boy last. Meanwhile, the kachina father who was taking care of the Runner kachinas at Awat'ovi had fashioned all the necessary prayer feathers for them and was waiting with the feathers in a tray. At the close of the race he was going to distribute these prayer offerings to the kachinas, whereupon they were supposed to return home. The Hömsona who had murdered the boy now got up. Approaching his partners, he motioned to them, "Come on, let's go!" With that all four Runner kachinas dashed off. They did not waste any time accepting the prayer feathers and prayer sticks but sped off as fast as their feet could carry them.

The kachinas were already far away, yet the boy who had challenged the Hömsona still was not back. The spectators began to worry. "Something must have happened to him. Maybe the Hömsona did something to him." These were some of the thoughts that crossed the people's minds.

A few of the spectators decided to go and check. They went along the same course where the runners had raced and found what they were looking for. The boy was lying in his blood, dead. They exclaimed, "The Hömsona must have killed him!" They informed the other spectators. "He was killed!" they shouted. The ensuing commotion was tremendous. "Let's go after them. Let's kill them," said the boys and men, whose voices could be heard as they ran to their houses for weapons. Grabbing any weapon they could find, they rushed after the fleeing kachinas. Some of those who owned horses mounted them and galloped off in pursuit of the fugitives.

The chase was on. Sure enough, the kachinas could be seen hurrying down to the plain below Awat'ovi. Upon reaching level ground they sped on, one behind the other, following the contours of a wash. They were moving along the southeast side of Walpi, past Huktuwi, when the Hömsona began to tire. Soon it happened to all of them. The kachinas were getting tired. A little while later they came to a place where the Hömsona who killed the boy could not keep up with the others any longer. It was at this place where the riders from Awat'ovi caught up with the kachina. They quickly surrounded him and killed him by shooting their arrows into him. No sooner had they cut him down than they resumed their pursuit of the others. They had just reached a little hillock and were nearing its base when the Angwusngöntaqa was caught. He was dispatched in the same manner. The men surrounded him and shot him to death. Then they went after the remaining two. At a place in the southwest, northeast of Mishongnovi, there is a large wash. The pursuers were approaching this wash when they caught up with the Leetotovi. Again they dealt with him in the same way. Now only the Sikyaatayo was left. He had reached the wash by now and when he looked back, he saw that his pursuers were not too close yet. He took off his mask and discharmed himself by swinging it repeatedly over his head. Four times he did the discharming act, then placed the mask on a bush, jumped down into the wash, and climbed out again on the other side.

This happened exactly according to the plan the leaders from Shungopavi and Awat'ovi had hatched out. Should any of the kachinas be caught before reaching the wash, they were to be killed. In case one managed to cross the wash, however, or even if all of them should do so before the pursuers' arrival, they were to be spared. This is what the two headmen had agreed upon. Apparently, the leader from Awat'ovi had instructed the boys and men to this extent before they took up their pursuit. "If the kachinas cross the wash before you, you are not to harm them. They can return home. But if you catch up with them before one or all of them escape across the wash, you may kill them all. The one who crosses the wash, however, you are not to chase after any longer." This is what Ta'palo had impressed on the men prior to their departure.

The Sikyaatayo had just crossed the wash when his pursuers reached the place where he had left his mask. They found it perched on a bush. They said, "It looks like he got across. As you recall, we are not supposed to follow him any longer." With that they stopped their pursuit and headed for home. Thus the Sikyaatayo was the only one they failed to catch. He alone was not killed.

Meanwhile, the boy who had impersonated the Sikyaatayo kachina had returned to Shungopavi. The village leader said to him, "Thank you for coming. I'm grateful they did not kill you. This is how it will be now. You can live here now."

That same night the village leader from Shungopavi was clearly expecting a visitor again. Once again he had bedded down, but he was not asleep. Sure enough, it was not long before the headman from Awat'ovi arrived. As on the previous occasions the Shungopavi leader stoked the fire, then he said, "Well, you must be around for a reason."

"Yes," Ta'palo replied, "you did indeed do what I asked you to do. We killed three kachinas from your village, you killed one of our boys. We did just as agreed." The Awat'ovi leader continued, "I'm happy the way things worked out. So tomorrow I want you to come to the village and round up my children. You can gather the women and girls. The men, young and old, however, you must kill. I'm glad you consented to my plan and did exactly what I asked you to do. I'm happy that it shall be this way now."

When the leader from Shungopavi heard this, he just sat there, speechless, mulling things over in his mind. Finally, after a long pause, he spoke. "No," he said, "we killed one of your people, a handsome boy. You, on the other hand, killed three of my relatives. So we are even. We did the same thing to one another. No more killing. I refuse to do that to your people. I can't bring your womenfolk over here. That's not what I wanted. I simply can't do that."

Now the Awat'ovi leader sat there, all surprised. "Too bad, indeed," he replied. "It seems we committed the same crime, so I thought you would agree to my scheme. It's my desire that my village get erased from the earth. For this reason I came up with this plan. I was under the impression that you were for it. But now, I think, this was all in vain." With that, Ta'palo got up and left for home.

This is the reply the Awat'ovi leader received in Shungopavi. Understandably, he was unhappy. Upon arriving home, he mulled over the situation. As he was wondering what to do, it occurred to him to try the Oraibis. That same night he headed over to this village. Upon reaching his destination he went straight to the village leader's house. The two headmen exchanged the customary smoke. When they were done, the leader from Oraibi said to the headman of Awat'ovi, "Well now, you've come a long distance. This must be for a reason. You can't just be walking around. What's on your mind?" he asked.

"I certainly have a reason," the Awat'ovi leader replied. He then gave an account of what he had done so far. "The first place I went to ask for help was Walpi, then Shungopavi. But they both declined. You're my friend and partner. I need someone's help, so I selected you. That's why I came here." Ta'palo went on, "My children over in Awat'ovi are out of control. They have no respect for people nor do they listen to anyone. The elders are nothing to them. They are ravishing the women and girls. Our shrines and ceremonies are in shambles. They don't mean anything. These Spaniards, nothing but sorcerers and witches, are hoping to settle here for good. That's why they came. The same thing took place when we still lived in the underworld. Now I want my village erased from the surface of the earth. It is to disappear completely. If you assist me, therefore, you can have everything. You can bring women and girls here. They can help you to increase in number. If you plant our fields, they will yield large crops for you. I'll let you have all these things if you help me. After all, you're my older brother. Awat'ovi is to be no more." This is what Ta'palo said to the Oraibi leader. The latter, in turn, reflected on the proposal.

When he was done thinking he said, "All right, so this is what you want. What you said refers to your children. Does one kill one's own children?" he asked.

"Yes, I do," Ta'palo replied. "That's the way I want it. It will be my responsibility, no one else's. I'll find out what will happen to me. But life in my village cannot go on the way it is. Life there is bad."

By responding in this manner Ta'palo showed his determination to follow through with the deed. He was willing to have Awat'ovi totally destroyed. It was his desire for the village to disappear. Now the Oraibi leader accepted. "But I don't want your land. It's too far away. I'll take the girls and women. Also, I can't do this alone. This is an enormous task. I can't be the only one. I must have partners in this," he said to the Awat'ovi leader. "The other villages will probably support me."

Ta'palo replied, "The Walpi headman refused, explaining that this was not their custom. I think the two of us should go there. We'll go together and see what he has to say." With that the two headed over to Walpi. But instead of going to the village leader, they sought out the warrior chief.

Once again they first smoked. Upon completion of the smoking ritual the warrior chief inquired about the reason for their coming, and Ta'palo explained. He repeated what he had told the Oraibi leader, that he had offered him the Awat'ovi womenfolk and fields. That the Oraibis were not interested in the fields because they were too far away. That it was going to be that way. He could have the girls and women. If the Walpis were to help, they could have the Awat'ovi land.

At this point the warrior chief agreed. "All right," he said, "let it be this way. You can count on me. I'll help you. So let's go to my leader." Thereupon they went to the village chief. After completion of the customary smoking ritual, the warrior explained to the leader what they had planned, that the Oraibis had agreed to the attack and that they would assist Ta'palo in wiping out the people of Awat'ovi.

Once more the Walpi leader asserted his position. "This is not our custom. We would be raiding Hopis. This would mean killing our people, our very own people. That's not our tradition. But you are in charge, you are the warrior chief. If you have no objections, there's no way out for me." The Walpi leader was forced to go along now. He did not want to interfere with his warrior chief, which meant that he had agreed to the undertaking. He too threw in his support. In return, the Walpis were to be awarded the Awat'ovi land, its fields.

All three of them had discussed the matter now and they were of one mind. Because the warrior chief consented, the village leader had no other choice but to obey him and go along with his decision. This is how they talked there, and then the three men parted, each going home in his own direction.

What had been agreed upon was that four days hence, at dusk, they would come over to Awat'ovi, both from Walpi and Oraibi, and would hide along the boulder-strewn slopes there. Once the people of Awat'ovi were asleep, Ta'palo would let them know about it or give them a signal. Therefore, with four days at their disposal, the three departed for home. They would need to work on their weapons, such as bows and arrows, and ready what it takes to hide out. Everything that relates to killing and war had to be prepared.

As soon as the Oraibi leader arrived back home, he gathered his warrior chiefs. Having done so, he told them that the Awat'ovi leader had requested their assistance. He shared every detail with them. "Start at once to get your weapons ready. We'll march in four days. So go to work," he bade his warrior chiefs.

Next, the Oraibi leader decided to send two of his nephews to Mishongnovi and Shungopavi. He told them, "I want you to go to these villages and ask them to join our forces. Tell them to come with us to help the Awat'ovi leader. He needs us. If you inform them at both places and they agree to help us, we can all fight together." This is what he ordered his nephews to do, and then he sent them on their way. The village of Shipaulovi did not yet exist at that time.

One of them headed to Mishongnovi, the other to Shungopavi. The Mishongnovis were all for joining them. They agreed right away. "Sure, you can count on me," said their leader. He consented without hesitation. The Awat'ovi leader had, of course, already been to Shungopavi in the very beginning. Upon receiving the messenger from Oraibi the Shungopavi chief said to him, "As you recall, the race we staged with its tragic ending was a terrible thing. Beyond that I can't agree to anything. I won't go. I don't want to bring the Awat'ovi girls and women here. I will not allow them into this village. Let every man here decide for himself. If someone is so evil and bad that he wants to join in with you and the others, let him do so. I, for one, will not go." He absolutely refused to be part of the attack. With that he gave his people permission to decide for themselves. This is what the Shungopavi leader did. He remained steadfast.

From that day on the men concentrated on their weapons, knowing full well that they only had four days. Soon the fourth day, their deadline, arrived. Now they were getting ready. It was toward late afternoon when they were about to set out on the warpath. The Oraibi leader made it a point to meet with the warriors where they had assembled. He was grateful to them. "Thank you all," he said. "With happy hearts go forward to your destination. Go in strength," he encouraged them. "I'll be waiting here for you. Don't worry about anything as you go along. It was the Awat'ovi leader who wanted it this way." After these words the Oraibis started out. There was a huge number of them, boys and men.

The same happened at Mishongnovi. The men there, too, dressed and then, in turn, marched off. Most likely, their headman had addressed them prior to their departure, and the same was probably true for the leader of the Walpis. By sundown the warriors reached the hiding place below Awat'ovi that Ta'palo had pointed out to them. It was about dusk by the time all of the contingents had assembled. What a huge throng they made up, the Oraibis, Mishongnovis, and Walpis. Their number was incredibly large. It was nightfall now and the men were encamped at the northwest side of Awat'ovi, next to a spring. Ta'palo, who was ultimately responsible for all this, now got his chief emblem out. In addition, he picked up his pipe bag and pipe. Then he descended the northwest side of the mesa accompanied by his wife, who carried a large bundle of piki. When the two arrived at the enemy camp, the Awat'ovi leader was elated. Looking about among the warriors, he saw that there were many of them. "Thanks," he exclaimed, "thanks for consenting to my wish. This is how I wanted it. But first you must eat," he said, whereupon his wife distributed the piki among the men. When they were satiated, he took out his pipe, and then they smoked, he and several of those with the rank of war chief. Ta'palo was overjoyed. "Thanks again," he said. "Thank you for agreeing to my plan and for gathering in such large numbers. I want my people wiped off the surface of this earth, and I see that all of you assembled here share my desire. I'm most happy," he explained.

When the smoking ritual was over, Ta'palo said to the warrior chiefs, "I'd like you to remain here for the time being. Later, while it's still dark but getting closer to daylight, climb up to the trash piles on the ledge." With that he pointed out to them precisely where that location was. "After the sun rises, I'll be sitting on top of my kiva. Watch me carefully. The minute I get up and wave my blanket, I want you to launch the attack," he said. "Run up to me first, grab me, and throw me inside the kiva. I don't care to live any longer. For it is my wish that this village here become a ruin. These sorcerers must all die. As soon as you have thrown me in, take the ladder. Then run from kiva to kiva and at each one, pull out the ladder. We're just celebrating the eve of the Wuwtsim ceremony, so the men and boys are bound to be sleeping in their kivas. And then when you are up there, divide the village among yourselves and spread out. Pick up chile bundles, set fire to the wood stacks on top of the roofs, and, after lighting the chile, cast it into the kivas. Lots of men will be inside. Then kill the men who are there. That done, herd the women and girls together at the village dump; include the children also. Tie them there at the dump. Tie up their hands behind them. Be sure you leave no one out. Having accomplished that, you Oraibis can have first choice of the women and girls. Put aside how many you want and which ones. Then let the others have their pick," he said. "I'm content now. Therefore, let me give you this." With that Ta'palo presented them with his chief emblem. "Here, have this. It's supposed to be mine symbolizing my children. But I'm fed up with them. That's why I let you have it. With it in your possession and happy in your hearts I hope you'll make it to the new day." This is what Ta'palo said to them. Thereupon he ascended the mesa with his wife, returning to the village.

Mindful of these instructions, the attackers were encamped there now, waiting for the moment when he would give them the agreed upon signal. The men whiled away the time checking their weapons. Some sharpened the points on their arrows, others the blades of their stone axes. They made sure their gear was tight and strong. Dressing for battle, they painted their faces, putting red ocher along their eyes above the nose. From the nose down across both cheeks they drew lines with black hematite. Next, to be more powerful they tied white eagle plumes in their hair. Now they would be light of weight and would be able to run with great speed in pursuit of the enemy. By the same token, these plumes would ensure that they would not tire easily. Finally, the day began to break. By the time the sky showed the first signs of grayish dawn, the attackers had reached the designated trash piles along the ledge. There the warrior chief once again admonished his men: "Be sure you don't hold back now. Give it all you can. If you're without fear and fight hard, you'll survive, and nothing will happen to you. The Awat'ovi chief wants it this way. Don't show mercy to anyone." This is how he admonished his men.

Just as the sky turned the colors of the yellow dawn, Ta'palo rose to his feet on the kiva roof. He waved his blanket in the air, whereupon the attackers climbed to the top of the mesa and began the assault. There were many of them, so many in fact that they filled the village of Awat'ovi. They exactly followed the orders they had received. Running from kiva to kiva, they found that the men were inside. Immediately, they pulled out the ladders, thereby depriving those inside of any chance to escape. Now, all of them had come to Awat'ovi with finely shredded juniper bark and greasewood kindling. Upon removing the ladders, they lit the bark. The attack took place, of course, on the very eve of the Wuwtsim ceremony. This meant that the women still had their roasting pits going. With fire from those they ignited the juniper bark and the greasewood kindling, which they hurled into the kivas. Next, they set the wood stacks on top of the kivas aflame and threw them down through the hatches. Then they shot their arrows down on the men. The latter had been completely unsuspecting and had no weapons whatsoever. Now the raiders stormed into all the houses. Wherever they came across a man, no matter whether young or old, they killed him. Some they simply grabbed and cast into a kiva. Not a single man or boy did they spare.

At that time the Spaniards used to grow a lot of chile at Awat'ovi. The Hopis had of course obtained seeds from them, and since there was plenty of water there, they also harvested great quantities of this spice. Bundles of dry chile were hanging on the walls outside their homes. The attackers pulverized them. They simply grabbed the pods, squeezed them in their hands, and scattered the powder into the kivas, right on top of the flames. Then they closed up the kiva hatches everywhere. As a result, the smoke could not escape. The chile caught fire and, mixed with the smoke, stung most painfully. There was crying, screaming, and coughing. After a while the roof beams caught fire. As they flamed up, they began to collapse, one after the other. Finally, the screams died down and it became still. Eventually, the roofs caved in on the dead, burying them. Then there was just silence. All of the people inside the kivas had perished. This is what happened to them.

To make sure that they had not made a mistake, the raiders now, once more, went from house to house. Wherever they found an old man, they cut him down. Old women they killed too. Younger women and girls they herded together at a place by the dump. Some of the Oraibis, Mishongnovis, and Walpis had positioned themselves along the mesa edge and made sure no one was able to descend. Anyone who attempted to escape was killed. Some tried to sneak away secretly. They were shot. Others they simply grabbed and hurled over the mesa edge. They allowed no one to get down. When all the survivors had been rounded up, they attacked the houses themselves. Whatever would burn, they set aflame, the buildings and their wood stacks. Awat'ovi presented a terrible sight. It had been turned into a ruin.

Evidently, a handful of Awat'ovi men and boys had managed to hide somehow and had not been discovered. However, the number of those who were not found and survived the killing was small. Meanwhile, the Oraibis and Mishongnovis were getting ready to go home, taking the women, girls, and children with them. At this point, a few of the Awat'ovi boys and men who had remained alive emerged from their hiding places and, searching the houses, gathered whatever arms they could get hold of. Then, small though their number was, they set out in pursuit of the enemies. At some place they came upon them and attacked. However, those on the Oraibi side far outnumbered them and quickly overpowered them, killing them all. Having killed them, they cut off their heads and gathered them in a pile. The place where this happened came to be known as Masqötö or "Skull." It is still known under this name today.

These are the terrible events that took place during the sacking of Awat'ovi. While the attack was going on, some of the Walpis and Mishongnovis had already begun to round up some of the womenfolk for themselves. As they were leaving with the others now, they took their captured women and girls along. The Oraibis, however, who had concentrated on the fighting, had not been able yet to pick out a lot of women. After all, it had not been planned this way. They were not supposed to make their selection before the end of the battle.

They now realized that the Walpis and Mishongnovis had already selected some of the more attractive ones and were returning home with them. While doing so they had been attacked by the pursuing Awat'ovis, who in turn were all killed in the attempt. They had attacked to free the women, but instead all lost their lives.

By now they were all bound for home, each group with the women they had picked. At a place on the southwest side of Walpi the contingents from Walpi, Mishongnovi, and Oraibi came together, all with the women and girls they had gathered. There the Oraibis protested, "Remember, this is not the way it was to be. Ta'palo wanted it otherwise. We were to have first choice and were to pick whatever women and as many as we wanted. Then you Mishongnovis were to have your turn. You Walpis were to be rewarded with the land. So what you did was not right. We therefore demand that you give us back the women. They belong to us. Those that we leave over, you can have."

The Walpis and Mishongnovis, however, did not agree. "No," they cried, "we've already chosen these for us, so we'll take them along. These are ours. We won't give them back to you."

The three groups argued back and forth, urging one another to do what was right. But they could not come to terms. The Walpis and Mishongnovis simply refused to give up their women. Thereupon one of the Oraibis exclaimed, "In that case no one shall have them. Let's get rid of them. If we kill them all, nobody can have them."

No sooner had this been proposed than they started slaughtering the women and girls. They would just grab one and kill her any old way, either by stabbing her or shooting her. Some of the women and girls, poor wretches, were crying, "Let me go with you. Don't kill me. I'd like to go with you." But they were pleading in vain, and a great number of them were killed. As the massacre continued, one of them cried, "Some of us women are initiates of a society. We know how to make rain. We'll teach you the art of rain-making if you spare us and take us along."

At this point they showed mercy to some of the society initiates, such as the members of the Maraw and Lakon societies. But others who they did not murder they injured severely by cutting off their arms or legs. Some men who interceded on behalf of the women they mutilated by severing their penises and testicles. In some cases they also cut off the women's breasts. Finally, they showed some mercy to a few who were versed in certain skills and put them aside. Those who had been wounded they left where they were. One after the other the poor things perished there miserably. This is how they dealt with their female captives. A large number of them, women and girls, were murdered. The children they did not harm.

Now they distributed the remaining prisoners in equal lots. The group from Oraibi even took one man from Awat'ovi along because he was familiar with peaches. For this reason lots of peaches are now harvested at Oraibi. The contingent from Mishongnovi found someone who owned the sweet corn. That's why they always raise lots of sweet corn. The Walpis must have found some women who had the knowledge of making pottery, for they know how to make pots now. This is what took place there when so many women were massacred. For this reason the location is called Mastsomo (Death Mound). Ever since that day it's been known that way.

This is what happened there. All the captives had been fairly distributed now, and none of the groups took an excessive number. And because of this distribution descendants of the Awat'ovis live in our villages here.

The next day those Oraibis and Walpis who had participated in the raid returned to Awat'ovi. They wanted to be sure that no soul was living there anymore. Upon arrival they checked the village ruins. Only smoke was rising in the air. Where a building still happened to be standing, it was demolished. Freestanding walls were toppled over. Pots were smashed and ladders burned, metates broken into pieces. Looms, beams to hang things on, they set afire as they went along. Once in a while a man would put a precious thing aside for himself, such as a knife or a necklace, a bowguard, metal-tipped arrows, or a nice bow. They also appropriated bells and lances. These the members of the Al society still have in Oraibi. There was nobody around anymore. As the men walked about they only heard each other talking. Not a soul anywhere. There was only silence. This is how Awat'ovi was destroyed and leveled to the ground. Those villagers who had been led away were warned never to show any longing for the place, never to think of returning to it. The ruin was to stay the way it was. Being that way, they wanted no trace of it to be left. This had been the village leader's express wish. Ta'palo had, of course, lost his life together with the others.

Thus the village leader Ta'palo sacrificed his own children to get rid of this life of evil, craziness, and chaos. In this endeavor he was helped by the other villages. Together they laid waste to Awat'ovi. Throughout these villages there must still be living some of their descendants. But Awat'ovi no longer exists. Ta'palo's plan came to pass. Because they killed his daughter and seduced his wife, he wanted the village to disappear from the earth. In getting his wish fulfilled he lost his own life. He succeeded in eradicating Awat'ovi, for the village is no more. Only a few remnants of its walls are left. And here the story ends.

NOTES

1. According to Yava, the bodies of the murdered children "had been rubbed with cornmeal before they were thrown into the fire" as a symbolic gesture "that whatever might be planted in Awatovi would never grow" (1978:94). In the song, as it is presented here, Sakwyeva, the oldest of Pavayoykyasi's sons, himself smears his body with the germs of maize. I assume that this signifies that he is withdrawing his powers of germination.

2. Pövöngvi, the name of the sorcerer kiva at Awat'ovi, is etymologically obscure. Fewkes, who lists Pü-vyüñ-o-bi as the name (1893:365), cites an explanation from Stephen, according to whom it is derived from the plural of *powaqa* (witch). This analysis is not tenable, however, since the plural of *powaqa* is *popwaqt*, which is too far removed from the sound structure of the name.

Glossary

Al Society Members If a Hopi man intends to be initiated into Wuwtsim and he has an Al or "Horn" member as a godfather, he is initiated into the Al society. The Al society member is distinguished by two horns on his head. In addition, he wears a buckskin mantle. Each leg has a tortoise rattle attached, and he walks barefoot. In his hand he holds the *mongko* (chief stick). Both sides of his chest are marked with white dots. White dots are also on his arms and legs.

The (Two) Horn society members are considered guards, and when the ceremony takes place on *astotokya* (hair-washing eve) they guard the kiva. Should an intruder try and peep in, they will first try and chase him away. If he fails to comply and resists their efforts, they kill him.

Aliksa'i A storyteller usually begins with *aliksa'i*. In reply to this formulaic introduction the listeners utter, "*Oh.*" As the narrator continues with the story, we keep acknowledging the story with this same response. But not all Hopis begin their tales in this manner. We, who trace our ancestry to Oraibi, follow this custom, while some living in the distant villages of the other mesas commence by saying "*Ituwutsi,*" which means, "It is my story."

Altar For an altar to exist there must be a religious society. Any society that has an altar sets it up as soon as its members enter the kiva to hold their ceremony. Praying, and sometimes also the singing of prayer songs, takes place at the altar. The makeup and paraphernalia of each altar vary from one society to another.

Angwusngöntaqa (kachina) Angwusngöntaqa is one of the Runner kachinas. He wears a ruff of crow feathers, hence his name Angwusngöntaqa (The One That Has Crow around His Neck).

Apoonivi (place-name) Apoonivi is an elevation that lies somewhere southwest of the Oraibi mesa and slightly to the northwest. Of whitish appearance, it is an important place for the Hopi. When individuals die, they first ascend this peak and then, after making their descent to the northwest side, continue their journey to Maski (Home of the Dead). There are steps leading up to Apoonivi, two on the southeastern and northwestern flanks of the elevation. At its very top is a house. Only the deceased can see this house.

Arrow To manufacture an arrow one first needs to collect the necessary wood. Desirable are branches that are both very straight and very strong. Apache-plume is said to make beautiful arrows, but men going after this plant generally have to travel far. Others use greasewood or cliff-rose to construct their arrows. As a first step, the wooden shafts are straightened out as much as possible. Next, one end of the arrow receives a point, while on the opposite end a groove is cut across the top. Into this groove is inserted the bowstring, which, when drawn, projects the arrow. Directly below this grooved end, three split feathers are attached that are held tightly in place by means of sinew wrappings. The other ends of the feathers are also bound to the shaft with sinew. Should a man intend to decorate his arrow, he does so, of course, prior to mounting the feathers.

The arrow that comes with a child's bow is painted red at the lower end. The portion where the feathers are mounted has its own distinct decoration, and the bottom tip is painted blue-green. The very first arrows a baby boy ever receives are fashioned from a small reed. One arrow from this first bundle is set aside for his umbilical cord, which is tied to it and then stuck into the ceiling at the home of his birth.

In former days the Hopi used to coat their arrows with rattlesnake poison. When such an arrow was shot at a foe and penetrated the body, the poison would spread within that person's system and bring on a quick death. In former times when the arrow was one of the few Hopi weapons, they also used shaft-straighteners to align their crooked shafts when necessary. This implement was made from some hard material and had three or four perforations. How exactly it was employed has been forgotten, however.

Atsamali (place-name) Atsamali is situated at a point northwest of Oraibi. This is the place where the Buffalo dancers are taken during the rest periods of their public performance. Here too they are sent home after the last dance.

Northeast of Atsamali a line is drawn. At the time of the schism of Oraibi, Yukiwma intended to start out from this point and therefore drew the line. In starting out from there he was going to claim the land beyond this mark.

Awat'ovi (place-name) Awat'ovi used to be a big settlement, on the mesa southwest of Pongsikya or Keams Canyon. The Bow clan had established its village there, but it fell into ruin, as is well known. When the people of Awat'ovi allowed the Christians into their community, the Hopis of the other villages became so angry that they attacked them and wiped them out.

Bacavi (Third Mesa village) Bacavi was the last Hopi village to be founded. When during the schism of Oraibi the "hostiles" were driven out, they first settled in Hotevilla. Some of them tried to return to Oraibi but were not admitted. It was then that they established themselves at Bacavi. Kuwannömtiwa, a member of the Sand clan, was the one who built the village there for his followers.

Baked Sweet Corn *Tuupevu* is sweet corn baked in a pit oven. After removal from the underground oven it is strung up and then dried in the sun. Once the *tuupevu* has hardened and people want to eat some, they need only boil it for it to return to its moist state. A kachina always includes *tuupevu* when he comes bearing gifts.

Begrudging or Envying Good Fortune Whenever a Hopi does something spectacular or acquires something valuable or good, another person is bound to be envious. The person will begrudge the former this good fortune because the blessing went to someone else. In such cases, the persons who are jealous will almost always put the fortunate ones down in some way. They may label the others as sorcerers or even claim that a fortunate person sold a corpse to gain the things of value. In these ways Hopis typically slander one another.

Blanket Hopi blankets are manufactured by the Hopis themselves. As a rule, it is the men and boys who do the weaving. They also carry out the spinning themselves. They definitely spin a white yarn, and if a weaver wants to create a blanket with varicolored stripes he dyes the yarn. Then he weaves it in different colors. Normally a blanket is woven in narrow consecutive bands. These bands are usually black and white, but occasionally a blue-green stripe is also part of the design.

Bow To make a bow one first sets out to get the necessary wood, which needs to be strong and rigid. Oak is most suited for this purpose. Upon returning from one's collecting trip, one first prepares the wood by hewing it properly. Then it is lashed to something so that it will attain the desired shape in the drying process. Once the wood is thoroughly dried, one fashions the bowstring. Generally, the string attached to the bow is of animal sinew, which one twists while it is still moist. Some bow makers also place sinew along the back of the bow in order to give it more strength. Such a bow is referred to as "one that carries sinew on its back." A sinew-backed bow does not break even when drawn with great force and curved in a sharp arc. When the bowstring is drawn hard, the arrow is released with great velocity. The bow described above is not flat like the child's bow. Rather, its wood is slightly rounded.

Unlike the adult bow, a child's bow is decorated with an array of colors. The place where it is held is painted white; this area is flanked on both sides with blue-green. Next comes a red section followed by yellow. The outer ends are painted purple. The blue-green and yellow color zones are spotted with either three or four black dots. The back of the bow is colored red, as is also the entire length of the string. Some bows have blue-green zigzag designs painted on their backs. While the designs are applied on a black background, the rest of the inside from the handle outward is yellow, which is also true for the bowstring. Children's bows are given to the young, uninitiated boys during the Powamuy and Niman ceremonies.

Butterfly Hairdo When a girl reaches a marriageable age, her mother styles her hair in a way termed *poli'ini*. First she brushes her hair thoroughly before parting it in the center. Then, using a wooden hoop for support, she fashions a whorl on each side of her daughter's head. When the girl's hair is long and luxuriant, she will inevitably have large whorls. A girl wearing her hair in this fashion is most attractive in the eyes of the Hopi. The similarity of the whorls in the girl's hairstyle to the wings of a butterfly accounts for its appellation *poli'ini* (butterfly hairdo).

Pre-pubescent girls, on the other hand, have a hairdo referred to as *naasomi*. The *naasomi* is worn on both sides of the head above the ears and is not as large as the *poli'ini*.

Cape The *atö'ö* (cape) is about the size of the smaller of the two wedding robes woven for a Hopi bride. The bottom and the top portions of the cape are bordered by two stripes: a narrow outer black one and somewhat narrower inner red one. The field in the middle is pure white. This garment is worn only on special occasions, mostly by young girls and women. However, some kachinas also use it, either in the form of a wrap around the shoulders or in the form of a kilt around the waist.

Cicada The cicada is supposed to have the knowledge of producing warmth. This is why the Hopi hold it in high regard. It is said that when the cicada plays its flute, warm weather arrives. Members of the Flute society pray to the cicada, among other things, when conducting their ceremony. Long ago when the Hopi had not yet come to their destined land but were still engaged in their migration, the owners of the Flute ritual reached the northernmost spot on earth. They tried in vain to melt the ice there, using their knowledge of producing heat, before they arrived in Hopi country.

Corn Corn is ever present in the life of a Hopi. At a child's birth, a perfect ear of white corn represents the symbolic mother of a child. From corn a variety of items are made: food, sacred cornmeal, flour. Wherever a special event is going on, corn or its byproduct is never missing. Corn is so precious that whenever it is incorporated into a Hopi's song, it is spoken of as "Mother." At death, a path of cornmeal is made along which the deceased travel wherever they are destined to go.

Cotton   Long ago the Oraibis used to grow cotton along with everything else they planted. For this reason there still exists a place northwest of Oraibi that is called Pitsinvastsomo (Cotton Field Hill). Here cotton was grown. Wedding robes were fashioned from the cotton for all the daughters-in-law. In former times the weather used to get quite hot; that's why people were able to grow this crop. Nowadays the climate is not as hot anymore, so no one is planting cotton.

Once there was a saying that went like this: "If you never let go of the cotton and keep rubbing it (i.e., to weave wedding robes), you will cause the summer to become shorter. You won't have much of a warm season any more." This is what the old people used to say. Evidently it is true. There are always weddings taking place today, one after the other, both in winter and summer. That's why the warm season is short now.

Coyote   The Hopi have no use for the coyote whatsoever; therefore, they do not prize him. It may be that the ancient Hopi benefited from him somehow, but no one has ever mentioned anything along these lines. In many stories Coyote believes everything he is told. As a result, he gets into all sorts of predicaments, and people laugh at him. Any person, therefore, who is equally easily duped is labeled *ihu* by the Hopi, which denotes both "coyote" and "sucker." Coyote also has to imitate everything. In other tales he gets himself into sticky situations because of his lecherousness. Once in a while, however, he will do something beneficial for people.

Farmers certainly do not appreciate the coyote. After all, it roams their fields destroying their watermelons and muskmelons. Thus, long ago people used to organize coyote drives to get rid of these pests. However, neither its pelt nor its meat was ever used.

For some Hopi the coyote constitutes a clan totem. Consequently, they refer to themselves as belonging to the Coyote clan.

Coyote Clan Member   Coyote clan members take their existence from the coyote. A few affiliates of this clan still live in Hotevilla. There are also some in Oraibi. They are together in one phratry with the Kookop clan. Having the coyote as a clan symbol, they must have found something good in the animal to take him as their clan ancestor. The coyote is, of course, a good hunter. Also, when he plans to do something, he first ponders every aspect of the situation carefully. Next, he makes several attempts, and finally he executes his plan. For this reason the Coyote clan has the animal as a clan totem.

Crier Chief In the past the person in charge of public announcements came from the Greasewood clan. Whenever the *kikmongwi* commissioned him to make an announcement, he would do his bidding. If a date had been set for a certain event such as the Niman ceremony or if there was to be a hunt, the *tsa'akmongwi* would announce it publicly. After he had been instructed as to the announcement, he would carry it out verbatim. If the *kikmongwi* cleared his voice at a certain spot or coughed, the crier would do likewise.

Crystal A crystal is a stone that is transparent. The "crystal gazer" or shaman employs it in his diagnosis by looking through it. He can see if something is wrong with a patient. Then he informs the patient about this.

Dance Day The day called *tiikive* can refer to two things: it either marks the last day of a given time span set by an individual or it constitutes the last day of a ceremony. If the latter is to include a public performance, it occurs on that day. Several activities conclude with *tiikive*.

When those who are congregating in secret rituals have come to their last day, *tiikive* is the day on which they dance. This applies to the initiates of the Snake, Flute, Wuwtsim, and Maraw societies. When the day set for the Niman kachinas arrives they likewise perform their dance on *tiikive*, but on this occasion no secret rites are performed. In a similar way, the social dancers do not engage in any secret rituals, but they also close their public performance as soon as *tiikive* comes. Thus, public dances mark the completion of the ceremonies for all these various groups.

Dust Devil A dust devil is a wind that comes along in a circulating motion, carrying all sorts of debris with it. Occasionally a small dust devil may directly move toward a person walking about. When this happens, the person lays one hand on the heart, the other on top of the head. In addition, the mouth is tightly closed. For it is said that the dust devil will tear out a person's heart. This is the reason the Hopi are afraid of the dust devil.

Once in a while someone will flip a finger at the wind. This prevents it from approaching the person. People claim that sometimes the dust devil is someone's long deceased uncle or younger brother. It may be a sorcerer walking around in this guise. For this reason people won't let a dust devil close to them. Frequently a tiny dust devil can be seen whirling up to children that are at play.

Enemy An enemy is someone who causes other persons harm or grief or is not friendly toward them. In a war the enemy is the one who raids the other side. Of course, even one's own tribe member can be one's enemy. Long ago such tribal groups as the Navajos, Apaches, Comanches, Kiowas, Chemehuevis, and Yavapais came to raid the Hopi villages and, consequently, were the Hopis' enemies of old.

Famine A famine is a very tragic event, causing people terrible suffering whenever it occurs. Its initial phase is usually marked by crop failure. As time passes, all the stocked corn reserves are slowly depleted. At the point when nothing is left to consume anymore, the famine is on. And not until a god has compassion with the people, and rights the wrong committed by them, can recovery begin. The Hopi have experienced famines on many occasions.

Female In-Law *Mö'wi* is a kinship term reserved for the female who marries a man that is related to her clan-wise. Thus, the wives of the men of a certain clan are *mö'wi* to all members of that clan and the phratry it belongs to. When a son marries, his wife is also a *mö'wi*. But in this case only the father and his male clan relatives consider her as their *mö'wi*.

Because a *mö'wi* is generally very revered, we do not address her by name. However, anyone who mentions her by her given name is said to be taken along by the setting sun. Why this saying exists, no one knows.

Fire Pit Within a kiva the fire pit is always situated just beneath the entrance ladder. It is in the area northwest of this fire pit that most activities take place. The ancient fire pits were usually square and slightly dug into the floor. Its side walls consisted of flat rocks. The fuel was always kept in stock underneath the ladder. The person who looked after the fire was known as *tsoylan'aya* (fire tender).

Flute Society Members Long ago, the members of the Flute society used to entertain the people in Oraibi with their ceremonies. There were two groups, the Gray Flutes and the Blue-Green Flutes. In Oraibi they performed every other year, taking turns with the initiates of the Snake society. Some of the Flute members used to play a flute with a broad rim at the end. They were usually the ones walking along the outer sides of the group as it made its procession into the village. They were beautifully costumed, dressed in kilt and embroidered kachina sash, and wore a *pavayoykyasi* (moisture tablet) on their back.

Flying Shield In stories powerful beings, such as gods, are bound to own a *paatuwvota* (flying shield), which they employ as a mode of transportation. With it they reach any destination in no time because they can fly about with the shield. The shield is made from cotton and is woven in the manner of a Hopi wedding robe. The owner of such a vehicle needs only to climb aboard, tug on something, and utter a command, whereupon the shield rises in the air and takes the rider to any place desired. When the being wishes to descend, the procedure is repeated.

Fog Fog usually comes after the rain has cleared off. People are not happy about the fog because it is said to dry up the land, the peaches, and plants. Also, there is no light when it is thick. Each time the fog is really bad, the last child of a family, the one referred to as *sisipi* (chamber pot) can blow at the fog. As a result, it generally burns off then.

Fox The Hopi make use of fox pelts in many ways. They employ the skin as a pendant in the back from the waist down when dancing. For example, boys and men wear it in this fashion when they dance the Butterfly dance. Most of the kachinas do likewise. According to Hopi mythology, the sun god emerges from his kiva in the morning carrying a fox skin. He puts the skin up on top of his kiva, at which time gray dawn appears. This particular fox is called Gray Fox.

Grinding Corn When a woman or girl intends to grind corn, she first shells the amount of corn she wants and then winnows it so that the chaff and worm-eaten kernels can be separated. Next, she puts the corn kernels into the coarse grinding stone and there begins to crush them, coarse grinding everything. This done, she brings the corn back up in the slanted metate and grinds it repeatedly to make it finer. Finally, the corn becomes cornmeal, and when it is the desired texture, she scoops it from the grinding bin. Next, she builds a fire under a roasting pot, and dry roasts the cornmeal until no trace of moisture is left. Then she places the corn in a finer metate, spreading it out there to cool off, at which time she grinds it fine. This accomplished, she sifts the cornmeal to remove any remaining chaff and, if she wishes, grinds it once more.

Hehey'a (kachina) There is one particular kachina whose name is Hehey'a. One type, known as Kuwanhehey'a (Colorful Hehey'a) is very handsome. Hehey'amuy Taaha'am (the Uncle of the Hehey'a), on the other hand, is very homely and speaks backward. He has hair consisting of lamb's wool and adorns his head with a bunch of red peppers. His face is black with a distorted mouth. For a nose he has a corncob in whose top is inserted a turkey wing feather. His eyes are sad-looking. Kaolin is used for his body paint, and red deer hoofs are depicted on both sides of his arms and thighs. His whole upper torso is clad with a goat skin, and his waist is girdled with a silver concho belt. In addition, the uncle wears a kilt and footless black stockings that go up to the knee and are tied to the shin by means of narrow woven belts. His brown-colored moccasins are decorated with embroidered ankle bands, and from his hips dangles a rattle made of antelope hoofs. Wherever the uncle arrives in the company of the Kuwanhehey'a, he acts as their side dancer and mimes the words of their chants. During the performance of the Sa'lako puppet drama, a pair of Hehey'a uncles participates, toting on their backs the grinding stones of the little puppets. During the actual dance of these two marionettes, the two uncles act out the words of the song in pantomime and also check the fineness of the sweet cornmeal the puppets are grinding. More than one Hehey'amuy Taaha'am also comes with the So'yoko ogre kachinas. In this role, they carry ropes.

Homol'ovi (place-name)   Homol'ovi is an ancient Hopi village on the bank of the Little Colorado. For some reason it fell into ruin, and the people living there became scattered all over Hopi land. I don't know what clans own the ruin. But they say that those who were from the ruined settlement of Palatkwapi stayed in Homol'ovi for a while until they became absorbed into the Hopi villages.

Hopi   We Hopi settled here ages ago and we are still here. But the land is not ours. We are here only as tenants. We made our emergence from the underworld at the Grand Canyon with all sorts of other people and from there migrated into all directions. The being who first inhabited this upper world gave us certain instructions, and we are the only people that still live in some ways by these instructions. Tradition has it that at first we undertook a great migration before arriving here in Hopi country. Along the way we left many ruins, which still exist. It is as if we marked the land area that is ours in this way. Some of those who went through the migration are Hopi just as we, but when they arrived at certain locations, they settled there permanently for some reason. Yet our destination was a place called Tuuwanasavi (Earth Center), and only after reaching this place were we to settle for good. These were our instructions, though they were not followed by the others.

It seems as though a Hopi does not do any evil, thus the name Hopi. But some of us are evil.

Hovi'itstuyqa (Mount Elden)   Hovi'itstuyqa is a promontory situated southeast of the San Francisco Mountains. Several ruins can be found at its foot. The Hopi are well familiar with this place and claim that the people who lived there in ancient times are some of their forebears. The Hopi remark that people are not all physically built the same, some having more prominent buttocks than others. As one looks at Hovi'itstuyqa, it resembles a person's buttocks jutting out, and for this reason the Hopi refer to the mountain feature as "Buttocks Sticking Out Point."

Hömsona (kachina)   Hömsona is one of the Runner kachinas. Whenever he challenges someone to a race and catches up with him while they run, he cuts some of the loser's hair off. That's why the kachina's name is Hömsona (Hair Craver). He always carries a knife or some sort of scissors. Upon catching up with a person in a race he flings him to the ground and on occasion may cut off his entire hair knot; once in a while, he only snips off a lock from the hair.

The kachina's face is black, and he has a snout. On his head he wears feathers arranged in a cross-wise fashion. Around his neck is wound a yellow fox ruff. In addition, Hömsona is clad in kilt, embroidered sash, and Hopi belt.

Huk'ovi (place-name) Huk'ovi is a butte southwest of Oraibi. There is a ruin there. It seems to be windy there all the time. For this reason the location is referred to as Huk'ovi (Windy High Place).

Kachina A kachina is something very special to a Hopi. Although the kachinas live unseen, they appear in person when one calls them at Hopi country. At that time they are visible. Upon their arrival, they entertain us all day long. They visit us with intentions that everything will be good. They bring us gifts, which consist of foods prepared by their sisters. At the conclusion of their dances we present them with prayer feathers and pray to them that they will take our messages into every direction so that we may be constantly visited by rain. But the Hopi do not pray solely for themselves; they pray for everyone who is thirsty, including animals and plants. They pray to the kachinas for rain for all things.

The kachinas inhabit a variety of places. They reside where springs surface. They travel about by way of clouds, and that is the mode they use when they visit us.

Way back in the past the Hopis did not carry out the kachina ceremony on their own. At that time it was the real kachinas who came to the Hopi. Because some Hopis were evil, however, and began to show disrespect for the kachinas, the kachinas abandoned them. But before they departed, they turned over their secrets to the Hopi. From that time forward the Hopi had to carry on the kachina cult on their own. As a result, they endure hardships whenever they do so.

Kachina Father The kachina father takes care of the kachinas. Whenever they dance during the day, he sprinkles them with sacred cornmeal and takes them to their resting place at the Katsinki (Kachina shrine). He also leads them back to the plaza for the next dance round. In this fashion he takes care of them.

As soon as the kachinas are ready to dance again and start stomping, he sprinkles them with the cornmeal. To do so he comes along the rear of the dance line until he reaches the song starter. Here he calls out to the kachinas, exhorting them. Having done that, he steps up to the last dancer and, scattering his cornmeal as he goes from kachina to kachina, moves along to the front end of the dance line. Stopping in front of the first dancer, he then lays out a cornmeal path on the ground.

Kachina Sash The *mötsapngönkwewa* (embroidered kachina sash) is an article of Hopi clothing that is not worn every day. Put on only on special occasions, it is a part of the attire of some kachinas. However, it is also worn by the men in various ceremonies. The Maraw society, whose members are women, makes use of it, too. The sash consists of two identical pieces that are sewn together at the middle, which accounts for its overall length. The person wearing this sash girds it around the waist once and lets the remaining portion hang down to the right side of the body.

Both above and underneath are fairly narrow bands of black color decorated with paired markings of white generally referred to as *pöqangwkuku* (Pöqangw tracks/warrior tracks). Right in the center of the sash is a blue-green area said to represent the earth. Its middle portion has red design elements that represent flowers, the idea being a desire for fields covered with flowers. The designs, flanking each side of the flower elements, are *haruveni* (bean markers) and symbolize a newly sprouted bean plant. The broad black sections at the very bottom and the very top of the sash, finally, incorporate so-called "tooth marks."

Katistsa (place-name) Katistsa is a community somewhere at the Eastern Pueblos along the Rio Grande.

Kawestima (place-name) Kawestima is a ruin situated under an overhang somewhere far away northwest of Oraibi. When Tawakwaptiwa threw out Yukiwma during the Oraibi split, the latter chose Kawestima as his destination. But he never reached the place. Instead, he settled at Hotevilla.

Kilt The kilt, which is woven by the Hopi men themselves, forms part of the native apparel. Whenever it is worn by the kachinas, it is nearly always embroidered. The only exception is Sootukwnangw, who dresses in one that is unadorned. Such a plain kilt is called a *kwatskyavu*. Properly worn, the kilt is open on the right, where the decorated side also shows. On certain occasions the embroidered sash known as a *mötsapngönkwewa* is worn over the kilt.

The embroidered kilt has a narrow black border all along the bottom edge. In the past, above the border there used to be a somewhat broader band of blue-green, but kilts like this are not made anymore. Also located right above that black edge are about three or four pairs of vertical marks that are called *pöqangwkuku* (Pöqangw tracks/warrior tracks). Each end of the kilt is decorated with embroidery. In the very bottom field are alternating white and red stripes in vertical alignment that symbolize the rain falling from the clouds. Hence, above them is a design depicting a cloud. The design, which is entirely black inside and resembles the steps of a staircase, is enclosed by a white border while the background up to the rainfall symbols is red. Below the red is a narrow band that separates the red from the rainfall pattern.

Kiva Many different kachinas hold their dance performances in the kivas. But they are not the only ones who make use of the kiva. When the initiated members of a secret society are to hold their ceremonies, they also assemble within these underground structures. For example, the men stage their religious activities here during Wuwtsim. In addition, the Powamuy, the Flute, and the Snake societies, to mention only a few, congregate here for their secret endeavors.

Since the women, too, have rituals of their own, the Maraw, Lakon, and Owaqöl societies also carry out their ceremonies in a kiva. So these religious chambers are not occupied solely by men. Social dancers, too, use the kivas to practice. In winter men and boys occupy the kivas and engage in whatever activities are assigned to them. Thus, one may bring his weaving to the kiva and set up a loom there. For Powamuya, kachina dolls, bows and arrows, and other items of this nature are manufactured. A kiva is off limits only to uninitiated children. It is not until the month of Paamuya and the night dances following the Powamuy rites that these children, accompanied by their mothers or grandmothers, are allowed to witness the dances. On these occasions they watch the dances, together with the women, from the raised area to the southeast of the kiva's interior. At one time even young girls who had been initiated were not permitted to witness dances unaccompanied. The same was true when they went there to practice for a social dance.

The ancestors of the Hopi all lived in kivas once. Thus, in the eyes of the Hopi, the kiva is also a home. However, it was not like the dwellings we inhabit today; it was simply a hole dug in the ground with a cover on top. Entering the kiva was, therefore, only possible by descending a ladder.

Kooyemsi (kachina) The Kooyemsi is a kachina for both the Hopi and the Zuni people. His head is painted with reddish-brown ocher; small globes are attached in place of his ears and on the top and back of his head. This accounts for the appellation Tatsiqtö (Ball Head) occasionally applied to him. From the balls hang turkey feathers. The kachina's mouth and eyes can take on various shapes. Around his neck some sort of cloth is usually tied. For a kilt he wears a folded woman's dress, and his waist is adorned by a silver concho belt. On his legs and feet he wears footless black stockings and brown (sometimes white) moccasins. At times he may also go barefoot. In his right hand the Kooyemsi carries a rattle that has its own distinctive style, and in his left hand he holds an eagle wing feather with which he motions while dancing. A second feather is tucked into his kilt on his back.

A Kooyemsi can fulfill more than one function. While not considered a clown, the kachina will perform in funny ways similar to a clown. In the past he acted in this role only during dances performed by kachinas classified as *taqkatsinam* (powerful, manly kachinas), such as the Hoote, Hooli, and Tsa'kwayna. Today, he no longer clowns for the *taqkatsinam* in any of the villages. Only at Zuni does he still carry out this function. Whenever a kachina group requires a drummer, the Kooyemsi will also take on this task.

In the days when the Hopi men still herded sheep, a shepherd participating in a kachina dance might once in a while not have the time to prepare an elaborate mask. He would then simply put on a Kooyemsi mask and join the dance group. A Kooyemsi could therefore appear in conjunction with such diverse costumes as those worn by the Long Hair kachina or the Hoote. The dancer would dress exactly like the other kachinas except for the head, which would represent a Kooyemsi.

There are occasions when a large group of Kooyemsi will sing as a chorus for the other nonchanting kachinas. Also, each time clowns are part of a kachina plaza dance, a few Kooyemsi always act as *Kipokkatsinam* (Raider kachinas). Hence they are named Kipokkokoyemsim (Raider Kooyemsi). Also in the past they used to arrive in the village during the month of Ösömuya (approximately March) to challenge the girls to all sorts of guessing games in the dance court. Occasionally, they would also come during kachina nighttime performances for this same reason.

Koyaanisqatsi The concept of *koyaanisqatsi* stands for all states of life that are negative. When people reach the state of *koyaanisqatsi,* life in its entirety breaks down. Respect for others disappears. People do not heed the words of the elders and leaders. Their ceremonial rites and beliefs are forsaken. No opportunity is omitted that people can't use to set themselves against each other. When the youngsters encounter an elderly person, they pester him. Mutual love is nonexistent. People compete for leadership positions. They become so crazed that they abandon their children for a life of amusement. Therefore, no good comes with *koyaanisqatsi,* this "life of turmoil and disorder."

Koyaanisqatsi did not begin at this present time. The Hopis first encountered this sort of life while they were still living in the underworld. When they did not come to their senses, someone who intended to set them right did away with some of them. At first it was with fire that he destroyed them. The second time it was with a flood. For those who were pure of heart he sought a new life on this present world. Hence those first people went along in these ways and then emerged into this world. But here again they experienced *koyaanisqatsi* many times over. And each time they did this, there was always something to correct this situation.

Kwan Society Members   An affiliate of the Kwan (Agave) society is thought to hold the highest rank among the four Wuwtsim groups. Long ago when the kivas were still entered for the performance of the Wuwtsim ritual and when the ceremonies were still intact, the various Wuwtsim groups would go to the Kwan kiva first to ask there for permission to dress in ceremonial garb. The Kwan members had the Al (Horn) society initiates as helpers. The latter would do things for them. Thus, when the Kwan members were in session during Wuwtsim and an Al member wanted to make fire for all the Wuwtsim groups, he would first go to the Kwan kiva and get glowing embers there. From there he returned to his own kiva and lit a fire for his own group. Then he would visit the remaining societies and build fires for them before reentering his own kiva. Next, all the societies went to get food.

In appearance the Kwan member is distinguished by one horn. He wears a buckskin for a mantle and carries a lance in his right hand. In his left he holds the *mongko* (chief stick) and a bell. His face is daubed white, and on both sides of his chest dotted lines run down his body. Arms and legs are also covered with dots.

Kwiptosi (dish)   To make *kwiptosi* one first shells as much white corn as desired. The corn is then boiled. After its softness is checked, a kernel is cracked every so often with one's teeth. Before the corn is completely soft, it is taken out and the water is allowed to drain. Next, a kettle for parching corn is put on the fire. It is filled with dune sand, and when the latter is hot, some of the boiled corn kernels are put inside. Now everything is stirred. Once the kernels start popping and are done and slightly browned, one places them into a sifting scoop and sifts them. Once all the corn is parched, it is spread out to dry for a while. As soon as it is slightly dry, it is heaped on the coarse grinding metate. Now everything is ground to a coarse flour. This in turn is sifted to eliminate the chaff. Next, the coarsely ground cornmeal is roasted in a vessel over the fire. Then the fine-grinding process is completed on the fine-grinding metate. The resulting flour is now sifted once more, thereby removing tiny pieces of chaff. Then it is finally *kwiptosi.*

Ladder   Long ago, when doors in the modern sense did not yet exist, the only way the ancient people entered their homes was by means of ladders. In those days, therefore, one had to ascend to the rooftop first either by way of steps or on a ladder and then climb indoors, again, by using another ladder. But now that the Hopi have acquired doors from the white man, they enter a house only through them. Even for kivas this entrance mode is the preferred one today.

Lakon Society Members   The Lakon ritual is a women's ceremony, quite similar to the one performed by the Maraw society initiates. Like the latter, they announce the ceremony for a length of eight days. At the halfway mark the members enter the kiva, and on the eighth day they stage a public performance. Proceeding to the plaza, the Lakon initiates stand in a circle. Upon beginning to sing and dance, they motion with the wicker plaques they hold in their hands.

The two Lakon girls who come to throw gifts into the crowd arrive after the dancers. As the Lakontaqa (Lakon man) guides them to the plaza, he draws cloud symbols for them on the ground. Onto these the Lakon girls cast their hoops, whereupon they cast darts at them. First the yellow one, next the blue-green one, then the red one, and finally the white one. In this fashion the two Lakon girls enter the circle of the dancers. After putting their hoops and darts aside, they pick up a couple of things to throw into the crowd of spectators. The girl who entered from the southwest takes up her position at the southeast; the other who entered from the southeast places herself at the northwest. Next, both bow to each other with their gifts, whereupon they hurl them to the young men and boys who grab for them.

At noontime all the young men who are strong runners descend from the mesa to the plain below. From their gathering place then the Lakontaqa sends them off in a race. There is a coiled plaque that is a short distance away and others that are far away at the plaza in the midst of the dancers. These plaques the runners earn as prizes.

Lance   One of the Hopi weapons in the past was the lance. Lances come in various lengths. One type is very long; another is quite short. The lance is fashioned from agave stalks but also from other material that is both straight and sturdy, frequently oak. Its head is tipped with a large piece of flint held tightly in place with sinew wrappings. This particular sinew is peeled off the spine of an elk. Some men also tie an eagle tail feather to the weapon. While the longer lance is simply hurled into the midst of the enemy, the shorter version is used to stab at a foe from close range.

Leetotovi (kachina)   Leetotovi is the name of one of the Runner kachinas. His face and body are painted black. Across the eyes and the mouth of the kachina run bands of red color. On his head the Leetotovi wears a yellow fox pelt that hangs down to the back. When Leetotovi challenges one of the male spectators to a race and catches up with him, he beats the loser with his yucca whip.

Löhavutsotsmo (volcanic hills northeast of Flagstaff) Shortly before reaching Nuvatukya'ovi (the San Francisco Mountains) as one comes from Hopi, there is an area with a series of hills and mounds in close proximity to each other. These elevations are known to the Hopis as Löhavutsotsmo (Testicle Hills). When looking at these hills on one's way from Kaktsintuyqa, they closely resemble testicles, hence the name.

Low-Class Person A *söqavungsino* (low-class person) is one who is destitute and poor. Such persons have no possessions of their own and are not recognized as bona fide members of the community. People of this status live along the refuse area of the village.

Maraw Ceremony The Maraw is basically a women's ceremony, although a few male initiates also belong to it. When the Mamrawt (Maraw society members) are in session, these men participate in some but not in all phases of the ceremony. The Mamrawt begin their rites in the month of Paamuya (approximately January), at which time they make prayer feathers. In the course of that night, kachinas arrive and perform their dances within the various kivas. Then, during the month of Angukmuyaw (approximately September) they conduct a second, much longer ceremony. While setting their public dance performance date sixteen days in advance, they spend the last eight days confined within their kiva. During this fall ritual, the Maraw participants make their novices, or ceremonial children, fully initiated members.

It is at this occasion that Maraw members take turns showing their thighs publicly as they don their kilts. The initiated member wears her kilt much higher than is the norm, which accounts for her thighs being exposed. A design that runs along the bottom border of the kilt girds the woman exactly around the high points of her buttocks. Right above her knee is a horizontal stripe, and another circles the thigh a little farther up. These two stripes, in turn, are connected by four vertical lines. The right leg below the knee is decorated with blue or green body paint, while the lower left leg is painted yellow. And since at this occasion the Maraw initiates sport their kilts so high, the men all go to ogle their thighs. This public display is also known as Qastikive (Thigh dance).

Mask Whatever someone wears over the head to hide the face constitutes a *tuviku* (mask) for the Hopi. Another term for such a device is *kwaatsi,* which literally translates as "friend." Although merely a mask, it becomes alive the minute it is put on. And when the living mask detects something negative about its wearer, it will take revenge on him. Thus, during a particular ceremony, a dancer may become weary before the day is over. Another may complain that the mask is hurting him. He may feel fine in the morning, but then all of a sudden the mask may turn on him. If the wearer of the mask then changes his attitude, the mask quickly ceases to cause him pain. Consequently, a mask must not be upset or toyed with under any circumstances, and it is imperative to have a pure heart when engaging in a kachina ceremony.

Traditionally, the kachina impersonator wishes for various foods while adding the various attachments to the bare mask. Typically, he will say, "Let this ear be a peach as it goes on here. Let this eyeball be a grape as it gets tied on here. Let this snout become a squash as it is attached here." Thoughts of this kind cross the impersonator's mind while he is mounting all the pieces that form part of the mask.

Generally, masks are kept at home and out of sight. Sometimes they are also stored at a kiva. On *totokya,* the day before a dance ceremony, the masks are first assembled properly and then fed with honey. A drop of honey is placed right into the mouth hole. At times people may put the honey in their own mouths, mix it with saliva, and then spray the mixture over the mask.

Long ago, when the kachinas did not wear masks yet, they used to hide their faces with Douglas fir. As a result, children never attended a dance performance in those days. Today, Tuutukwnangwt (Cumulus Cloud kachinas) still do not don masks but conceal themselves behind an array of turkey feathers held together with twine. Others, such as the Paavangwt (Mountain Sheep kachinas), may do the same at times. In the Eastern pueblos along the Rio Grande, kachinas still disguise their faces with Douglas fir. Such kachinas are termed *piniitom* by the Hopi. To this day, the Hopi kachina known as Tsito covers his features in this manner with fir branches.

Matsonpi (place-name) Matsonpi is a ruin situated at the northeast corner of Hotevilla. The ruin, which lies on a small mound, is said to have perished in a fire. For this reason it was abandoned by its inhabitants.

Medicine Man There is more than one type of Hopi medicine man. One is the bone doctor who treats or cures only maladies of a person's bones. Another one is the herb doctor, knowledgeable in the use of all medicinal plants, who performs his remedies by means of them. The last is the crystal gazer or shaman who has his own method of treatment. Looking through his crystal, he will diagnose the ailment of a person and then instruct him in the appropriate treatment. At other times he will remove the object causing the sickness. For instance, he may draw out a thorn or a shell implanted in the patient by another person. Moreover, if the shaman detects that someone has unknowingly violated a taboo or committed some other wrong act, he will enlighten and instruct the person in the remedy that should be applied. These shamans no longer exist, and with them has died the knowledge of their practice.

The Hopi also perceive the badger as a great healer. Medicine men in general rely on some animal as they serve their patients. Sometimes a medicine man may choose a powerful being such as a bear to be his symbolic father to help him practice his skills.

Metate   A Hopi woman utilizes corn flour on a daily basis. Consequently, in the past it was a must for her to possess her own grinding stone or metate. There are two types of grinding stones. One is a coarse-grained slab, and the other is a fine-grained one. Sometimes the coarser metate is equipped with two hand stones or manos, implements with which the grinding is performed. Generally, the woman first shells her corn, then grinds it down to the proper size in the coarse grinding bin. By repeating this process she produces flour with a coarse texture. After she removes the flour from the bin, she dries it in a hot kettle. Next, she places it on the finer stone slab, where she regrinds the entire amount two or three times.

The metate proper forms an enclosure with four sides of thin flat stone slabs. In the front of the grinding stone is a narrow channel referred to as *matavuva*. A similar channel runs along each side. These channels, about equal in width to the front one, are sloped upward. Along the top there is still another channel that is also termed *matavuva*. Overall, the top end of the metate is positioned somewhat higher than the bottom part, so that the person grinding is compelled to make downward strokes only. The place behind the grinding bin where the grinding is carried out in a kneeling position is referred to as *mataptsö* (metate corner.)

As the process of fine grinding the corn goes on, the finished flour is placed into a pottery vessel where it is firmly packed down. Not all the flour can be removed from the slab, however; a small amount always remains. So the person grinding takes a brush, licks it in order to moisten it, and with spittle removes the small amount remaining by touching it with her brush. In this way all the flour is cleaned off the metate.

People are told not to step inside the grinding bin. Should someone do so, according to a saying, one's colon will protrude from one's anus.

Mishongnovi (Second Mesa village)   When the Mishongnovi people arrived here, they first settled on the southwest side of Kwangwup'ovi. In due course, when they expressed a desire to become integrated members of the village of Shungopavi they approached the *kikmongwi* to ask his permission. Tradition has it that they were very loquacious and that they spoke quite aggressively. Whenever the *kikmongwi* said something, they were quick to give a negative reply. But the *kikmongwi* of Shungopavi spoke to them as follows: "There is no way that you can live with us here in Shungopavi. We have become quite numerous here. If your heart is indeed set on living here with the Hopi, build your own settlement at that butte off to the east. There I have my seeds stored. If you really want to settle here among us go to that place, establish a village, and guard my seeds." The Mishongnovis consented and did exactly that.

Mixed Hunt The concept of the mixed hunt is based on the fact that on this occasion young men and girls go hunting together. As soon as the event has been announced, the girls prepare food on the day they intend to go. Whoever plans to participate in the hunt mixes her batter early in the morning to make *somiviki*. As soon as she is done cooling her food, she wraps it up in a bundle. Then a girl's father, older brother, or uncle saddles a burro or horse on which she can ride out. The girls then join the hunters at their gathering place.

Upon setting out on the hunt, the girls pay close attention to the hunters. Wherever one of them kills a cottontail or a jackrabbit, the girls race for it, competing with each other. The one who gets there first thanks the boy for the kill and takes it away from him. The girl also keeps track of from whom she acquires rabbits and how many. Upon her return to the village the girl's mother then makes piki for her daughter. This piki the girl distributes among the hunters. After that the mixed hunt is over.

Number Four A Hopi always does things four times, or in multiples of four, for example, eight and sixteen times. Thus, when a group of people is engaged in a ceremony that is planned to run its entire length, it will be in session for the full sixteen days. At other times the ceremony may go on for only eight or even four days. By the same token, when the Hopis seek a response to their inquiries, they will ask only four times and then quit. At that point they will be given answers if they did not receive answers right away. Thus, there is not a single thing in Hopi culture that does not require the number four as a determiner. Likewise, the creator has now purified us thrice. If the creator cares to repeat this purification and cleanse us once more, thereafter we will live as we should.

Nuvakwewtaqa (place-name) A mountain range known by the name of Nuvakwewtaqa lies a short distance southwest of Homol'ovi (Winslow).

Therefore, the Hopi know where it is situated. After a snowfall it is as if this elevation had a belt of snow, and for this reason it is called "That Which Wears a Snow Belt."

Nuvatukya'ovi (San Francisco Mountains) The mountain range to the southwest of Hopi land is known by the name of Nuvatukya'ovi. We go to that place during our ceremonials such as the Niman and also occasionally on Powamuya to gather evergreens. Since there are shrines at that location, those who go to gather these evergreens deposit paho at these sites. In our belief the San Francisco Mountains are one of the homes of the kachinas; therefore, there is a kiva on top of one of its peaks. Nuvatukya'ovi is also one of the boundary markers of Hopiland.

Old Spider Woman Old Spider Woman is a personage extremely talented in all creative arts. For this reason, whenever a Hopi girl or woman wishes to acquire a certain skill, she turns to her in prayer. For example, one may want to learn how to make piki or to become skilled in pottery making or wicker plaque weaving. On each occasion one prays to her. Since she is the grandmother of the Pöqangw Brothers, Pöqangwhoya and Palöngawhoya are just like her, versed in many things. In stories Old Spider Woman helps anyone in need. Thus, she has ways of doing away with a person's enemies. Also, she always gives a person advice on what to do.

Oraibi (Third Mesa village) According to some, the Hopi first settled at Shungopavi. There the *kikmongwi* and his younger brother are said to have differed over some matter. As a result, the younger brother left, headed north, and started his own community at Oraibi. However, not everyone shares the same version of this event. Some others say that the Hopi, after their emergence at the Grand Canyon, first embarked on a migration before they established their first settlement at Oraibi.

Then, in the more recent past, the people there clashed again due to different views regarding the white man's way of life, in particular, schooling. This led to the banishment of those who rejected the Anglo way of life. In turn they established the village of Hotevilla. After renewed differences there, some people settled at Bacavi. Next, several of those who wanted the way of the whites and had remained at Oraibi moved below the mesa and founded another village where they worked for the government. Today that place is known as Kykotsmovi. Yet others for some reason migrated to Moencopi, where the Oraibi people had been going on foot for a long time already because they owned fields there. Thus, as a result of the banishment, several villages now exist northwest of Oraibi.

Ösömuya (month) Ösömuya (approximately March) is the lunar month following Powamuya (approximately February). Its name, "whistle-month," is attributed to the fact that the wind blows constantly at this time of the year. Ösömuya is also the time for night dances.

Paamuya (month) The lunar month of Paamuya (approximately January) follows Kyaamuya (approximately December). In the eyes of the Hopi Paamuya is a happy month, for as soon as the moon appears and people spot it, they start beating their drums. Drumming and singing can be heard in all of the kivas then. Whenever some of the men decide to bring girls into the kivas for social dances, they do so.

Paayu (Little Colorado River) The river that flows past the southwest side of the Homol'ovi ruins is called Paayu by the Hopi. The river that flows through the Grand Canyon, however, which is much larger, is referred to as Pisisvayu (Colorado River).

Paiutes The Paiutes are a native people with a culture quite different from that of the Hopi. For ages they sought out the Hopi country on their raids. Generally, they arrived from a northwesterly direction. Today, during the event of a social dance, the Hopi also disguise themselves to resemble other tribes, including the Paiutes.

Pavayoykyasi (deity) They say that very early in the morning Pavayoykyasi walks about asperging the crops in a Hopi's fields. And, indeed, just as one arrives at his field, there are drops of dew clinging to the crops. People describe Pavayoykyasi as a handsome youth who is always dressed very nicely.

The term *pavayoykyasi* is also used to mean "moisture tablet," which is worn, for example, on the back of an Eagle kachina. A member of the Flute society also carries one.

Piki (dish) Piki is an ancient food of the Hopi. When a woman plans to make it she begins by heating up her stone griddle. She then boils some water and pours it on the blue flour. That accomplished, she adds wood ashes mixed with water, which gives the batter its hue. As soon as her stone griddle is hot enough, she spreads ground melon seeds over it and allows them to burn into the stone. After she bakes each piki, she removes it and spreads a new layer of batter over the griddle. The previously baked piki is placed on top of it and becomes moist from the steam of the new batter. The completed piki can then be rolled up for storage. From that point on she continues rolling and stacking one piki on top of another.

It is said that Old Spider Woman is skillful and talented in many things, so someone eager to learn to make piki prays to her. Old Spider Woman also resides somewhere southwest of Oraibi. Thus, whenever a girl wishes to learn the art of making piki, she takes some wood to her abode and leaves it there for her along with some sacred cornmeal.

Piktotokya (ceremonial day designation)   *Piktotokya* occurs two days before *tiikive* (the day of the public dance performance). *Piktotokya,* in turn, is preceded by the day *suus qa himu* (once nothing day). On *piktotokya* the women are traditionally busy preparing piki, hence the name *piktotokya* (piki *totokya*).

Pipe   The pipe is made out of clay. Any potter who fashions bowls makes pipes along with other pottery. Whoever needs a pipe simply places an order with the potter. Sometimes the men also make their own. The mouthpiece that is added to the pipe generally consists of a reed.

Pivanhonkyapi (place-name)   Pivanhonkyapi is a ruin southwest of Oraibi, on the northeastern side of Apoonivi. The ruined village lies close to the mesa rim. There are holes in the bedrock along the southeastern edge. Into these holes the people of Pivanhonkyapi used to insert poles whenever they wanted to perform the ladder dance. A dancer would climb up the inserted pole and then jump to the next pole over. This spectacle must have been awesome to behold, for the holes are far apart. In addition, the southeastern side has a steep cliff.

Plaza   The plaza is usually situated somewhere near the middle of a village, hence it is used as the dance court if a ceremonial activity is taking place, for example, and kachinas have come. Various other dances are also performed in the plaza. The Snake, Lakon, and Kwan societies, for instance, carry out their dance performances there.

Houses are erected on all four sides of the plaza, and alleys lead into it. In the past, when certain items were to be traded, someone would make a public announcement on behalf of the vendor, who would then sell the goods at the plaza.

Powamuy Ceremony   During the Powamuy ceremony people are being purified. That is the reason for its name Powamuya. It is the Powamuy leader who does the purifying. He purifies people from everything, especially the desire to perform in social dances. During this month the kachinas harvest bean sprouts and bring them to the children on the morning of *totokya* (the ceremonial eve). That same night there are kachina dances in the kivas that uninitiated children are not permitted to watch.

Prayer Feather   A *nakwakwusi* is fashioned to the accompaniment of a prayer. Then it is also smoked upon. This type of prayer feather has more than one function. It can be the symbol of a path laid out, but it can equally well be worn on the head. It also serves to represent symbolically the breath of life. A *nakwakwusi* is produced from the downy breast feather of an eagle together with hand-spun cotton twine.

Prayer Stick/Prayer Feather   A paho is not only made from a variety of items, but it is also fashioned in many different ways. While it is never made from the breast feather of the eagle, it can be made from turkey feathers. Paho can be found hanging from the ceilings of kivas. For example, when kachinas are to return to their homes, they are given paho. The members of the Kwan, Al, and Wuwtsim societies each fashion their own unique paho. A great diversity of paho are made at the time of Soyalangw. It is said that those for whom the paho is intended are elated upon receiving it. A paho carries with it a person's most intense wishes and prayers. A medicine man who has treated you takes what ails you along with a paho and goes to deposit that. In fact, there is nothing for which the Hopi do not make a paho. They make it for the sun, the moon, deities who exist unseen and all the other beings that they rely upon for their existence.

Public Announcement In the past when the Hopi wished to inform fellow villagers of certain things, they would petition someone to make a public announcement on their behalf. At other times, a formal announcement could be made by the *tsa'akmongwi,* or official village crier. To broadcast his message, the crier always climbed on a rooftop. The opening formula of his announcement usually sounded as follows: "Those of you people out there heed my words." The conclusion was equally formalized: "This is the announcement I was instructed to make known to you. That's about it." Whenever the crier shouted out his announcement, he typically drew out the last word of each sentence.

Qa'ötaqtipu (place-name) Qa'ötaqtipu is a ruin site somewhere on the northeast side of Bacavi. Burned corn was discovered there, hence the appellation Qa'ötaqtipu (Burned Corn).

Qömi (dish) *Qömi* is made from *toosi* (ground, roasted sweet corn). After baking sweet corn in an earth oven, people usually string the cobs up, whereupon they let them dry. When the drying process is complete, people shell some of the baked sweet corn and grind it up. It now becomes *toosi.* The *toosi* is placed in a pottery bowl, into which water is added. Both ingredients are now stirred and kneaded. When the mixture acquires the desired consistency, it is *qömi* (sweet corn cake). Having made the *qömi* in this way, one eats it cold.

Occasionally, a girl will fashion little sweet corn cakes and take them into the kiva on a flat tray during a night dance in the month of Powamuya. Also, in the old days, when a girl had a sweetheart and wanted to let the boy's parents know about this, she would stack a small amount of folded piki on a tray, place some sweet corn cakes on top, and take this to the boy's house. If the parents were not in favor of the girl, they simply put some meal on the girl's tray and took it back to her.

Rainbow The rainbow is an evil force. They say it exudes a terrible stench, which is one of the reasons why the clouds are afraid of it. Thus, if the clouds are on the way to some destination and a rainbow arches under them, they retreat. As a result, they cannot bring rain to the people. That's why one commonly hears that a rainbow is bad. People say that it closes in the clouds. "They can't come to us now. It's not going to rain. The rainbow closes the clouds in." And it is true; they fail to come then.

Ritual Requiring Initiation Whatever religious practice a Hopi is initiated into, by means of a hair-washing rite, constitutes that person's *wiimi*. The Hopis engage in many rituals, and no one Hopi is familiar with the esoteric practices for all of them. Some rites are exclusively for men; others are only for women. The first exposure to a *wiimi* takes place when a child is initiated into the kachina cult. Thereafter, the Hopi can learn about the ritual of another society. Usually, it is the society that is affiliated with one's kachina godfather or godmother.

Long ago people were involved in a great variety of rituals conducted by special societies, some of which have become extinct. For example, the Nakya rites and the clown ritual no longer exist. Also, the Momtsit do not carry on their ritual anymore. Only the initiates of the Powamuy, Wuwtsim, Soyal, Al, Kwan, Taw, Snake, Antelope, Flute, Lakon, Owaqöl, and Maraw societies still conduct their esoteric practices in some villages.

Runner Kachinas Runner kachinas typically come during the month of Ösömuya (approximately March). As a rule, they appear without anyone's prior knowledge. They bring all sorts of gifts with them as they proceed to the location where they plan to challenge people to a race. Some of the kachinas' kiva partners know about their arrival, of course, and dress up in fanciful ways. They then go in this guise to where the Runner kachinas are and challenge a Runner kachina to a race. But the kachinas will also pull in a spectator if they fancy challenging one to run with them. Taking their victim to a line, the latter usually dashes off as soon as he reaches the line. The kachina then sets out in pursuit of him.

There is great variety among Runner kachinas. They all have different names. Tatsiipölölö, for instance, throws his ball at the loser, Tsöqaapölölö metes out his punishment with balls of clay. Tsilitosmoktaqa, upon catching up with his victim and grabbing him, force-feeds him chile powder. The Kwitanono'a, on the other hand, feeds his victim excrement. Aykatsina (Rattle kachina) whips the loser with yucca strips. Nahoyleetsi'ytaqa does the same. The Kokopölmana, finally, flings her victims on the ground as soon as she catches them. Then she flattens out on top of them and executes several pelvic thrusts into her victims.

Sacred Cornmeal   Sacred cornmeal was once used by the Hopi on an everyday basis. Each morning as one went out to pray toward the rising sun, one made it a habit to pray with *hooma*.

The kachina father, that is, the man who tends the kachinas, also uses it as he takes care of them during their dances. When the kachinas are to change dance positions, the father makes a cornmeal path for them. He ceremonially feeds them with the cornmeal, whereupon they commence dancing. In the evening, at the conclusion of their performance, sacred cornmeal is again an ingredient in ritually preparing the kachinas for their journey home.

On the occasion of a wedding, after the ceremony is completed and the bride is to return home, a cornmeal path once more is marked on the ground for her. Again, when there is a ritual in progress and prayers are being conducted, cornmeal is involved. On *astotokya,* the climactic night of the Wuwtsim initiation, a member of the Kwan society uses cornmeal to seal off the paths leading into the village. Finally, when one goes to deposit a paho one always takes cornmeal along. Before the paho is deposited, one first prays to it using the cornmeal. This accounts for the expression *hom'oyto* (to go to deposit cornmeal).

Shaman   In times past a small group of medicine men were capable of removing foreign objects that had been implanted into a patient by sorcery to cause an ailment. A medicine man of these qualifications was referred to as a crystal gazer or shaman. He would diagnose the patient through a crystal, and if there was a problem, he would point it out to the patient. When he discovered the foreign object responsible for the ailment, he removed it. Once in a while someone would seek out a medicine man to test his powers and would self-administer the insertion of this foreign object. If the medicine man found it, he gave it to the patient with instructions to get rid of it.

Shipaulovi (Second Mesa village)   The village of Shipaulovi is an offshoot of Shungopavi. It is said that if ever Shungopavi becomes extinct, the people of Shipaulovi are to carry on its ceremonies. But as Shungopavi still exists, the inhabitants of Shipaulovi go there to be initiated into the necessary societies, such as the Wuwtsim and the Maraw. Consequently, the altar pieces of the Snake society are also kept at Shungopavi.

Shungopavi (Second Mesa village)   Shungopavi lies approximately southeast of Oraibi. According to the traditions of some, the Hopi established their first settlement there.

But they did not settle on top of the mesa then. To that location they migrated much later. Tradition also has it that two brothers, the *kikmongwi* and his younger brother Matsito, had differences of opinion that resulted in the latter's moving to Oraibi. He took some people along and founded Oraibi. For some unknown reason the people of Shungopavi and the people of Oraibi do not speak the same dialect, even though they are both Hopi.

Sikyatki (place-name) Sikyatki is a ruin northwest of Walpi. The place was first settled by the Coyote clan. Then, for some reason, the members of this clan moved away, and now they have spread throughout the Hopi villages.

Smoking Long ago the Hopi prayed every day, and while they did this they always smoked a pipe. Also, whenever the *kikmongwi* had a caller, he had to offer the guest his pipe. Likewise, when one plans to participate in a kachina dance and goes to the kiva from which the impersonators will come, the person in charge of the ceremony must first offer you a smoke before you can join in. When a ceremony is in progress, there is a round of smoking at the beginning and at the end of the ritual. As soon as your neighbor has finished, he hands you the pipe. You now take a few puffs and address him in the manner according to which you are related to him. If he is your father, you would say, "My father." When his turn comes to reply he would say, "My child." In the past all people knew how they were related to one another. If one is not familiar with one's neighbor and that person happens to be older than you, you may address him as "My father." And if he is not much older than you, the proper form of address would be "My elder brother." If one does not wish to use this expression, an alternative form of address is "Companion of my heart."

The person smoking first prays fervently from his heart, before he exhales the smoke, that things will turn out beneficial for him and that he will prosper. This smoke then carries one's prayers to those who are more powerful. This is what ritual smoking means to the Hopi. Thus it is little wonder that whenever they are engaged in a certain endeavor, tobacco and pipe are ever present.

Somiviki (dish) *Somiviki* is made from the batter of blue corn flour. It is wrapped in a corn husk and then tied in two places with yucca strips. After being packaged in this way, it is boiled.

Songs In the past, when the Hopi were to do something, they usually did it to the accompaniment of a song. For example, long ago a man would go to the fields singing. The reason for the singing was to alert his crops of his approach. He wanted them fully awake before his arrival. And as he walked among his plants, he also sang. Likewise when a woman or a young girl grinds corn, she does it to the tune of a song. That is a grinding song. With the accompaniment of a song her work is not so tedious; therefore, she also sings while grinding. Whenever a woman puts her child to sleep, she also sings it a lullaby. When we were playing as children, we did so while singing a song. Also while we swam, there was still another song.

Even evil persons have a song at hand, a song that makes you go crazy. With it they can cause someone to go wild when they desire that person sexually.

All rituals are complete only with song. Thus, the members of the Wuwtsim and Maraw societies, the kachinas, the social dancers, and even the clowns all have their individual songs. There is also the Snake dance song, the Flute ceremonial song, and the Kwan song.

People who played the guessing game *sosotukwpi* also had songs of their own. Players sang as they competed against one another.

At times when women are weaving wicker plaques, they weave while singing the Owaqöl (Basket dance) songs.

Finally, it seems that folktales generally included a song, but some of them have been forgotten. It is said that the Hopi is a mockingbird. That is why the songs are composed using the languages of many other people. Thus, one song might be in the Zuni language, another in Navajo. As a matter of fact, songs always include words from other Indian groups. Some are so ancient that the meaning of the words is completely obscure.

When Coyote sings within a story, he always does so in a very deep voice. He never sings in a high-pitched tone. He bellows the song out.

Sorcerer/Sorceress A sorcerer is the equivalent of an evildoer. For this reason we, the Hopi, did not inform the sorcerers that we wanted to ascend to this upper world. Somehow, however, the sorcerers found out about it and made the emergence with us. They are reputed to congregate at a place called Palangwu. Sorcerers and witches do not live on their own. They lengthen their life span through the lives of their own relatives. All witchcraft activities are carried out only at night. Whenever sorcerers seek to extend their own lives, they extract a person's heart with a spindle. Sorcerers are also said to go about in the guise of some animals.

Sometimes when a Hopi acquires something through hard work, another person who is envious and looks upon the former with disfavor will label that person a witch. If it is true, the person will never admit it of course. A witch who is caught red-handed performing acts of witchery will try to entice his captor to accept some valuable possession (in the case of a sorcerer) or even her own body (in the case of a sorceress). This is to keep the captor from revealing the sorcerer's identity.

Sosotukwpi (game) *Sosotukwpi* is a Hopi game. It is generally played in the kivas during the winter month of Paamuya (approximately January).

The competing players assemble in two groups on the northwest side of the fire pit. One group sets up the four *pakwsivu* (gaming cylinders), which are fashioned from cottonwood. The group that actually begins starts up a chant. Next, the players of the group who will be doing the guessing cover themselves up with blankets. That done, a member of the singing group hides the *soomoki* (the object to be guessed) under one of the cottonwood cylinders. The other group now takes off its blanket covers, and one of their members steps up to search for the hidden object. This person moves one hand back and forth over the cylinders searching for the hidden piece, concentrating while doing so. "Maybe it's here or here, or here," the player keeps thinking. From the cylinder containing the hidden object a breeze seems to be emanating toward the player's hand, which may reveal the location. The guesser then picks up the cylinder and shows it to the others. If there is nothing underneath, it is put aside. If the guesser is lucky and by the third try picks up the right cylinder with the hidden object in it, that group wins. However, if the player fails to guess correctly three times in a row, that side loses. When a player knocks over the right cylinder the very first time, they say the hidden object comes out of the cottonwood cylinder at once.

Now the winners set the game up again. The losers in turn send one of their group over. While the guesser moves a hand over the cylinders, the winners start up a song again to distract the others. That is how *sosotukwpi* is played.

In stories the game is always described as one in which men and women play together. They get so involved that they compete until daybreak the following morning. Not before sunrise do they go eat breakfast. Long ago, life was like this, way back in time. Nowadays the game is not played anymore.

Soyalangw (Soyal ceremony) Soyalangw is a ceremony that takes place during the winter, not long after the Wuwtsim ritual. This entire event lasts sixteen days. During this time the Sosyalt (members of the Soyal society) carry out esoteric rites in their kiva, and they fashion prayer feathers of various kinds for everything from which the Hopi benefit. It is also at this time that the sun reaches its winter home. From that point on it journeys toward its summer home, and the days grow increasingly longer. In addition, Soyalangw marks the beginning of the new kachina season with the appearance of the Soyal kachina. Somewhat later, the Qööqöqlö kachinas arrive to ceremonially open all the kivas so that the other kachinas, too, are now able to make their visits.

Spider For some Hopi the spider constitutes a clan totem. To those who are not of the Spider clan, a spider has no significance whatsoever. Thus, when one comes across a spider in the home, one kills it. It is also commonly believed that if a spider urinates on you, you will break out in sores.

There exists an old woman in Hopi mythology who assists the Hopi in many ways. She is very compassionate and very powerful. The giver of all life created her before the animals were created, even before this world was made. This woman is known as Kookyangwso'wuuti (Old Spider Woman) by the Hopi. But it is not known for sure why she is referred to in this way.

Spring Ages ago, when the Hopi were still on their migratory route, it was customary for them to take a water vessel along. Each time they intended to settle at a site, they buried the vessel in the ground, whereupon a spring emerged, affording them a source of water supply. When they finally arrived at Hopi country, they established settlements at places situated close by springs. As soon as they became familiar with the springs in the area, they gave them names. Thus, the discoverers of newly emerged springs would name them according to their clan totem.

Some springs are inhabited by kachinas, so the Hopi go to these sites to deposit prayer feathers to ask for rain. Obviously, water is most precious to the Hopi. For this reason they conduct communal spring-cleaning parties that take place every year.

The elders also remind children that Paalölöqangw, the Water Serpent, inhabits every spring and that one should therefore not play around these locations. The Serpent is said to make his appearance there exactly at noon. When someone wants to drink from a spring, he should not do so by bending over it. Instead, one should ladle the water out. If a ladle is lacking, the cupped hands should be used to take a drink. A third taboo relating to pools of water forbids sexual intercourse in or near the water. A consequence of breaking it is that the girl will be impregnated by the Serpent.

Tiikuywuuti (deity) Tiikuywuuti is a being with greater-than-human powers. She died giving birth when her child did not come out. Hence her name "Child Sticking Out Woman." She makes her home just about anywhere and is the mother of all the game animals.

Tiikuywuuti is a female deity endowed with a mask. Underneath this mask is a beautiful woman. She is said to resemble the Qötsamana. Just like this kachina she wears a ruff and her face is daubed white. Attached to the face are flat bones featuring eye holes. Above her eyes are a number of dots that represent the brows. Tied to both sides of her head (in *naasomi* hair style) is galleta grass. From the *naasomi* hang the pods of the grass.

A Hopi who is not a good hunter prays that Tiikuywuuti may have intercourse with him so that he can become a good hunter. Whenever the goddess comes to someone and he is not brave, he freezes with fright. As he is petrified with fear, he is not aware of her coupling with him. Upon coming to again, the man looks for tracks. Occasionally he will find some, but only the tracks of a jackrabbit. Those are the tracks Tiikuywuuti leaves behind. Tuwapongtumasi (Sand altar clan's woman) is another name for the goddess.

Tiiponi (ceremonial object) All religious societies must possess a *tiiponi*, which is a very important item. It is made from eagle feathers and the feathers of all the other birds. At its base the resulting feather bundle is wrapped with cotton string. Inside the wrapping are also the seeds of all types of grasses, which are set aside as food for the birds. The owner of a *tiiponi* regards it as a mother, addressing it as "My mother." It is stored in the house of the religious leader who owns it. When it is placed on the altar, the initiates of a given society pray to it with sacred cornmeal.

Toosi (dish) Whoever wants some *toosi* (ground, roasted sweet corn) shells some sweet corn that was baked in an earth oven and then grinds it. After fine-grinding the latter, it is sifted and heaped on a tray. In this form it is eaten by taking pinches from it.

Torch A torch consists either of finely shredded cedar bark or of other sticks that are bound together. Hence its Hopi name *kopitsoki*, literally "dry sticks bundled together." To light a torch one uses a flint on a material such as cotton. Once the cotton is ignited, one can take the light from it. In the days when matches were not yet available to the Hopi and when someone's fire went out, one simply took a torch to somebody else's house and used it to borrow fire there.

Totolospi (game) *Totolospi* is a game that the children of long ago used to play. One must first find some sort of rock slab or a wooden board, which is then marked with charcoal. Along the border of the gaming board a not-too-narrow band is drawn. On this band, which outlines the gaming board, lines are marked. First five lines, then a number of little circles. This intermittent design band leads to an opening from which it moves inward somewhat like the tail of a snake. This tail, too, is marked with segments of five lines and circles all the way to its tip. This band is the path on which the gaming pieces are moved.

Next, one searches for something to be used as gaming pieces. Anything can serve this purpose. Sometimes it is a little pebble or the tip of a corncob. Just anything of this sort will do. Finally, one splits a reed down the middle. The two halves, which serve as dice, may be painted on their back, sometimes with a zigzag design.

To actually play, as a rule three or four people band together. The starting point is in the very center. That is where the gaming pieces are placed. Then one grabs the reeds in such a way that they stick up. When released, they usually fall sort of inward. If both reed halves come to rest with their open side up, it counts five points. When the split reeds land upside down, the throw is worth ten points. Since there are groups of five lines and circles marked on the *totolospi* board, one advances in multiples of five. With both reeds showing the flat, open side, one moves five times. With both the curved sides up, one gets ten points and can advance ten places. However, should one split reed land upside down and the other with the flat side up, one loses one's throw. The player must now quit and the one next in line has a turn. As one leaves the center area of the gaming board, one can move one's gaming piece either to the right or left. Any route is fine. However, if one player catches up with someone else's gaming piece and lands right on top of it, the former takes the other contestant's place and sends that piece all the way back to the starting line at the center, the tip of the snake's tail. Now one has to begin all over. The player who first succeeds in entering back into the center without any problems beats the others. This is how *totolospi* is played.

Turds (derogatory label for sorcerers)   Since the beginning of time the Hopi have been speaking of certain people as "turds" or "feces." They represent sorcerers and witches and are almost a necessary force in a narrative. Sorcerers frown upon benevolent people and, for this reason, conjure up schemes to harm or destroy them. They particularly dislike a man who marries an exceptionally beautiful girl in their village. They then plot how to take his wife away from him. Eventually, however, the man harmed by them overcomes his evil opponents with the help of a more powerful being. Nevertheless, these turds are said to be very potent themselves, for they have at their disposal a multitude of ways and means of doing things.

Tuutsiitsiklawqa (kachina)   Tuutsiitsiklawqa is one of the many Runner kachinas in the Hopi kachina pantheon. Whenever he comes to race, he competes with someone. He catches up with the chosen one, grabs the loser, and tears this person's shirt. This is the reason for his name, "One Who Keeps Tearing the Clothes of Others."

Tuutukwi (place-name)   The place-name Tuutukwi refers to the area of free-standing volcanic plugs somewhere southeast of Oraibi. They are quite tall, hence the name Tuutukwi (Buttes).

Urge to Defecate   Often in a story, when the hero or heroine is either on the way to an unfamiliar destination or is being taken somewhere by an evil being, Old Spider Woman knows about it. If she then intends to show herself to them, she will in some magical way cause in them the urge to defecate. As soon as the urge is felt, the male or female protagonist will step aside, and before they can empty their bowels, Old Spider Woman will speak to them. She typically begins by saying, "Phew! Can't you move farther away and then defecate?" Next she instructs them to enter her abode after they have finished with their business. The reason that Old Spider Woman employs this method to reveal herself to a mortal only at a time like this may be that at that moment one is all alone.

Vent Hole   The ancient dwellings were never without vent holes. Because the Hopi did not have windows in those days, vent holes were there for the same purpose. In summer, when the weather was hot, it was through this opening that a cool breeze entered the house. Then it was not so hot in the interior. The room where a person ground corn was always equipped with this opening. Through it a suitor talked to his girlfriend while courting her.

Village   Whenever the Hopi established a village, they settled there with the intention of staying permanently. As soon as some sort of disaster struck the community, however, they usually moved on in search of a place with better living conditions where they could found another village. Unlike some other Indian groups, the Hopi, therefore, were not nomads. Homes were built using only stone and mortar, except for the roof, which was constructed from log beams covered with brush and mud. Wherever a village was erected, a village center or plaza had to be part of it. In general, the northwestern end of the plaza was occupied by members of the Bear clan, who constituted the Hopi elite. The three remaining sides of the plaza were open for anyone who wished to build there. Within the village were several rows of houses that were often multistoried. They consisted of rooms especially built to store corn and other crops, a chamber where piki was made, and of course an area that served as living quarters.

Village Leader   The *kikmongwi* (village leader) of old came from the Bear clan. In a given village he is supposed to be the father to all. Therefore, in the olden days, he was the first to rise in the morning and the last to retire at night. The *kikmongwi* never gives orders. He does not think of himself only when he does things. On the contrary, his only concern is that as an end result his children will benefit. Therefore, he is not alone when he takes on a task. He seeks advice from his fellow leaders as he works on it. Obviously, a white man's "chief" and the *mongwi* of the Hopi are not synonymous.

Walpi (First Mesa village)   Walpi is an old village. The people of Walpi may have settled at this location approximately during the same period as the people of Oraibi and Shungopavi, but one cannot say for certain where they came from. Just as the Shungopavi residents, they used to live below the mesa. But because of the constant raids of enemy groups they moved to a site above the original settlement where they were better off. In time, some relocated to a place northeast of Walpi and founded another village, which is known as Sichomovi. Finally, people from a Rio Grande pueblo arrived and settled at the northeasternmost end of the mesa, just southwest of the Gap. That village is referred to as Hanoki by the Hopi.

Wedding Robe The *oova* (wedding robe) comes in two sizes, one being quite a bit larger than the other. The large one is woven for the bride so that she can journey to Maski (Home of the Dead). As the robe constituted a married woman's vehicle to make her descent to the underworld, she was not supposed to sell it. In previous times when the *oova* was never sold, the woman would sometimes fashion a sack from it. People also used the garment as a sitting mat. It was also not supposed to be decorated. Embroidery would have added weight to it and not permitted the dead woman to ride it down the Grand Canyon on her way to the underworld.

The bridal robe is further said to function as a water sieve. With its help the clouds sift their moisture to produce the very fine rain. In Hopi belief, upon one's demise a mortal is transformed into a cloud personage, and whenever a woman checks on the people she left behind, she employs the *oova* as a sieve. By using the *oova* to sift the rains, a fine drizzle is produced instead of hail. Hail is dreaded by the Hopi because it ruins the corn crops and smashes holes into muskmelons and watermelons.

One of the corners of the wedding robe has sixteen stitches of red yarn. They symbolize a young woman's menstruation. Also attached at this corner is a corncob. This corncob is not a real cob but is made from varicolored yarn. However, it closely resembles a corncob.

White Thigh A woman or girl possessing light-complected thighs is sexually most desirable to the Hopi male. When men or boys know of a female with this asset, they spread the word. By the same token, men are attracted to a female who is, overall, lighter skinned than average. The term for a woman like that is *sikyavu,* which, literally translated, means "yellow person."

Wukoqal Butterfly Dancers *Wukoqalvoliit,* literally, "big forehead Butterfly dancers," are Butterfly dancers whose foreheads are clearly visible because they are not covered with hair bangs. That's how they got their name. Some of them have a flower made of yarn attached on one side of their head and a horn on the other. Another type is distinguished by bundles of turkey feathers worn at the side of the head. A third group, finally, sports wicker plaques tied to both sides of the hair.

Wupatki (place-name) On the northeastern side of Nuvatukya'ovi (the

San Francisco Mountains) lies a ruin named Wupatki. People say that long ago Hopis used to live there.

Wuwtsim Eve   The members of the Wuwtsim society plan their ceremony for a duration of sixteen days. At midpoint the Wuwtsim leader enters the kiva, and whoever else wants to go in with him, does so. They then live, eat, and sleep in the kivas in pursuit of the day on which the public dance takes place. From day four on, the men keep track of the days by marking each day off with a line. There is now one more set of four days. The first is termed suus qa himu (once nothing); the second piktotokya (piki eve); the third totokya (eve); and the last one tiikive (dance day). On totokya (eve) at night the society members are not allowed to sleep. Instead, they keep dancing all through the night. The following day they stage their public performance.

Yellow Fox   The Hopis make it a habit to hunt the yellow fox. They stalk the animal for its pelt. After stretching the hide out on the ground, they let it dry. The kachinas then wear the pelt dangling from the rear waist. Some kachinas also employ it as a ruff. According to Hopi mythology Taawa, the Sun god, places the yellow fox skin on a ladder pole at his house. At that time it gets to be yellow dawn.

Bibliography

Baker, Shane A. 1994. "The Question of Cannibalism and Violence in the Anasazi Culture: A Case Study from San Juan County." *Blue Mountain Shadows* 13:30–41.

Bandelier, Adolph F. 1976 [1892]. "Final Report of Investigations among the Indians of the Southwestern United States, Carried on Mainly in the Years from 1880 to 1885." *Papers of the Archaeological Institute of America. American Series,* vol. 4, pt. 2. Cambridge: Cambridge University Press. Reprint New York: AMS Press.

Bartlett, Katharine. 1934. "Spanish Contact with the Hopi: 1540–1823." *Museum of Northern Arizona Notes* 6(12):55–60.

Bascom, William R. 1955. "Verbal Art." Journal of American Folklore 68:245–252.

Beaglehole, Ernest, and Pearl Beaglehole. 1935. "Hopi of the Second Mesa." *American Anthropological Association Memoirs* 44:1–65.

Benedict, Ruth. 1959 [1934]. *Patterns of Culture.* 2d ed. with a new preface by Margaret Mead. Boston: Houghton Mifflin.

Bourke, John G. 1984 [1884]. *The Snake-Dance of the Moquis of Arizona.* Tucson: University of Arizona Press.

Brew, John Otis. 1941. "Preliminary Report of the Peabody Museum Awatovi Expedition of 1939." *Plateau* 13(3):37–48.

———. 1979. "Hopi Prehistory and History to 1850." In *Handbook of North American Indians,* vol. 9. *Southwest.* Alfonso Ortiz, ed. Pp. 514–523. Washington DC: Smithsonian Institution.

Colton, Harold S. 1959. *Hopi Kachina Dolls with a Key to Their Identification.* Albuquerque: University of New Mexico Press.

Colton, Harold S., and Edmund Nequatewa. 1932. "The Ladder Dance: Two Traditions of an Extinct Hopi Ceremonial." *Museum of Northern Arizona Notes* 5(2):5–12.

Colton, Mary-Russel Farrell, Edmund Nequatewa, and Harold S. Colton. 1933. "Hopi Legends of the Sunset Crater Region." *Museum of Northern Arizona Notes* 5(4):17–23.

Courlander, Harold. 1970. *People of the Short Blue Corn: Tales and Legends of the Hopi Indians.* New York: Harcourt Brace Jovanovich.

———. 1971. *The Fourth World of the Hopis.* Greenwich CT: Fawcett Publications.

———. 1982. *Hopi Voices: Recollections, Traditions, and Narratives of the Hopi Indians.* Albuquerque: University of New Mexico Press.

Curtin, L. S. M. 1971. "Spanish and Indian Witchcraft in New Mexico." *Masterkey* 45(3):89–101.

Curtis, Edward S. 1970 [1922]. *The North American Indian,* vol. 12. *The Hopi.* New York and London: Johnson Reprint Corporation.

Darling, J. Andrew. 1999. "Mass Inhumation and the Execution of Witches in the American Southwest." *American Anthropologist* 100(3):732–752.

Dittert, Alfred E., Jr., and Fred Plog. 1980. *Generations in Clay.* Flagstaff AZ: Northland Press.

Ediger, Donald. 1971. *The Well of Sacrifice.* Garden City NY: Doubleday and Company.

Eliade, Mircea. 1964. *Shamanism: Archaic Techniques of Ecstasy.* Willard R. Trask, trans. Bollingen Series, 76. Princeton: Princeton University Press.

Farmer, Malcolm F. 1955. "The Identification of Ho-vi-itsi-tu-qua Pueblo." *Plateau* 28(2):44–45.

Fewkes, Jesse W. 1893. "A-wa'-to Bi: An Archeological Verification of a Tusayan Legend." *American Anthropologist* 6(4):363–375.

———. 1895. "Preliminary Account of an Expedition to the Cliff Villages of the Red Rock Country, and the Tusayan Ruins of Sikyatki and Awatobi, Arizona, in 1895." *Smithsonian Institution Annual Report,* 557–588.

———. 1896a. "The Prehistoric Culture of Tusayan." *American Anthropologist* 9(5): 151–173.

———. 1896b. "Preliminary Account of an Expedition to the Pueblo Ruins near Winslow, Arizona, in 1896." *Smithsonian Institution Annual Report,* 517–540.

———. 1898. "Archaeological Expedition to Arizona in 1895." *Bureau of American Ethnology, 17th Annual Report for the Years 1895–96,* pt. 2, 519–742. Washington DC: Smithsonian Institution.

———. 1903. "Hopi Katcinas, Drawn by Native Artists." *Bureau of American Ethnology, 21st Annual Report for the Years 1899–1901,* 3–126. Washington DC: Smithsonian Institution.

Fewkes, Jesse W., and A. M. Stephen. 1893. "The Pá-lü-lü-kon-ti: A Tusayan Ceremony." *Journal of American Folklore* 6:269–284.

Geertz, Armin W., and Michael Lomatuway'ma. 1987. *Children of Cottonwood: Piety and Ceremonialism in Hopi Indian Puppetry.* American Tribal Religions, 12. Karl Luckert, ed. Lincoln and London: University of Nebraska Press.

Gimbutas, Marija. 1989. *The Language of the Goddess.* San Francisco: Harper.

González Torres, Yolotl. 1985. *El sacrificio humano entre los mexicas*. México DF: Instituto Nacional de Antropología e Historia. Fondo de Cultura Económica.

Hammond, George P., and Agapito Rey. 1929. *Expedition into New Mexico Made by Antonio de Espejo, 1582–1583, as Revealed in the Journal of Diego Perez de Luxan, a Member of the Party.* Los Angeles: Quivira Society Publications.

Hargrave, Lyndon L. 1930. "Shungopovi." *Museum of Northern Arizona Notes* 2(10):1–4.

———. 1931. "First Mesa." *Museum of Northern Arizona Notes* 3(8):1–6.

———. 1935. "The Jeddito Valley and the First Pueblo Towns in Arizona to Be Visited by Europeans." *Museum of Northern Arizona Notes* 8(4):17–23.

———. 1937. "Sikyatki: Were the Inhabitants Hopi?" *Museum of Northern Arizona Notes* 9(12):61–66.

Hartmann, Horst. 1975. "Alosaka und Muyingwa." *Baessler-Archiv* 23:293–346.

Haury, Emil W. 1986. "Tree Rings: The Archaeologist's Time-Piece." In *Emil W. Haury's Prehistory of the Southwest.* J. Jefferson Reid and David E. Doyel, eds. Pp. 61–72. Tucson: University of Arizona Press.

Hodge, Frederick Webb. [1969] 1910. *Handbook of American Indians North of Mexico.* Smithsonian Institution, Bureau of American Ethnology, Bulletin 30. 2 vols. New York: Greenwood Press.

Holterman, Jack. 1955. "Mission San Bartolomé de Xongopavi: One of Arizona's Forgotten Missions." *Plateau* 28(2):29–36.

Hooper, Mildred, and C. R. Hooper. 1975. "Awatobi: High Place of the Bow." *Outdoor Arizona* 47:18–19.

James, George Wharton. 1901. "The Storming of Awatobi." *Chautauquan* 33(5): 497–500.

———. 1917. *Arizona the Wonderland.* Boston: Page.

James, Harry C. 1974. *Hopi History.* Tucson: University of Arizona Press.

Kabotie, Fred. 1982. *Designs from the Ancient Mimbreños with a Hopi Interpretation by Fred Kabotie.* Flagstaff AZ: Northland Press.

Langley, Dama Margaret (Mrs. White Mountain Smith). 1939. "When the Hopi Deserted Their Ancient Gods." *Desert Magazine* 3(1):16–18.

LeBlanc, Steven A. 1999. *Prehistoric Warfare in the American Southwest.* Salt Lake City: University of Utah Press.

Lekson, Stephen. 1999. "Chaco." *Archaeology* 53(3):67–73.

Leonard, Jonathan Norton. 1967. *Ancient America.* New York: Time.

Luckert, Karl. 1975. *The Navajo Hunter Tradition.* Tucson: University of Arizona Press.

———. 1976. *Olmec Religion: A Key to Middle America and Beyond.* Norman: University of Oklahoma Press.

Malotki, Ekkehart. 1983. *Hopi Time: A Linguistic Analysis of the Temporal Concepts in the Hopi Language.* Trends in Linguistics. Studies and Monographs, 20. Werner Winter, ed. Berlin, New York, Amsterdam: Mouton Publishers.

———. 1991. "Language as a Key to Cultural Understanding: New Interpretations of Central Hopi Concepts." *Baessler-Archiv,* n.s., 39:43–75.

Malotki, Ekkehart, and Michael Lomatuway'ma. 1987a. *Earth Fire: A Hopi Legend of the Sunset Crater Eruption.* Flagstaff AZ: Northland Press.

———. 1987b. *Maasaw: Profile of a Hopi God.* American Tribal Religions, 11. Karl Luckert, ed. Lincoln and London: University of Nebraska Press.

Mindeleff, Cosmos. 1891. "Traditional History of Tusayan." In "A Study of Pueblo Architecture: Tusayan and Cibola." Victor Mindeleff, ed. *Bureau of American Ethnology, 8th Annual Report for the Years 1886–87,* 16–41. Washington DC: Smithsonian Institution.

Mindeleff, Victor. 1891. "A Study of Pueblo Architecture: Tusayan and Cibola." *Bureau of American Ethnology, 8th Annual Report for the Years 1886–87,* 3–228. Washington DC: Smithsonian Institution.

Montgomery, Ross G., Watson Smith, and J. O. Brew. 1949. "Franciscan Awatovi." *Papers of the Peabody Museum of American Archaeology and Ethnology,* 36. Cambridge MA: Harvard University Press.

Nequatewa, Edmund. 1938. "The Destruction of Elden Pueblo: A Hopi Story." *Plateau* 28(2):37–44.

———. 1967 [1936]. *Truth of a Hopi: Stories Relating to Origin, Myths, and Clan Histories of the Hopi.* Mary-Russel F. Colton, ed. Bulletin of the Museum of Northern Arizona, 8.

Parsons, Elsie Clews. 1926. *Tewa Tales.* New York: American Folk-Lore Society.

———. 1939. *Pueblo Indian Religion.* 2 vols. Chicago: University of Chicago Press.

Pilles, Peter. 1991. "Elden Pueblo: The Frustration of Following Fewkes." Paper presented at the 56th Annual Meeting of the Society for American Archaeology, New Orleans, April 26.

Pringle, Heather. 1998. "North America's Wars." *Science* 279:2038–2040.

Rawson, Philip, ed. 1973. *Primitive Erotic Art.* New York: G. P. Putnam's Sons.

Renaud, E. B. 1938. "Petroglyphs of North Central New Mexico." *Archaeological Survey Series, Eleventh Report.* Denver: University of Denver, Department of Anthropology.

Ross, Anne. 1973. "Celtic and Northern Art." In *Primitive Erotic Art.* Philip Rawson, ed. Pp. 77–106. New York: G. P. Putnam's Sons.

Schaafsma, Polly. 2000. *Warrior, Shield, and Star: Imagery and Ideology of Pueblo Warfare.* Santa Fe NM: Western Edge Press.

Shannon, Elaine. 1983. "Lost Idols of Shungopavi." *Newsweek,* January 31:32–33.

Shorris, Earl. 1971. *The Death of the Great Spirit.* New York: Simon and Schuster.

Simmons, Marc. 1974. *Witchcraft in the Southwest.* Flagstaff AZ: Northland Press.

Smith, Watson. 1952. "Kiva Mural Decorations at Awatovi and Kawaika-a." *Papers of the Peabody Museum of American Archaeology and Ethnology,* 37. Cambridge MA: Harvard University Press.

Stephen, Alexander M. 1894. "The Po-boc-tu among the Hopi." *American Antiquarian and Oriental Journal* 16(4):212–214.

———. 1929. "Hopi Tales." *Journal of American Folk-Lore* 42(163):1–75.

———. 1936. *Hopi Journal of Alexander M. Stephen.* Elsie Clews Parsons, ed. 2 vols. Columbia University Contributions to Anthropology, 23. New York: Columbia University Press.

———. 1940. "Hopi Indians of Arizona—III." *Masterkey* 14:102–109.

Titiev, Mischa. 1942. "Notes on Hopi Witchcraft." *Papers of the Michigan Academy of Science, Arts and Letters* 28:549–557.

———. 1944. "Two Hopi Tales from Oraibi." *Papers of the Michigan Academy of Science, Arts, and Letters* 29:425–437.

———. 1948. "Two Hopi Myths and Rites." *Journal of American Folklore* 61:31–43.

———. 1956. "Shamans, Witches and Chiefs among the Hopi." *Tomorrow* 4(3):51–56.

Tozzer, Alfred M. 1957. "Chichen Itzá and Its Cenote of Sacrifice: A Comparative Study of Contemporaneous Maya and Toltec." *Memoirs of the Peabody Museum of Archaeology and Ethnology,* 11–12. Cambridge MA: Harvard University Press.

Turner, Christy G., and Nancy T. Morris. 1970. "A Massacre at Hopi." *American Antiquity* 35(3):320–331.

Turner, Christy G., II, and Jacqueline A. Turner. 1999. *Man Corn.* Salt Lake City: University of Utah Press.

Tyler, Hamilton A. 1964. *Pueblo Gods and Myths.* Norman: University of Oklahoma Press.

Underhill, Ruth M., et al. 1979. *Rainhouse and Ocean: Speeches for the Papago Year.* American Tribal Religions, 4. Karl Luckert, ed. Flagstaff: Museum of Northern Arizona Press.

Vecsey, Christopher. 1988. *Imagine Ourselves Richly: Mythic Narratives of North American Indians.* New York: Crossroad.

Voth, Henry R. 1905. "The Traditions of the Hopi." *Field Columbian Museum 96,* Anthropological Series, 8.

Walker, William H. 1999. "Witchcraft." *Discovering Archaeology* 1(3):52–54.

Wallis, Wilson D. 1936. "Folk Tales from Shumopovi, Second Mesa." *Journal of American Folk-Lore* 49(191–192):1–68.

Waters, Frank. 1963. *Book of the Hopi.* New York: Viking Press.

White, Tim. 1992. *Prehistoric Cannibalism at Mancos 5MTUMR-2346.* Princeton: Princeton University Press.

Whiting, Alfred F. 1939. *Ethnobotany of the Hopi.* Bulletin of the Museum of Northern Arizona, 15. Flagstaff AZ: Northland Press, 1966.

Wilcox, David R., and Jonathan Haas. 1994. "The Scream of the Butterfly: Competition and Conflict in the Prehistoric Southwest." In *Themes in Southwest Prehistory.* George Gummerman, ed. Santa Fe NM: School of American Research.

Willard, Theodore A. 1926. *The City of the Sacred Well.* New York: Grosset and Dunlap.

Wilson, John P. 1972. "Awatovi—More Light on a Legend." *Plateau* 44(3):125–130.

Yava, Albert. 1978. *Big Falling Snow: A Tewa-Hopi Indian's Life and Times and the History and Traditions of His People.* Annotated by Harold Courlander, ed. New York: Crown Publishers.

CPSIA information can be obtained
at www.ICGtesting.com
Printed in the USA
LVHW08s1032011018
591997LV00013B/137/P